# KIPLING'S INDIA

# KIPLING'S INDIA: UNCOLLECTED SKETCHES 1884-88

*Edited by Thomas Pinney*

Schocken Books   New York

First American edition published by Schocken Books 1986
10 9 8 7 6 5 4 3 2 1    86 87 88
Editorial matter and selection © Thomas Pinney 1986
Text © The National Trust for Places of Histroic Interest or Natural
Beauty 1986
Published by agreement with The Macmillan Press Ltd, London and Basingstok

Library of Congress Cataloging in Publication Data

Kipling, Rudyard, 1895 – 1936.
Kipling's India.

Includes index.
1. India — Literary collections.  2. India —
Description and travel — 1859 – 1900 — Addresses, essays,
lectures.  3. British — India — Addresses, essays,
lectures.  I. Pinney, Thomas.  II. Title.
PR4854.K7   1986    828'.809       84 – 22242

Printed in Hong Kong
ISBN 0 – 8052 – 3962 – 6

# Contents

## Contents

# Acknowledgements

I would like particularly to acknowledge the assistance of the American Philosophical Society for a grant to help pay for the costs of photocopy. My student Vikram Chandra was indispensable in working out the glossary of Indian words, and Joyce Thompson cheerfully undertook a heavy part in preparing the manuscript.

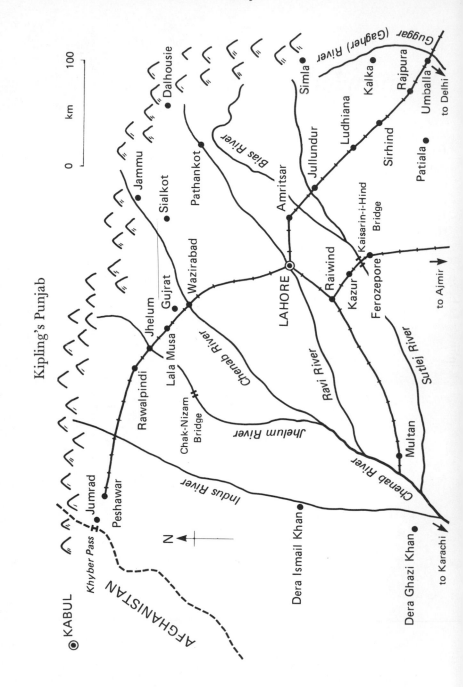

Kipling's Punjab

# Kipling's Lahore

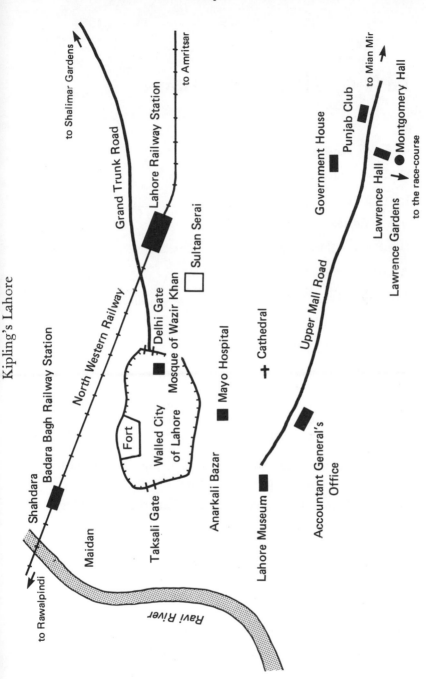

to Shalimar Gardens

to Amritsar

Lahore Railway Station

Grand Trunk Road

Sultan Serai

North Western Railway

Delhi Gate

Mosque of Wazir Khan

Mayo Hospital

+ Cathedral

Walled City of Lahore

Fort

Anarkali Bazar

Taksali Gate

Badara Bagh Railway Station

Shahdara

Maidan

to Rawalpindi

Ravi River

Lahore Museum

Accountant General's Office

Upper Mall Road

Government House

Punjab Club

to Mian Mir

Montgomery Hall

Lawrence Hall

Lawrence Gardens

to the race-course

# List of Illustrations

The illustrations in the text are by Kipling's father, John Lockwood Kipling, and originally illustrated his *Beast and Man in India*, Macmillan, 1891.

The Author and Publishers wish to acknowledge, with thanks the following plate illustration sources:

Plate 1   Rudyard Kipling, c 1882, at the beginning of his Indian career
         by courtesy of the National Trust

Plate 2   The Office of the *Civil and Military Gazette*, Lahore, from the *Kipling Journal*, No. 16, December 1930
         by courtesy of the Kipling Society

Plate 3   Front page of the *Civil and Military Gazette*, Lahore, Wednesday, 11 February 1885
         by courtesy of the Trustees of the British Library, (India Office)

# Introduction

This book presents a selection from the newspaper articles of Rudyard Kipling written in India from his nineteenth to his twenty-third year, 1884 to 1888. All of them are previously unknown and unidentified, and none of them has been reprinted before.

I

The young Rudyard Kipling who went out to India in the September of 1882 to join the staff of the *Civil and Military Gazette* in Lahore was still more than three months short of his seventeenth birthday. Properly speaking, it was a return to India, for Kipling had been born in Bombay and had lived there surrounded by native servants until, after the fashion of the English in India, he had been sent to England for his education. That was in 1871, when he was not yet six; now, eleven years later, he was returning, practically as a stranger, to the land of his birth and to the parents whom he knew only from their rare visits to England.

His appointment to the *Civil and Military Gazette* (hereafter the *CMG*) had come about through his father, John Lockwood Kipling, a ready and agreeable writer himself, who frequently contributed to the Indian newspapers and was well known to the editors and publishers of the English community in India. Kipling's mother, too, sometimes wrote for the *CMG*, in the form of letters describing the summer life of the hill stations. And Rudyard had already demonstrated a knack for journalism. He had been put in charge of his school magazine in 1881 and had filled it with work of his own. By early 1882 he had begun to write news items for the weekly paper in Bideford, just over the hill from his school at Westward Ho! Thus, when the question of what to do with an uncommitted but promising young man had to be faced, journalism seemed a clear answer. Kipling's erratic school performance and the comparative poverty of his parents put Oxford or Cambridge out of the question. For a time Kipling had played with the notion of a career in medicine, but this idea was not carried far. He had fallen in love and was not eager to leave England, but by the time his school days ended in the summer of 1882 the matter had been settled for him, and he dutifully sailed from London to take up his new work.

The *CMG* was published in Lahore, the capital of the Punjab and the centre of British administration for the northwestern frontier regions of India (as it was then) generally. Kipling's parents had been in Lahore since 1875, when his father was appointed head of both the newly-founded school of art there and of the Lahore museum. The size of the British community in Lahore was surprisingly small — perhaps a few hundred civil servants and military officers, not counting the rank and file of the troops stationed at the fort and in the nearby cantonments at Mian Mir. The popular idea of the British in India during the high days of Empire does not usually offer a very distinct realisation of how few their numbers actually were. All of the servants of the *Raj* could be, and were, enumerated each year in an official directory, complete with a statement of annual salary, that required only a modest shelf space. Immigration from England was discouraged, and the fixed practice of the administrators was to return to England on retirement. Thus there was little growth in the numbers of Britons in India year after year, and those who were there did not look upon the country as home but as a place of labour in exile. Unless these facts about the British community in India are clearly grasped — that it was a very tiny group set apart from a vast anonymous multitude, and that it saw itself as living in exile from home — one is likely to misunderstand the assumptions and the peculiar self-consciousness that identified the group for which Kipling wrote during his Indian years.

To take a trivial but revealing instance of the psychology involved, Kipling, in describing the illuminations at Lahore for Queen Victoria's Jubilee in 1887, compares the light shining on the exotic outlines of the night-time city with 'such a light as one sees at night playing over Brighton from far away on Lewes Downs' (18 February 1887). Does that comparison legitimize the scene at Lahore? Kipling is partly writing to himself: he knew that coast and those downs from family homes, and he was later to return to the region to make it his own home. But he is also writing to an audience who might be expected to approve the comparison.

The *CMG* was the property of a larger paper, the *Pioneer* of Allahabad — for which Kipling was afterwards to work — and though the *CMG* had a considerable plant, where a large job-printing business was carried on, the paper itself was a modest enterprise. Kipling was, as he wrote in *Something of Myself*, 'fifty per cent of the "editorial staff" of the one daily paper of the Punjab' (40); the other fifty per cent was the editor, Stephen Wheeler. Wheeler was only a few years older than Kipling, but he was comparatively a hardened journalist and certainly a severe taskmaster. He mistrusted 'original' or 'independent' writing, and for a long time refused to allow Kipling to do anything of his own. The best account of the demanding and unrewarding routine to which Kipling was now subjected is in a letter he wrote to a former teacher during the first weeks of his job:

I write, so to speak, between the horns of the gum pot and the scissors. For the last two hours I have been putting together the bulk of our paper and correcting proofs of all kinds but just at present there is a lull for tiffin so I am free to write to you. . . .

My working hours are from 10 till 4.15 or earlier if I can manage it. One isn't working all the time but it is necessary to be on hand for special telegrams and visitors between those two times. Besides this there is a lot of work out of office hours, telegrams come to my house at any time of the day and night. These have to be seen to. Special telegrams are generally full of abusive matter which might land us in a libel case and so on. One of the first things a sub editor has to learn is to altogether give up original writing. I have not written three words of original matter beyond reports and reviews since I have joined the staff. The actual business which I am learning is intensely interesting and does not become monotonous in any way for you never meet the same thing twice. Some thirty papers go through my hands daily — Hindu papers, scurrilous and abusive beyond everything, local scandal weeklies, philosophical and literary journals written by Babus in the style of Addison. Native Mohammedan, sleepy little publications, all extracts, Indigo papers, tea and coffee journals, jute journals and official Gazettes all have to be disembowelled if they are worth it. Moreover I am responsible for every scrap of the paper except the first two pages. That is to say, I bear the blame of correspondents' blunders — it is my duty to correct them; misprints and bad lettering — it is my business to find them out; vulgarities, bad grammar and indecency — we get that sometimes! have to be looked to carefully and I have a large correspondence all over India with men of all sorts. All local notes come to me and have to be digested, and I must pick up information about approaching polo matches, garden parties, official dinners and dances, to insert in the local column (to Willes, 17 November 1882: MS, Dalhousie University).

This routine was heavy enough; added to that, the content of the paper gave Kipling little chance for independent writing. The *CMG*'s first responsibility was to give the official news to a readership of officials: the proceedings of the government, national and local, the speeches of the Viceroy, the expositions of administrative authorities, the reports of various agencies, and all information of that kind. Then came telegraphic news from around the world, but mostly from Europe, and pre-eminently, from England. Long columns were filled with accounts of public, social, artistic and sporting life from the homeland to which the Indian exiles were all looking. The ups and downs of French political life were closely reported, perhaps to give the Indian civil servants a satisfied sense of their own comparatively orderly and useful activities. And the proceedings of Russia were recorded in detail — every Indian official would of course be expected to know what the Czar and his agents were up to and to have a notion about what the Imperial response should be. When these interests had been met, the market quotations, the results of racing and other sports that Anglo-Indian gentlemen took an interest in, and the weather — always the weather — had to be dealt with. Only then did local news get a chance to be heard from. 'Local' of course meant the English community almost exclusively. A murder, a religious

festival, or a race riot in the native quarter might get a summary
notice, and the misdoings of natives up and down the country
offered standard fare for editorial comment, but beyond that
the lives of the Hindus and Muslims and Sikhs of Lahore went
mostly unnoticed by the *CMG*. Local news tended, like the
national news, to have a strong official flavour: a levée at
Government House, a military ball at the Lawrence Hall, or a
letter from a Lahore administrator on some topic of government policy were standard items. After all these things had been
served, not much remained for indulging one's own line, or for
developing new lines of interest in the paper's coverage, or
even for any 'reporting', as we understand that term, of the
most ordinary sort.

Any account of Kipling's career as a journalist in India must
also stress the sheer physical discomfort of the life. Kipling tried
to give some idea of it to a reporter in San Francisco, where he
was interviewed as an interesting visitor on his way from India
to England in 1889:

An editor in India has a hard time of it until he gets ac-
climated, or salted, as we call it, and it takes from one to
two years to do that. The thermometer from March to
October during the day hovers at about 116 in the shade.
At dawn it is 84, and all through the night, after the air has
been pumped through wet reeds.

Outside during the day everything is dusty and redhot.
I have seen the blackness of midnight occur at midday from
the dust storms. The editor must have green paper on the glass
of his windows to keep out the glaring light. If he drinks he
will drink the national drink there called the *peg*. This consists of a little whisky in soda nine inches high, with ice. You
drink there for the liquid, and not for the liquor, and the
minute you drink it you feel it coming out through your shirt.

The editor in India, as he sits writing at his desk, has to
have every piece of paper about him weighted down, else
the fans which are ceaselessly going to prevent suffocation,
will blow everything away. Oftentimes the cholera strikes
these cities. It is worse now since we have the railroads.
Everybody who can then gets away to the mountains, but
somebody must stay and run the paper, and consequently the

attachés must be all-around men, who can turn their hands to anything, and keep things going (*S. F. Chronicle*, 2 June 1889).

Or, as Kipling put it laconically many years later in his auto-biography, 'a daily paper comes out every day even though fifty per cent of the staff have fever' (*Something of Myself*, p. 40).

There was a positive side, too, one should add. Especially at first, the boyish Kipling was delighted to enter into the privi-leges of adult life: he was being paid, he had responsibility, he belonged to a club. It was not long before he was given an office of his own, and he purchased a dog cart in which to drive between home and office. Though he lived with his parents, his comings and goings were determined by his own purposes. During Wheeler's frequent illnesses Kipling was in entire charge of the paper and of the printing plant, and he knew at a very precocious age what it was like to have 'about seventy men to bully and hector as I please', as he wrote on his seventeenth birthday (to Price, 30 December 1882: copy, Lorraine Price). The novelty of these things could not last long, however, and when the novelty was gone so was the pleasure.

When Kipling had proved to his disciplinarian editor that he could perform his routine soberly and capably he was, little by little, allowed to give his irresistible urge to write some exercise in other forms. By December of 1882 (and probably earlier) he was writing some of the miscellaneous editorial notes called 'scraps', brief items only a few paragraphs long at most, that made up the *CMG*'s front page after the telegraphic news had been accommodated. These scraps were based on topics from current news, and, though they might combine editorialising with description, and were sometimes facetious, they were not very adventurous.

No doubt Kipling also had some experience of writing all the other forms of editorial contribution — leaders, reviews, summaries, and the like — for we know that he sometimes had to do the whole duty of the paper whenever Wheeler was ill. We also know, from Kipling's plaintive recollection, that Wheeler considered translation an excellent discipline for his assistant, and regularly set him to translating from the Russian news contained in the official French of the *Journal de St. Peters-borough* or the *Nouveau Temps*.

Kipling's first venture into topical verse began in 1884 — one poem appeared in January, another in April, another in May. These were the first in a series that would continue throughout Kipling's stay in India and whose main memorial is *Departmental Ditties*.

Meantime, Kipling had been given his chance at what was to become the most distinctive form of his Indian journalism. In March of 1884 he had been sent to Patiala, a native state some 200 miles southeast of Lahore, to be 'special correspondent' for the *CMG* covering the state visit of the Viceroy, Lord Ripon, to open the Mohindar College. 'I was told to write as much as I could', he confided to an aunt (4 April 1884), and he responded by producing four long accounts of the cere-monies and the city (*CMG*, 20, 21, 22, 26 March) a total of about 10,000 words. This performance seems to have been accepted as proof of Kipling's fitness, for, as he wrote shortly after returning to Lahore, 'I have won my spurs as a descrip-tive special correspondent and even elicited approval from the far off Simla hills where my proprietors dwell' (4 April 1884). Other special assignments followed, the most demanding of which took Kipling in March and April of 1885 to the mouth of the Khyber Pass to cover the meeting of the Amir of Af-ghanistan with the Viceroy, Lord Dufferin; the result was a twelve-part series running over a three-week period. On his return from that assignment he was off to Simla, where, from June to August of 1885, he sent a steady flow of 'Simla Notes' to the *CMG*. And in November of that year he went on assign-ment to Ajmir to report the opening of the Mayo College by the Viceroy. Two years later, when Kipling was transferred from the *CMG* to its big sister, the *Pioneer* of Allahabad, his reputation as a special correspondent prompted his employers to put him on such work almost exclusively, an assignment that produced the articles collected in *Letters of Marque* and *The City of Dreadful Night*.

To return to Kipling at the beginning of his significant journalism early in 1884; it appears that Wheeler considered that his sub-editor might be allowed to exercise his abilities at home as well as abroad, for in May of 1884 Kipling began to write a weekly column called 'A Week in Lahore'. This ran irregularly for the next two years, trying to make something mildly interesting out of such stories as might be generated by the staid activities of municipal and official life. He also began to write accounts of local or near-local events such as native fairs, or the visits of theatrical troupes and other entertainers, or municipal celebrations, both English and native. One notable assignment led him through the cow-byres of the native quarter of Lahore to see at first-hand the origins of 'Typhoid at Home', as the resulting article was called. Apart from the fact that his 'special' assignments usually took him some distance away from Lahore, there is not much to distinguish them from his more local work: both show the same kinds of interests and powers at work in his writing.

Kipling may be said to have passed from his probationary state in 1884; by 1885 his production had become, compared with the trickle before that, a flood. Even within the limits of our seriously incomplete bibliographical knowledge it is clear that he was engaged in a copious production of quite varied material. The first of the short stories appeared as early as September 1884 ('The Gate of the Hundred Sorrows'), though it was not soon followed by others. He was also doing comic or descriptive sketches, more or less fictionalised, on such Indian topics and occasions as a bout of fever, or a Christmas day in exile, or a journey along the dubious roads of the hill country. These appeared either anonymously, as of course the great bulk of all that he wrote for the Indian papers did, or pseudonymously: his disguises might be ponderous, as in 'Hastings Macaulay Elphinstone Smallbones'; cryptic, as in 'Kingcraft' or 'Jacob Cavendish'; succinct, as in 'L. B.', or 'E. Y.', or 'S. T.', or, simply 'R'. The initials 'R. K.' began to appear at the end of some of these things in 1885, however, and by the end of his Indian career his name, without any further disguise or reticence, had become a valued means for selling newspapers. In 1885 too Kipling began sending contributions to journals other than the *CMG*, especially to the *Pioneer*, which was part of the family, but also to such publications as the *Calcutta Review*, the Calcutta *Englishman*, and the *Indian Planter's Gazette*.

As his professional achievements continued to grow, Kipling felt both undervalued and overworked at the *CMG*, where

Stephen Wheeler's initial mistrust of his new young assistant had never been fully overcome. A letter that Kipling wrote in 1886, when he had been on the staff for the better part of four years, makes vividly clear how he felt about the way in which he was used and, especially, about Wheeler's opinion that he, Kipling, was not reliable when it came to the labour of writing news paragraphs ('scraps') and of performing other routines (Allen in the passage that follows is Sir George Allen, founder of the *Pioneer* and a proprietor of the *CMG*):

About that notion which is abroad, that scraps delight me not nor routine work either. Allen said the same thing and then I sat tight, he being a full mouthed man and one [of my] owners to boot. Now I'll speak distinctly as the drunkard said. The whole settlement and routine of the old rag from the end of the leader to the beginning of the advertisements is in my hands and mine only; my respected chief contributing a blue pencil mark now and then and a healthy snarl just to soothe me. The telegrams also and such scraps as I or my father may write are my share likewise; and these things call me to office half one golden hour before, and let me out, always three quarters, sometimes a whole hour behind, my chief. My Sabbath is enlivened by the official visits of the printer and my evenings after dinner are made merry by his demands. So much for the routine to which I am averse. Of the scraps it is no profit to speak. They are pasted into a book with the days marked over them and are ready to be shown up the next time I have the 'aversion' brought officially to my notice.

On my word I fancy Allen must think I write my 'skits' in office hours. This is not so. You may bet your journalistic boots that if my worthy chief found any portion of the work which he did not conceive to be his share falling on his shoulders I should hear about it pretty sharply. The rhymed rubbish and the stuff like 'Section 420.I.P.C.' [the title under which 'In the House of Sudhoo' was first published] is written out of office for my own personal amusement — (I don't play tennis or whist or ride and my driving is no pleasure to me) — and then — O my friend — is damned as waste of time and only put in with a running lecture on the sinfulness of writing such stuff. Roughly speaking an extra half column of scraps

is necessary to prevent a talking to and ensure the reception
of a 'special'. Under these conditions is my 'play' writing
printed. When it is rejected — as happened in the case of my
'Other Side of the Question' I send it to the *Englishman* and
get Rs30. Otherwise of course I am not allowed to write for
other papers. I can't put what you call my 'higher flights'
aside any more than I/you can put aside the occasional
woman which is good for health and the softening of ferocious
manners. It's my amusement and like all amusements the
nicer for being discouraged. If you find the 'notion' floating
about any where you can combat it tell 'em like a good
fellow that if I *was* averse to routine and scraps they'd know
it in an unmistakeable way — from Wheeler, who would point
out that he was 'doing all my work', or else (his trump card)
'that I was making things hard for him'. He lives in nervous
dread of these things. I chuckle, because I am unregenerate.
He's a good man is my chief but he'll never burst a blood
vessel through hauling (to E. K. Robinson, 30 April 1886:
MS, University of Sussex).

Relief from the burden of Wheeler and his discouragements
came shortly after this letter was written, when Wheeler went
on leave and was replaced by Edward Kay Robinson, a young
man who had worked on the *Globe* in London and was now on the
staff of the *Pioneer*. He came to Lahore prepared not to inhibit
but to encourage his assistant's gifts, and it is from this period,
about the middle of 1886, that Kipling's career as a writer of
short stories began to blossom. Only two of the stories collected in *Plain Tales from the Hills*, Kipling's first book of stories,
had appeared in the four years of Wheeler's regime; within the
first half year of Robinson's new dispensation, ten of the stories
collected in *Plain Tales* had appeared, and they were only a
fraction of the total actually published in that time: many
remain yet uncollected. The two men made a major overhaul
of the paper in August 1887, partly designed to accommodate
and display Kipling's work. They bought new type, rearranged
the layout, and generally sought to brighten the looks of their
paper. On the revamped front page, now no longer devoted to
'scraps' but papered over with advertisements, the far right-
hand column was reserved for original contributions, and ran

over into the first column of page two. Items that appeared in this space came to be called 'turnovers', since one had to turn over the page in order to finish what began on page one. The space was not actually so captioned in the *CMG* itself, but when material from these columns was collected and published in a series of volumes by the *CMG*, 'Turnovers' was the title used for the series. These two columns of free space were shared by many contributors, but they were Kipling's special turf for the rest of his stay on the *CMG*. Between the first of August, when the paper's new design first appeared, and mid-November 1887, when Kipling left Lahore for Allahabad and the *Pioneer*, he filled many 'turnover' spaces with a variety of verses, sketches, skits, and stories.

It had long been clear to Kipling's proprietors — at least as early as his reports from Patiala in 1884 — that they had an unusually able property in the sub-editor of the *CMG*, and there had been talk on more than one occasion of translating him from the *CMG* to the *Pioneer* in Allahabad. The move was at last made in November 1887, and until his departure from India in March 1889, Kipling remained on the staff of the *Pioneer*. This paper, founded in 1865, was in Kipling's day regarded as the leading journal in all of India outside the presidency cities of Bombay and Calcutta, with whose papers it took at least equal rank. It was no small thing, then, to represent the *Pioneer*; it was all the more flattering to be made one of the paper's star performers, as Kipling soon was. At the beginning of 1888 the paper brought out a new weekly supplement called *The Week's News* and installed Kipling as its editor. He had been away on special assignment for the *Pioneer* when the supplement had been created, and his first knowledge of it was from the posters in the railway stations bracketing his name with that of Bret Harte as writers for the new weekly paper. *The Week's News* was, as Kipling wrote, largely a 're-hash of news and views' from the preceding week's *Pioneer*, but it also offered a page of fiction that it was Kipling's special business to fill. This he did with an astonishing energy and enthusiasm, providing week after week the stories that went into the books that first made his name with a public beyond India: *Soldiers Three, The Phantom 'Rickshaw, Wee Willie Winkie,* and the rest.

## II

Kipling's work on the *Pioneer* is, compared with that for the *CMG*, quite well documented: some things that he wrote remain unidentified; more still remain uncollected, but neither lot makes a large proportion of the whole. The case is quite different when we turn to his work for the *CMG*, with which this selection is entirely concerned (excepting one single item that first appeared in the *Pioneer:* 'Out of Society'). Until quite recently, the identification of Kipling's early work in India rested on a few very imperfect authorities. There was first the evidence of Kipling's own reprintings of his work; we know, for example, that he wrote 'The Gate of the Hundred Sorrows' in the *CMG* for 26 September 1884 only because he reprinted it in *Plain Tales from the Hills* four years later. Some of this reprinting was forced on him, notably in the case of the material in *From Sea to Sea* and *Abaft the Funnel*, first collected and published by American pirates and only then brought out in authorised editions. A second source of authorised identifications was created in 1896 when Kipling allowed (and presumably assisted) an editor to make extracts from his work for publication as *The Kipling Birthday Book:* a few of the items extracted in this collection came from previously unacknowledged writings for the Indian press and may be taken as certainly by Kipling. A third authorised source of identifications is the so-called Crofts Collection, a set of clippings of his work sent by Kipling to his old schoolmaster W. C. Crofts at different times in the 1880s, containing some twenty-two titles not otherwise identified. All told, Kipling identified by these direct and indirect methods some dozens and scores of his contributions to the Indian papers, but the body of work gathered into the canon in this way is of course a selection only. How rigid and narrow a selection could only be guessed, but once Kipling's fame was established at the outset of the 1890s there were many eager bibliographers and bibliophiles who were happy to guess. Files of the *CMG* and of the *Pioneer* were examined by professional bookmen, keen to find any track of Kipling across their pages. Promising titles, suggestive pseudonyms, characteristic subjects, notable turns of phrase — all suggested grounds for making attributions. Better-informed guesses were made by people who had some reason to know — friends, or colleagues, or interested comtemporaries. In this way, a very large list of conjectural attributions was built up. Two particularly enthusiastic collectors, the Englishman Captain Ernest W. Martindell and the American Ellis Ames Ballard, went to the expense of reprinting many of the items so identified, much to Kipling's annoyance (there is reason to think that Martindell, at least, had a commercial as well as an amateur interest in these reprints).

Kipling learned early to take a dim view of the bibliographers, for the same reason that he took a dim view of reporters: both were prying into things that he meant to keep private — his life, in the one case, and the unidentifiable body of his anonymous early work in the other. When an old friend who *did* know some of the secrets of his early work proposed that a selection from it should be published, Kipling at once demolished the idea: 'Well, a man does not like his boy-hood's play work (for that is what it comes to) being given to the public after nearly forty years' (to Mrs Hill, 18 February 1924: copy, University of Sussex). In that spirit, he steadfastly refused to assist the speculators, grimly accepting the annoying consequence that his silence would allow all sorts of unsupported attributions to go unchallenged. The most compendious record of this body of writings attributed to Kipling — almost all of it from the Indian years — is contained in the *Summary of the Work of Rudyard Kipling, Including Items Ascribed to Him* published by Admiral Lloyd H. Chandler in a limited edition in 1930. Following the guidance of Chandler and others, R. H. Harbord reprinted a good many of the early writings conjecturally attributed to Kipling in the first five volumes of his *Reader's Guide to Rudyard Kipling's Work*, privately printed, 1961—70. Inevitably, given the basis of their information, both Chandler's list and Harbord's reprintings contain many mistaken attributions.*

Kipling's more critical and cautious bibliographers, Flora Livingston in her *Bibliography*, 1927, and its Supplement, 1938, and James McG. Stewart in his *Bibliographical Catalogue*, 1959, treat the anonymous or pseudonymous Indian work very tentatively, accepting only a few items not identified in the

---

* Kipling left marked copies of Chandler's book and of Mrs Livingston's bibliography in which he denied the authorship of a great many items. The books are now at Wimpole Hall. Some of the things he denied he certainly wrote.

authoritative sources described above. Most of the careful
students of Kipling have been wisely content to accept the
guidance of Livingston and of Stewart. Louis Cornell, for
example, whose *Kipling in India*, 1966, is the most detailed
study yet made of Kipling's Indian work, confines himself
strictly to those items certified by Livingston and Stewart. At
the same time, it was obvious that Kipling must have written
far more than could be confidently identified. He had been,
after all, a working journalist in India for more than six years,
and the tale of his acknowledged writing bore no proportion
to what might certainly be expected from such a period of work.

Thus the matter stood until 1976. On the death in that year
of Kipling's daughter Elsie, Mrs George Bambridge, all of the
family papers in her possession passed to the National Trust and
were, a few years later, deposited in the University of Sussex
library. Among the materials thus laid open to public inspection
for the first time were the books of cuttings from Indian newspapers that had been kept by Kipling himself, and that preserved,
incompletely, but with a fullness unmatched elsewhere, the
record of his career in Indian journalism. There are four of these
scrapbooks, containing many hundreds of items from his pen,
almost all of them contributed to the Indian press between
1884 and 1891. Many of the cuttings are undated and without
any identification of the place where they first appeared. But
by a careful comparison of the materials in the scrapbooks with
the files of the *CMG*, the *Pioneer*, and other Indian papers, it
has been possible to assign almost every item in the scrapbooks
to a particular publication and a particular date. The writings
thus brought to light expand many times over the list of what
was previously known to be by Kipling during this period.
During his first two years in India, 1882 and 1883, Kipling does
not seem to have kept any scrapbook of his writings. The first
we have is from 1884, and it allows us to double the small list
of previously-identified items from that year. In 1885, the
quantity of newly-identified items multiplies many times over
what had been previously known or even conjectured. And so
throughout the rest of his years on the *CMG*. Altogether, the
four scrapbooks of Indian material contain 830 items not
previously attributed to Kipling. By far the greater part of this
total consists of 'scraps' for the *CMG*, the brief paragraphs on
the miscellaneous topics of the news that filled a part of the

front page of the paper under Wheeler and were relegated to the third page under Robinson. But besides 'scraps' there are among the new items some 140 original articles of all sorts: reviews, reports, sketches, stories, and leaders, on widely varying subjects, and ranging from the wholly impersonal to the highly characteristic. Four of the new items are translations from foreign news sources, and nine are verses. Of the 830 total items, fifteen come from the *Pioneer*, five from *The Englishman*; all the rest are from the *CMG*.

The original reason for keeping these scrapbooks appears to be that given in Kipling's letter to Kay Robinson of 30 April 1886: he wanted the ocular proof of his industry to show to anyone who might doubt his performance of routine or the quantity of his work. Once begun, however, the collection must have been kept going for its value to Kipling as well as for a defence against the complaints of his superiors. To judge from the evidence of revision made in Kipling's hand on a number of the clippings, he had some thought of using the scrapbooks as a reservoir from which he might draw reprintable items; in the event, however, he did very little of that. After he left India Kipling continued to keep a scrapbook record of his production: there are five further volumes among the Kipling papers at Sussex containing cuttings of his stories, poems, and articles, with an occasional typescript, from 1892 down to and after his death in 1936. They are not at all systematic, or complete, and one may guess that Mrs Kipling had more to do with their compilation than did Kipling himself. What they contain, with one or two possible exceptions, is well-known to the bibliographers, so that their interest is not comparable with that of the four scrapbooks from the Indian years.

Only a very few people seem to have known of the existence of these scrapbooks before the death of Mrs Bambridge brought them to public notice. No doubt Kipling's agents, A. P. Watt and his son A. S. Watt, had knowledge of them. There is evidence too that Kipling showed them, or at least made their existence known, to his first thorough bibliographer, Mrs Flora Livingston, though there was no question of her being able to make use of them. The two men who completed biographies based on the Kipling papers — Lord Birkenhead and Charles Carrington — both drew from the scrapbooks, but neither had time or occasion to straighten out the somewhat confused sequence of the

material, or to correctly identify the time and place of publication of the various cuttings.

To the record of the Indian scrapbooks the evidence from
two other sources has been added to extend the list of new
attributions from the Indian years: the diary that Kipling kept
in 1885, and the letters he wrote while in India. First, the
diary: Kipling left this document behind in Lahore by some
accident, and it ultimately passed into the collections of the
Houghton Library at Harvard. The entries are practically continuous down to the fourth of October, after which they
cease; there are some sections of personal interest, such as the
account of his walking tour in the Himalayas in May, but the
main business of the diary, and its main interest for us, is as a
record of his journalistic and literary work. In addition to its
list of writings already known, the diary confirms Kipling's
authorship of several items only conjecturally attributed to
him; most important, it identifies for the first time eighty-
one items contributed to the *CMG*: 59 scraps, 19 original items,
2 translations, and one verse. Incidentally, it establishes that
the Indian scrapbooks are incomplete, for it contains many
items missing from the scrapbook for 1885.

Kipling's letters written in India, the largest collection of
which is in the Kipling papers at the University of Sussex,
also add a few new items: ten original articles, and one set
of verses may confidently be attributed to Kipling from the
evidence so far discovered in his correspondence.

The total of newly-attributed pieces from Kipling's Indian
years arrived at through these three sources of information —
scrapbooks, diary and letters — is 927. The number of new
attributions is in fact greater than that, for there is evidence
in the letters for identifying some later works, but we are here
speaking only of the question of identifying new items from
Kipling's Indian years, and it is best to confine the discussion
to those limits. The task of accounting for all the new things
brought to light through the Kipling papers awaits the enter-
prising bibliographer who is prepared to overhaul and bring
up to date the pioneering work already done. But one may
note here that the list of uncollected items from Kipling's
Indian years in Louis Cornell's bibliography, which accurately
represents the state of knowledge before the Kipling papers
became public, gives a total of 118 (and a number of these are

not in fact by Kipling). The items now added to the list make an eight-fold increase; it is obvious that a new basis for the study of Kipling's Indian career is now available.

The quantity of new material now added to the body of Kipling's work is considerable; what about the quality? In and of itself it would never attract our attention now; it is interesting because it is Kipling's, and will be read for whatever it may have to tell us about the ways in which he might or did develop. The scraps, which are the most numerous of the new items, are usually written in editorial style and have little personal or expressive character. If one reads them *in extenso*, however, they do give a lively suggestion of the range of things that came under Kipling's notice and of the ability — essential to any journalist, no doubt — that he developed of saying something about nearly anything. George Eliot compares the journalist's art to that of the beater of gold leaf, whose business is to make the smallest possible amount of precious metal cover the largest possible area. Kipling certainly grew adept in that way. Perhaps it was in reaction to this demand of his newspaper life that he turned, in his fiction, to methods of rigorous exclusion and severe condensation. But there are many signs of the finished Kipling in these newspaper items, and if there is no single item that one would call distinguished, the effect made by a continued reading is of a vivid and distinct literary identity beginning to emerge through the routine forms of journalism.

## III

Very few people are likely to be able to sit down to a continued reading of this new material, unless they make a special trip to the University of Sussex to do so — and even there they would not find the nearly one hundred new attributions not included in Kipling's scrapbooks. Kipling could hardly have written for a less accessible medium than the *CMG*. Newspapers are ephemeral by definition and the Indian climate no doubt helped to confirm that definition; British India was not notable for its libraries, and in the west, where there were libraries, neither librarians nor readers were much interested in Indian newspapers. The consequence is that only two extensive files of the *CMG* are known to exist. One is in the India Office Library in London; the other, just recently brought back into public knowledge, is the file that belonged to the *CMG* office itself. The paper was suppressed by the government of Field Marshal Ayub Khan in 1963 and its building demolished to make room for new commercial development. For nearly twenty years the files were in limbo until, late in 1982, they were donated to the National Archives in Karachi. I have had no report on their condition, but it is likely that they suffered damage in their years of homelessness. There are short runs of the papers in a few libraries but nothing even approaching an extensive file. Practically speaking, then, there are only three places in the world where one may read what Kipling wrote for the *CMG* — London and Karachi for the paper itself, and the University of Sussex for the clippings in Kipling's scrapbooks. There are thus two kinds of practical difficulty in the way of reading Kipling's Indian journalism: inaccessibility and bulk. For the purposes of an unspecialised reader, a carefully-chosen selection would seem to be the best way to provide an idea of what that journalism is like.

As I see it, the articles here reprinted show that Kipling had two broadly different ways of looking at India. The first might be called the Official View, essentially paternalistic and administrative and not different from what one might suppose any responsible and mildly progressive Indian civil servant to have held. This is the view that urges on the native population the virtue of western education, of the improvement of the situation of women, and of good sanitation in the cities. This last was a favourite hobby of Kipling's, returned to again and again in the course of his Indian years: the outrageous stinks of the Indian cities, their dangerous and needless vulnerability to disease and infection, never ceased to work him up to good journalistic indignation, and the fervour of his preaching the gospel of good drains never diminished:

> Be it known to all men interested in so intensely important a fact, that the compiler of these notes will from the present date until further notice, in each issue of these notes, persistently and emphatically, in season, and out of season, abuse, vilify, scoff at, and bedaub with the mud of derision and the tar of opprobrium the slothful, unclean, reckless, negligent, stupid and irreclaimably perverse body corporate

known as the Lahore Municipality. . . . Lahore City is in as foul and as filthy a state as any city can be, which statement may be proved by standing to windward of the Delhi gate and gingerly sniffing the air therefrom. Further investigations in the narrow fetid gullies may be pursued at the risk of headache and nausea and graver distress. The gullies and bustees seethe and stink: the waterworks are out of order, and the end of these things will be disease and death (*CMG*, A Week in Lahore, 5 May 1886).

The official Kipling objected both to old-fashioned things like infant marriage, and to novel things like the native movement towards self-government, encouraged by the policy of Lord Ripon, the Viceroy. Here is a characteristic comment of Kipling's on the outcome of one experiment in self-government:

> The punishment of the Hoshiarpur Municipality has been extensively quoted by our contemporaries. The Bombay paper says justly: — 'The candle of Local Self-Government in Hoshiarpur has been blown out. The pity is that it was ever lighted in such an atmosphere.' As we know, the Municipality condoned appropriation of public land, because the filcher had erected a temple close to the sites in question. British justice and sense of corporate rectitude is shocked and scandalized; but the fault lies with that over-scrupulous weakness which has insisted on thrusting Western machinery into Eastern hands. The city fathers of Hoshiarpur acted according to their instincts and traditions. They would not have erred under the orders — not guidance but orders — of an English official, who took no interest in temples but a good deal in clear and clean roads. Left to themselves, they became themselves and that was all. . . . On the one side is a paper scheme. On the other all the influences of climate, caste and creed warring against the energy, impartiality and breadth of intellect which that scheme demands (*CMG*, 20 May 1887, p. 1d).

That is the paternalistic-official stereotype of the native fully developed: caste-ridden, venal, incompetent — a sort of larger child capable only of falling into trouble if left to himself. There is no reason to doubt that Kipling actually believed this.

He certainly repeated the account frequently enough in this newspaper manner without, so far as I can tell, any hint of doubt or irony. It may not be *all* that he believed on the question, however.

Allied to this view of the native is a frequently-expressed annoyance in response to 'ignorant' interference or judgements from 'home' — that is, the efforts of MPs and others to bring what they saw as 'reform' to India. Since they didn't 'know' India or the Indian, how could such interferings be anything better than dangerous nuisances? There is a lot of that attitude in the newspaper articles which need not, I think, be illustrated here. It is familiar enough from Kipling's stories. It combines a sort of orientalism — that is, a conviction that the natives are not suited by western forms — with a very western conviction that the English in India know best what is good for Indians. The inevitablity of contradiction in this position seems clear. But it expresses something more than simple contempt of the native in gross, for it includes the deeper distrust of democracy, and the fear of demagoguery.

But of course the natives were not the only topics of disapproval. If they had to be dragged into a world of sound drains and lighted streets, the other side of things was the failure of the English bureaucracy to provide drains and lights in a timely and efficient manner. Grumbling over the inadequacies of officialdom is a standard exercise in Kipling's journalism; again, it is too familiar from the stories to need illustrating here.

Perceptible under these perhaps superficial though powerful enough notions and responses is a sense of things that must have been in every English mind but could not be officially expressed. This was the anxiety of being alone in a world whose ways were not merely hostile — that was bad enough — but mysterious. So one could never be sure that one was getting anywhere. I think of two quite clear expressions of this. In 'The City of Evil Countenances' Kipling writes of an experience in which he was, for a moment, a lone Englishman literally surrounded by an alien crowd of northwest frontiersmen. The scene is so strange that it ceases to be human: 'Faces of dogs, swine, weazles and goats, all the more hideous for being set on human bodies, and lighted with human intelligence, gather in front of the ring of lamplight.' In this situation the only comfort is the appearance of the policeman, symbol of the English government, and the

sight of the 'magnificent drain and water main which runs
through the main streets of the city' — a kind of spiritual as
well as material plumbing. But then a splendidly savage Afghan
postures on a culvert, bringing western mechanics and eastern
barbarism into literal juxtaposition. And behind him there are
thousands more of the savages, whose language cannot be
understood and who, though they seem to accept restraint for
the moment, can never be reconciled to 'the white stranger
within their gates'. What hope of success can there be against
such odds? A variant of this perception, even more disturbing,
perhaps, occurs in 'Typhoid at Home', Kipling's repellent
discription of the conditions under which the city of Lahore
got its milk. As he penetrates deeper into the filth and darkness of the Lahore native quarter early on a February morning
he comes to a section which seems at first deserted but then is
suddenly revealed to him as concealing a multitudinous yet
indistinct and unformed life:

> But the dead walls, the barred and grated windows, and the
> high storeyed houses, were throbbing and humming with
> human life, as you may hear a hive of bees hum ere they go
> forth to their day's work. Voices of children singing their
> lessons at school; sounds of feet on stone steps, or wooden
> balconies over-head; voices raised in argument, or conversa-
> tion, sounded dead and muffled as though they came through
> wool; and it seemed as if, at any moment, the tide of un-
> clean humanity might burst through its dam of rotten brick-
> work and filth-smeared wood, blockading the passages below.

The combination of elements here is powerfully expressive:
ideas of disease, of teeming humanity, and of elemental force
come together in that 'tide of unclean humanity' against which,
when it comes, one will be quite helpless. Kipling, one imagines,
almost prefers the straightforward animal ferocity of 'The City
of Dreadful Countenances'. It is not fanciful to link such experiences as these to Kipling's persistent sense, expressed in so
many forms in his stories, of the fragility of civilisation, of the
unremitting need to defend the city against brute nature and
the barbarian.
The anxiety I have been describing belongs, I think, to the
official view of things in India, though it could not be given

official expression. For was it not just the perception that Indians were sunk in filth and barbarism that justified the English? Unluckily, the perception was thoroughly ambiguous, being both a call to action and at the same time a revelation that no action could make much difference or do much good.

Kipling's other view of India, the more personal and humane one, does not get so clear an expression as the official one does in his articles, but traces of it are there to be found by those who wish to look for it. It is in his accounts of the Amritsar fair, for example, in the alert and receptive interest he takes in the spectacle and its meaning. In sharp contrast to his response to the crowd in 'The City of Evil Countenances' and to the invisible crowd in 'Typhoid at Home', the response to the crowd in 'A Popular Picnic' is one of real pleasure, not least because the scene *is* alien: the men behave differently, the children behave differently, yet on their own terms and left to themselves they show both an impressive dignity and an attractive humanity. When the fair is over, Kipling's servant will return to his servant's role, and will no doubt be thoroughly unsatisfactory: 'But I saw another side of his character on the day when he piloted me through the packed tumult of the Chiragan fair of 1886. And it's very curious.' Does the irony of that last observation touch Indians or English more nearly? At any rate, when Kipling is rendering the Indian scene for its own sake, delighting in its variety and copiousness, and responding to the individuality of its people, he is very different from the Kipling who writes about India in relation to English purposes and English standards. Another instance of his attentive and sympathetic rendering of popular life is the description of maulvis and hajjis at the end of 'The City of the Two Creeds', an instance all the more striking by reason of the fact that Kipling himself seems to have had no liking for dogmatic religion in any form. Given the nature of his newspaper work and the clientele for which he wrote, his opportunities for this free rendering were not very many. But when he had them he took them.

Within the general subject matter of India there is plenty of room for many of Kipling's characteristic concerns. Children, for example, frequently catch his interested eye, whether they are the native children of 'A Popular Picnic' or the English children of 'Simla Notes', 29 July 1885. So do animals, which he is already able to present in his inimitable way as having an intelligent life without ever ceasing to be animals. The two extremes of English life in India that Kipling made particularly his own also appear: soldier life and Simla society. Several characteristic themes and special interests may be noted in these articles. The idea of the necessary breaking-in of the restive individual to a constructive discipline is given amusing expression — in animal terms — and with some real descriptive brilliance in the account of the imperturbable Captain Hayes and the fractious horse. Kipling's high admiration for technical competence appears repeatedly — in 'An Armoured Train', for example, and in the two very interesting accounts of bridges, 'The Sutlej Bridge' and the 'Chak-Nizam Bridge'. That admiration is part of a broader admiration, not just for the technician but for the professional or craftsman in general, and particularly to the sort of professional who can be seen as a version of the artist. Take the *Nats* of 'A Popular Picnic', for example:

> My friend the *chaprassi* said that the *Nats* who walk on slack ropes and balance themselves on bamboos, were the best part of the show. He was quite right. Their performances were very wonderful, and their tackle so insecure, that you expected a fall every minute from the rope to the stones below. On an average they collected two annas per performance, and they performed five times in three hours; but they never hurt themselves, which was what the crowd seemed to want.

The thing being done is quite trivial, but it is at the same time 'very wonderful'; and though the rewards are pitiful, there is a sense in which the *Nats* are beyond that consideration. Their skill is such that 'they never hurt themselves', and so disappoint the crowd's expectation; thus, though they are ostensibly striving to please the crowd, they also leave the crowd behind in the endeavours of their art.

Or take 'The Biggest Liar in Asia'. The mark of this artist is to choose the least profitable material and to transform it, and to do so without evident effort, his art concealing art. But, like the king who slew the slayer and shall himself be slain, he knows that his reign is never secure; his supplanter already exists and his defeat, in the fullness of time, is certain. Clearly, this is a man who works for no ordinary reward, but, like the *Nats*, seeks his recompense in the pure exercise of his art. The treatment of all these things is lightly comic, but the things treated are full of suggestion.

There is a connection to be made, perhaps, with another identifying theme in Kipling's work, that of self-sacrifice and the willing endurance of pain and fatigue in the service of one's responsibility — whether that be administration, or bridge-building, or dentistry in Afghanistan, or railway repair or newspaper work. This appears, not as an explicit topic, but as an assumption, a way of looking at all sorts of diverse things that arise in the course of journalistic reporting. Sometimes he writes about literal sickness. Fever, entailing struggle, horror and exhaustion, is the price that the Englishman pays for his position in India. In Kipling's treatment (e.g., 'De Profundis'), fever unites in a single symbolic experience the strains of official work with the sense of loneliness and abandonment in a strange land.

The astonishing descriptive skill for which Kipling is famous is evident, at least intermittently, at a very early point in these articles. Take this modest but characteristic sample from 'The Sutlej Bridge':

> Here the whole face of the country is scarred and scraped and scooped for the earth of the roadways. There is a faint feverish smell from the damp silt soil, and every where the eye falls on interminable processions of donkeys and donkey-drivers — laden beasts climbing up, and unladen ones going down. The sound of the thousands of little hoofs on the soft earth, and the never-ending 'thud' of the loads as they are tipped off, makes a bass drone, to which the rattle and thump of the donkeyboys' sticks supplies a staccato treble accompaniment.

The skill with which a large complex scene of movement and sound has been grasped and rendered rapidly but vividly is already highly developed.

But it is needlessly narrow to confine these remarks only to those things that Kipling later developed, or that critics have agreed upon to talk about in his work. It is not the least part of the interest of these early items to see Kipling trying out methods and manners that he did not go on with, or that belonged strictly to the earliest phases of apprenticeship. Nor should any editorial commentary be needed to bring out what is evident on the surface of these articles. The young Kipling was full of the joy of literature, eager to show his knowledge of books and authors through allusion and quotation; he took delight in imitation and parody, as testing his skill and showing his right to join the company of writers. And, as he looked alertly on the life presented to him, he added to it his own good spirits, his gift for phrase, his comic intervention, and his sympathetic interest in the variety of human responses to experiences of common concern. The articles presented in this selection from Kipling's Indian journalism must be read for what they are — the unpretentious productions of a young journalist writing his daily assignments — but they were, after all, the productions of no common ability, and they will, I think, enrich and confirm our perception of his more mature and ambitious accomplishments.

## A Note on the Text

All of the articles are reprinted here as they appeared in the *Civil and Military Gazette*. Written for a daily newspaper, they were necessarily subject to the pressures of haste. Moreover, the texts were set up, by hand, by men who did not know the meaning of what they set. The press-room staff of the *CMG*, except for the Scottish foreman, was all Indian, a mixture of Muslim, Hindu, and Sikh. The possibilities for error in carrying MS copy over into type were therefore far greater than would ordinarily be the case, and the ordinary case is bad enough. Kipling constantly complained about the state of the proofs that he had to correct.

In the circumstances, the standard of printing and proofing in the *CMG* is surprisingly good. Articles in the paper are nevertheless liable to the ordinary typographical errors, and sometimes to errors not so ordinary. Rather than perpetuate these I have silently smoothed out the text by replacing omitted particles, by adding missing marks of quotation or parenthesis, by supplying punctuation where the sense seemed to demand it, by deleting inadvertent repetitions, and by correcting the misspelling of standard names (e.g., Americian). Any other editorial alterations are signalled by being placed in square brackets [    ]. Many irregularities in spelling and punctuation remain, sometimes

because there was no certain solution to their mystery, sometimes because they seemed to me to offer no difficulty to the
reader.

# The Viceroy at Patiala

*Civil and Military Gazette, 22 March 1884*

**Attribution: Kipling to Edith Macdonald, 4 April 1884**

Lord Ripon, the Viceroy from 1880 to 1884, paid a state visit
to the Maharajah of Patiala on the occasion of the opening of
the Mohindar College in Patiala. The Maharajah, still a minor,
was the titular head of the most important of the Sikh states of
the Punjab, under British protection since 1809 and lying on
the plains of the Eastern Punjab some two hundred miles from
Lahore. The Mohindar College had been officially founded on
the occasion of another viceregal visit, by Lord Northbrook in
1875, to encourage education in a state notably backward in
that respect among the Punjab states. The Maharajah after
whom the college was named had died in 1876, however, and
progress had not been rapid thereafter. The things that Kipling
found furnishing the palace in such profusion had been standing
undisturbed in the eight years since the late Maharajah's death.
   This article is the third of four that Kipling wrote from
Patiala; the others cover the Viceroy's arrival, the ceremony of
opening the college, and the durbar that followed.

Patiala, March 20

This morning, at six o'clock, Lord Ripon and Staff went shooting to Bunnarhair, some six miles away. The party returned
about noon, having killed plenty of hare and teetur; a black
buck was also sighted, but escaped. Lady Ripon did not accompany the party, and spent the greater part of the day in the

Moti Bagh Gardens. At present, and until the evening, there is
nothing going on in the Viceregal camp. Tonight, as I have
already telegraphed, Lord Ripon returns the young Maharajah's
visit and holds a kind of Durbar in the palace. Preparations for
the Durbar are being made now, and the large hall in which it
will take place is worthy of description. Imagine a room seventy
yards long and thirty yards wide literally crammed with chandeliers and crystal fountains of white, red, and green glass;
throw in acres of mirrors, scores of alabaster statues, Persian
rugs, a gold kincob carpet five yards square, and two massive
silver-gilt chairs-of-state, and it is possible to obtain some faint
idea of the Durbar Chamber. Three of the big glass chandeliers
alone are said to have cost two-and-a-half lakhs of rupees. They
stand thirty feet high and hold about two thousand lights each.
But it would need the pen of Walt Whitman, the inspired auctioneer of the universe, to describe half the wonders of that
glittering room. In the daytime, with the vivid sunlight streaming
in upon thousands of rainbow-coloured glass drops, and sheets
of gold embroidery, it seemed as unreal as Alladin's Cave. What
it will be to-night, when the myriads of candles are lit, and the
floor is gay with native dresses, may be imagined.

Patiala Palace is an enormous white building, in the middle of
the city. This morning I explored as much as was open to
European visitors. The first object of interest, as the guide-
books say, is the Patiala State Museum, and the way in which
the museum was formed was as follows. When Mohindra Singh,
the present Maharajah's father, died, he owed various Calcutta
tradespeople close upon nine lakhs of rupess, and had, during
his life, dealt with them to three or four times that extent in
cash. (Those who are interested in the affairs of this state may
remember how the shop-keepers of Calcutta flocked to Patiala
as soon as the news of the Maharajah's death reached them, and
clamoured for payment in the Moti Bagh: the Council of
Regency, of course, satisfied all claims.) The Maharajah's method
of procedure was peculiar and expensive. Walking into a shop,
he would take 'all on that side the counter', or all in the shop,
as his royal fancy moved him, and, after his decease, his purchases formed the Patiala Museum. One room is called the arm-
oury, and contains the gold-mounted swords given to the
Maharajah by the Prince of Wales and Lord Lytton. In racks
round the room are hundreds of double-barrelled fowling-

pieces of the best make, and on a long table down the centre lie hundreds of gun cases that have never even been opened. Rook rifles, military sniders, gold-mounted Remington repeating rifles, breech-loading pistols, silver mounted revolvers, stick guns, and many other varieties of lethal weapons may be seen here in scores or dozens, just as they were bought, mixed up with Brown-besses, obsolete breech-loading rifles of a pattern twenty years old, and naval carbines. At present they are neglected and dusty, but I am told that, when the young Maharajah comes to power, they will all pass to him. Happy young Maharajah!

In another room are the State howdahs and palanquins and the silver carriage, which, I learn, was made entirely in the Patiala State. The cushions are purple velvet and gold, the whip ivory and silver gilt, and the body of the carriage silver gilt; everything being in perfect keeping, except a square of tawdry Brussels carpet at the bottom of the carriage.

Ascending many stairs we come to another department of the Museum. When His Highness bought any thing he did it wholesale, and everything is repeated many times over. I counted a hundred and fifty penknives, twenty or thirty nail-brushes of various patterns, and then gave it up as a hopeless task. At the risk of being tedious I will give a list of a few of the more prominent features of the department. Bolts, nuts, and screws in assorted cases, sheets of lead; wire net-work, zinc and tin, ten or twenty of each; albums in Russia leather, malachite, ivory, mother-of-pearl, silver, onyx and agate, piled anywhere and anyhow; dressing bags in scores; liqueur stands, riding whips, sausage-machines, champagne-tweezers, candle-sticks, and chimney-piece ornaments more than I could count; pictures of all kinds, piled face to the wall; twenty-seven brass parrot cages, and fourteen courier bags; an assortment of cigar and card-cases in tortoise-shell and gold; several telescopes and binoculars, dozens of glove cases in agate and onyx; then musical boxes as big as small organs, stereoscopes, patent medicines, patent inks, and a flock of India-rubber decoy ducks, flattened and dusty, butcher's scales, spring balances, and Bramah locks and children's toys, all of the newest and most expensive kinds. This is not a tenth part of the contents of that room, and it was a little depressing to see how everything was gradually being spoilt with neglect.

As I was leaving, an official asked me if I would care to see His Highness's dressing cases. I had seen nearly a hundred, and explained that it was all very grand, but a trifle monotonous. Then the official told me that the dressing cases he referred to had cost half-a-lakh each, and I changed my mind. Each case stood four feet high and was mounted in solid silver with the Maharajah's monograph 'M.S.S.' in silver half-a-foot long, on the outside. Inside was a complete service for dressing, dining, and writing, surgical instruments, and cheroot cases, all in silver with the Maharajah's monogram in blue and white enamel on each article. A complete set of plate in silver, and a whole stand of liqueur bottles made up the contents, which numbered over two hundred and fifty articles, all embedded in purple velvet. When I say that the toilet service was silver, I would be understood in the most literal sense. Every bottle and case was of solid silver throughout. Unfortunately the Maharajah died before the dressing-cases reached him from England — for which he is a good deal to be pitied.

They must be worth every rupee of the hundred thousand spent on them, and, however much I might write about them, I should fail to give any idea of their appearance. It would be worth while to visit Patiala to see those dressing-cases alone. In common with all the other things, they are sadly neglected, and one is so warped that the lock is hampered and will not open.

Further exploration of the Palace led to some curious discoveries. I had been close upon two hours in the building, and was only on the outskirts of it. Ten minutes' wandering across huge silent squares, baking in the sunlight, and through innumerable dark passages, brought me out to a second and smaller edition of the wonders I had left behind. More chandeliers, more statues and knicknacks, but all of a much older date, and covered with the dust of years. Two or three natives, who looked as if they had grown grey in the guarding of these treasures, salaamed wearily as I entered, and were good enough to leave me alone. Beyond these aged servitors not a soul was visible, though, all round the square, (it was the third I had entered) I could hear steps and the sounds of far off voices, and, now and then, the noise of suppressed laughter.

Here, too, were more albums, bound in blue velvet, but dusty and frayed at the edges, and holding photographs of Indian worthies long since dead or retired. None of them bore a later date than twenty years ago, and I discovered portraits of the Princess Beatrice in short dress and crinoline, the Prince of Wales, a young man with all his hair on: Lord Lawrence and his brother seated at a table, directing the affairs of our Province; General Chamberlain and the Strachey brothers; Lord Napier of Magdala, youthful and gay of appearance; Sir Donald Macleod; Sir George Grey and his Council, in the days when that gentleman was Lieutenant-Governor of Calcutta; all the heroes of the Mutiny and the capture of Delhi, and, lastly, the immortal Patti, a young and graceful *prima donna* with a huge chignon. Besides these, there were photos of regiments in India long ago, notably the Black Watch, the 90th Regiment, now the Scottish Rifles, and the 73rd Highlanders. One of the most interesting photos was a representative of a picnic under the walls of Jumrood twenty years back. The belle of the station wore a big crinoline, dressed her hair strangely, and all the lovely 'spins' of that period looked out of the soiled page like a collection of long-buried ghosts. It is more than possible that the only remembrance of that picnic remains shut up in the walls of the Patiala Palace — not often to be disturbed. Behind the album stood the grandfather of all the sewing-machines in the world — bobbin-less, rusty and paralyzed — adding not a little to the strangeness of the scene. Knicknacks from the Exhibition of 1861, a large steel engraving of the Queen's marriage, coffee-coloured anti-maccassers, and the gruesome wool-work in which our ancestors so delighted, all helped out the idea that I had suddenly stepped out of the life of to-day, and had gone back a quarter of a century at least.

When I left the dusty, faded purchases of the late Maharajah, I wandered, through more passages, into an assembly of grey-beards seated in one of the most charming looking-glass rooms I had ever seen. Gold leaf and coloured glass, in a strong sunlight, are apt to be garish and overbold in colouring; but time had toned down this small chamber till it looked like a very opal. Persian rugs were spread on the floor, and on these rugs sat five aged men in spotless white, doubtless discussing State affairs among themselves. As soon as they recognized the pres-sence of a Sahib among them, they rose *en masse*, and, with the greatest gravity, proceeded to 'shoo' me out of their presence as one might 'shoo' a strayed fowl. It seems that I had trespassed too close to the ladies, and as none of the five elders understood English, they had adopted this course in order to let me understand that it was as well to withdraw. I took the hint, and managed to rejoin modern civilisation in the shape of the barouche kindly placed at my service by the authorities in the great outer square. There appeared to be no end to the Palace, whose white walls go half across the city, and, in the old times, it must have seen many strange sights. All noises are stifled or dulled by the masses of brick and masonry, and any deed of violence committed in one of the thousand winding passages would run but little risk of being detected.

The elephant fight here has been postponed till to-morrow; one elephant only being *must* at present. It is to take place on the *maidan* outside the city, and promises to be a big thing of its kind.

# A Week in Lahore

*Civil and Military Gazette, 7 May 1884*

**Attribution: Sussex Scrapbooks 28/1, p. 68**

The articles that ran under this title, a series beginning with this item of 7 May and running irregularly until 2 June 1886, were apparently all written by Kipling, a total of thirty-six in all. The articles were notable in the *CMG*, since that paper austerely neglected most of the local news — the comings and goings, the amusements, the ceremonies, the casual triumphs, accidents, and disappointments of daily life as it unfolded among the English in Lahore. Kipling was assigned to the work rather than offering to do it, and his letters contain several complaints about the difficulty and tedium of the task. He signed them with the name of 'Esau Mull', or, simply, 'E.M.' A 'Mull', in Anglo-Indian slang, was a civil servant from the Madras Presidency, 'mull' being short for mulligatawny. What allusion Kipling had in mind, if any, I do not know.

Most of whatever interest these articles may have had orig-inally has long since perished with the little community to which they were addressed. Yet there are moments of observation and remark that may still engage us, partly for what they tell us about the India in which Kipling lived, and partly for what they tell us about Kipling himself. I have accordingly chosen to reprint not complete articles in the 'Week in Lahore' series but such extracts as I have judged to carry this double interest.

It is more than possible that the last paragraph of this item was written by John Lockwood Kipling.

Lahore — when almost all who can have taken their leave to the Hills, and the 'coppersmith' is busy all day tolling the knell of departed cold-weather delights — has no history of its own. You shall find it tastefully scattered round the band stand (at least thirty strong) on Friday nights, or lolling, like Tennyson's Godlets, who were so offensively remiss in their duties to mankind, over iced drinks in the Lawrence Hall Gardens. Yet the whole symposium in archaic carriages or cane-bottomed lounging chairs will not, from a newswriter's point of view, repay fifteen minutes' study. Lahore has, in fact, aestivated and will not awake again till October, when the rains have abated off the surface of the earth, and the voice of the returning Hill birds is again heard in the land. For such at home as believe that the Englishman in India spends his highly-paid days in slaying cobras and 'walking in the jungle' (this last is always insisted upon, after the returned Prodigal has explained that snakes are far from common in a Punjab station) the mournful spectacle of a dozen hot men, slowly absorbing cold drinks under the shadow of a red-hot Stucco palace, would be both healthful and instructive.

This deep peace of ours is only broken by the arrival of strangers from other, and hotter, climes — Mooltan *par exemple*. The vivifying coolness of our station acts like a charm upon these visitants, and a shower is to them pleasure unalloyed. Some few weeks ago a Mooltan man and a thunderstorm burst upon the station together. As the first big drops fell on the roof of the club, the Stranger abandoned his billiard cue and hurried out, with upturned face, into the compound, where he stayed, rapturously smiling at the clouds, till thoroughly wet. 'I haven't seen rain for three years', was the explanation tendered to a delighted bystander, and the moral of this story is that, in spite of the dead calm which broods over the station there are others worse off then we. [A paragraph on the Indian practice of adulterating wheat follows.]

A people whose tobacco is — well, what it is — cannot, in the very nature of things, be expected to set a high value on the purity of their wheat. It was once the writer's misfortune to watch some cheap tobacco in process of manufacture for the *chillum*. The tobacconist was old and withered — it must have been from long sitting on a cranky board over an offensive drain. At the edge of the roadway, where the dust of traffic blew densest, and the pariah dog took refuge from the passing *ekka*, lay the tobacco in dusty sheaves on a coarse cloth; and the buyer, a young and sprightly coolie, whose only clothing appeared to be a brass tooth-pick slung round the neck, was allowed — but not without much altercation — to take his choice from it. This he intimated to the Ancient with an expressive gesture of the toes and forthwith the bundle was triturated, soaked, rolled, and thumped in an evil looking cloth of doubtful parentage, till it oozed out on the board abovementioned, a brown sticky mass. The water, by the way, was hastily caught up in a *chatty* from the running stream below, and it must have been to counteract its peculiar bouquet that the Ancient stirred in what he said was 'attar of roses', from a dirt-encrusted beer-bottle. A little lime mixed with more water, a careful handful of something that looked like dried tamarinds and smelt like all Colognecity made the 'gruel thick and slab', and a few deft pats and punches slid it into a large dried leaf, fit for immediate use. Then it was revealed to me, as the coolie went away with this terrible compost in the folds of his turban, that India could never be great nor prosperous, nor enlightened, till her teeming millions were taught to respect the gift of the American dryad and to smoke their weed pure and undefiled.

We seem to be all agreed to praise our Railway management and nobody will deny that, if a Briton wished to swagger — and at times this duty is incumbent upon him — he might challenge the world to match our achievements in this line. But there are spots on the sun, and I humbly venture to submit that the native subordinate staff does not, as a rule, know its business. Why should a booking office clerk take six minutes and a half by a Shrewsbury clock, to get two first-class tickets and a third, to Amballa? Why should he tell passengers to go to distant parts of the station for tickets to Dinanaggar on the new Pathankot line, and why, oh why, does he make mistakes with your change? I am perfectly aware that you cannot buy an extensive range of accomplishments for fifteen rupees a month, but, surely, in an important station like Lahore, some pains might be taken to teach Nubbi Baksh his business. At the Punjab College, they teach Milton and Chaucer — and if report be true, squabble over these worthies at times — and other branches of learning may be studied at the High Schools, but nobody seems to give any instruction in Railway work. There are a number of decorative persons, mostly of the Eurasian persuasion, in Lahore Railway Station, whose business seems to be to emerge from the recesses of the Station building a few minutes before the arrival of a train, and to exist beautifully until its departure. Their duties consist, so far as one may see, in wearing caps with silver monograms, in brandishing lanterns — this is not often undertaken — and in discussing the affairs and festivities of the Punjab Rifle Volunteers. Nubbi Baksh does all the work with which passengers are concerned and he might be taught to do it a great deal better. He is docile enough, and, if closely looked after, willing. On occasion, too, he is affable, but affability is not a virtue included in the fifteen-ruppe-per-mensem contract, and Nubbi Baksh wisely sticks to the letter of the bond.

If I were a native third-class passenger, by the way, I should most certainly appear daily before Mr Parker or Mr Clarke, on charges of assaulting those decorative young persons with the lettered caps and lanterns. Native passengers are stupid, troublesome — anything you like — but they ought to be treated more like human beings than they are. The official swells at the head of affairs say that they are willing to deal promptly and severely with any cases that may be brought to their notice, but you can't cure the unnecessary rudeness and truculence of manner which I am sorry to say, has grown into a confirmed habit with many of the European and Eurasian subordinates on our Railways, by an official wigging. I give the following brilliant idea for what it is worth: — Let some of the Heads of Departments disguise themselves in the garb of the country, and, as cultivators or craftsmen, take their chance among the dingy crowds that are hustled, pushed, and driven, like bullocks into their pens whenever a train arrives. Surely, there is enough dramatic talent in the S.P. and D. Railway to work out this priceless notion, with a view to reporting on it afterwards [ . . . .]

It is a question for philosophers to settle whether the clouds of fine cinder dust blown up into the higher atmosphere by the Javanese volcano have moderated the sun's heat, as well as enriched his evening splendour with a crimson afterglow. This notion is seriously entertained by scientific observers in America, and, up in the Punjab, we are quite willing to believe that some influence has been at work to keep our air fresh and cool. But the tyrannous sun is not to be denied and, at last, the hot weather seems to be setting in. The untidy *siris* tree that scatters pods all the year round is now flinging abroad her scented plumes of flowers and unfolding her late leaves. The *shisham* is in full foliage with a wealth of that clear bright green which seems to defy the scorching heat. The mulberry's shabby fruit, and the mean, dry figs of the *pipal* have attracted immense flights of a pretty black and white starlings known to some as the 'mulberry bird', and every native who could get a gun of any sort has been out after them. In the Gurdaspur district, where mulberries are plentiful flocks of these starlings seem to stretch for half a mile across the sky, and they are netted in some numbers. In the great division of nature into things good to eat and things not good to eat, they stand in class No. 1; but they are not so tasty as snipe, nor so succulent as quail. The pairing time of most birds is about over. Our summer visitors have come and are taking toll of the insects. Bronze green bee-eaters, who will presently set up housekeeping in holes in dry banks, like sand martins and others, are hard at work thinning our winged plagues. The small Indian honeybee, not much larger than a house fly, is still rummaging the fading flowers and building her comb in the fork of a *ferash* tree, until the Department of Revenue and Agriculture shall issue instructions for taming and 'exploiting' her. The beautiful brown and yellow hornet blunders down your unstopped chimneys, and the pale yellow wasp, nimble on the wing but feeble afoot, has begun its summer course of crime. The brilliant ichneumon-fly, one of the most indefatigable workers of the insect tribe, is now fetching head loads of finely tempered mud, at the rate of one every two minutes, and building neat little grottoes, which she fills with fat-bodied spiders, preserved by some antiseptic

secret of her own, till the time when her infant successor shall
be ready to eat his way through their soft bodies to the shell of
his domicile, and so into the free air. The burly black and
yellow carpenter bee, who has the gift of drilling holes in timber
as round and smooth as if done by steel augers at the Railway
workshops, is driving his tunnels into all the dead wood he can
find and storing them with the dry, waxy *goor*like honey it is
his speciality to manufacture. The many kingdoms of the ant
world are in lively motion, and their highways are alive with a
harvest time of grass seed. Some of them, like two-legged cultivators, are threshing, and their chaff may be seen in large quantities. The omnivorous hoopoe is down on them, since she is
feeding her little hoopoes in their evil-smelling nest. This pretty
bird in her domestic interior is careless and dirty. All nature, in
short, seems to be alive and busy, while we must resign ourselves
to make as good weather of it as we can with the help of the
punkah, and, later, the thermantidote.

Esau Mull.

# A Week in Lahore

*Civil and Military Gazette, 21 May 1884*

**Attribution: Sussex Scrapbooks, 28/1 p. 71**

One of the main objects of Lord Ripon's vice-regal administration was to encourage local self-government in Indian cities. The
policy met with predictable suspicion and dislike among English
administrators, fully shared by Kipling: they called the idea
'lokil sluff', in derision of the native pronunciation of the
phrase 'local self-government'. Nevertheless, Lahore was one of
the cities to elect natives to its municipal council. Here Kipling
describes what the elections were like. The *Tribune*, referred to
towards the end of the sketch, was a native weekly paper in
Lahore.

Lahore Elections

Each ward (the City proper is divided into eight) is served with differently tinted voting papers, which must be brought up to the poll by the voters in person — a system which they wholly fail to understand. 'If Ram Singh *père* is sick,' say they, 'why on earth cannot Ram Singh *fils*, a fine growing lad of ten, bring up his Papa's vote?' In the beginning, all the various ward papers were white, but this led to so much queer dealing on the part of the candidates, and opened a way to so much quiet swindling, that coloured ones were substituted. Elections take place in the early morning, and, long before the hour of opening the poll, the ground is covered with a swaying many-voiced crowd, eagerly discussing each candidate's chances, and impartially accusing everyone concerned in the matter of flagrant bribery and corruption. At one ward election I noticed that every circle of talkers had a gay-turbaned, deep-voiced centre man, and by this centre man the movements of the circle were regulated — a faint adumbration, hereafter to be made perfect, of the 'boss' system in ward politics. He looked after the wavering among his followers, as a mother hen might guard her brood from the machinations of a kite, and secured them good places in the crowd. The appearance of a white face on the ground was the signal for a volley of complaints from Young India — aghast at the audacity of a mob which had dared to disregard his claims, and clamourous in denunciation of So and So's 'base tricks'. 'Let us,' cried one gentleman, clad in robes as snowy as his principles, 'let us lay aside our personal feelings and vote for an able man. But the mass of the people are not sufficiently educated for this.' And they weren't. They could understand voting for a man, be he Hindu, Mahomedan, or Sikh, who, in time of need, might sanction the enlargement of their *tharrahs* and wink at the blockade of the drain below. Also they could understand food and four-anna pieces, and, in place of these things, young India offered them principles and patriotism, and they heeded him not. They were not sufficiently educated.

The Munsiff's court house, where this election was taking place, was a small two-roomed bungalow, bare as the Mian Mir parade ground, if we except two green baize tables, two chairs and an indifferent punkah. Voters were to enter at one door of the frowsy little den, vote and pass out at another. Five candidates had presented themselves for election, and five iron files, each marked with a candidate's name, were drawn up in line on one of the tables, ready to impale the voting papers as they were given in. At another table, the votes were registered on paper and, when the poll closed, file and register were compared for accuracy's sake. Each voter was supposed to be identified at the door and had then to give up his name and voting paper to the Deputy Commissioner. As soon as this, official made his appearance, the crowd, now a thousand strong, closed up behind his steps, and the police, from the barrack hard by, linked themselves hand to hand, and, breasting the crowd as a swimmer might breast the sea, kept it, by main force, from overwhelming the verandah and spiking itself *en masse* on the voting files. Up and down the cleared space pranced a native Inspector Sahib, and, at his bidding, some twenty men at a time would be admitted into the verandah, formed into an orderly *queue* and sent, one by one, to vote. For two long hours the reeking policemen bore up against the pressure from without, and if at times, the blue and yellow line broke without the Inspector Sahib's order, let us say that it was from sheer weariness of muscle, and not as Young India — ever at one's elbow with grievances and objections — hinted, from the magic of any silver talisman. When the first *queue* was in position, a khaki-clad darogah threw open the doors of the court house, and the great machine that is to regenerate all Aryavarta began to work.

The darogah read out each man's name as he entered, and handed up the voting paper to the Deputy Commissioner. Then came the question '*kis ki wasti raz hai?*' ['who do you vote for?] and the voter, having recorded his vote, was motioned onward by two police men, and passed through the opposite door almost as swiftly as the coloured slip of paper could be stuck to its proper iron. That, in effect, was all. A machine which combined the swiftness and despatch of a Chicago sausage maker (for the voters slid through that court house at a rate varying from six to fourteen to the minute) with the mechanical freedom from error of Babbage's calulator. Its very simplicity, as it ground out the tale of votes in the bare evil-smelling little room, made it all the more impressive. The Deputy Commissioner, be it remarked, had to take the voting slips from each man and put them on their appropriate files, and his share of the proceedings seemed only second in point of unpleasantness to that of the straining, swaying policeman outside. Sometimes in the middle of a long 'break' of brown voters there would be a check — a minor had presented himself with his father's voting paper, or an aged father had come in place of his son. This would cause an interruption just long enough to scribble a note on the back of the doubtful paper, and to cut short the long account of that fever fit which had prevented Mahomed Din or Gopal Dass from attending in person. The expostulator passed out like the pig in the grip of the sausage machine, impelled by the current behind, and, almost ere he had time to realize the situation, was shot once more into the crowd without. Then the monotonous labour would commence anew, till the recurring *'kis ki wasti raz hais'*, the crisp sound of the voting papers as they slid down the file, and the hum of the waiting crowd, wove themselves into a sleepy sort of song, broken at long periods by the detection of a 'doubtful vote', and its banishment to a distant corner of the green table. Some of the voters produced the white papers that had been originally issued, vowing that they had received no others; others who had voted for other wards turned up to try their luck a second time; were dropped on and swiftly dismissed. How on earth the lynx-eyed registrar of the votes could be sure of his men, will remain a mystery till the crack of doom, but the culprits owned up and passed on with a propitiatory smile, and seemed in no way disconcerted. Now and then too, the barrier of police outside would give way and had to be reconstructed with yells and evil language, for the crowd was helplessly jammed and had to be thrust back *en masse*, while the heads of the circles, mentioned before, waxed purple in the face in their efforts to keep their constituencies out of the reach of the evil communications that were corrupting good voters on every side. Young India, still to the fore, and babbling of 'appeals to Lord Ripon', 'telegraph to Viceroy', &c., pointed out a gap in the row, where an Honorary Magistrate, he said, was 'using his influence' to get his men passed through by the police. How this would affect the result of the elections one whit, I was not told; it was sufficient that 'influence' had been used, and our Empire in the East was tottering to its fall therefore.

The first two hundred voters seemed men of good education and position; after this, the quality deteriorated, and voters came in more and more scantily clothed and, in some cases, scarcely knowing for whom to decide. One aged Sikh, whose raiment would have scandalized a western constituency, expressed his willingness to vote for any one the Sirkar might please, or, failing this, for both ward candidates at once. His readiness to oblige was unappreciated. Another old gentleman, who seemed far too poor to have any stake in the ward, announced, with an angry glance at the assembly behind him, that he would vote for ' — Singh *and no one else, so help him*'. Had any canvasser been bringing pressure to bear on him, I wonder? Episodes of this nature were, however, few; for the whole system seemed to be too thoroughly 'understanded of the people' to admit of them. Between the hours of seven and nine nearly a thousand men had recorded their votes, and the atmosphere of the court house had risen about as many degrees. By nine every registered voter had been disposed of. Ten minutes later the Deputy Commissioner had counted the voting slips, compared them with the register and announced the result of the poll to the eager assembly without, and, amid the screeches of the winning side, and the rough banter of the losers, the ward election came to a close.

What impressed an on looker first, was the sublime distrust every one had for every one else at the polls that morning, and the lofty morality of the Baboos. It is wrong and wicked to hold meetings before the elections, it is sinful, they argue, to give feasts, and it is crime unspeakable to buy votes. Let the would be Municipal Commissioner stand or fall by his own merits, and move neither hand nor purse throughout the elections. The late lamented Mr Barlow would have protested that it was a vastly fine idea, and so says the Baboo; but it is an idea that a few hundred years electioneering at home have never worked out and that Lahore has yet to wait for.

Taking the whole business of the elections all round, one thing certainly strikes us, and that is the fact that, in spite of the difficulties in their path, the local authorities have done wonders. The time allowed them was short, but an enormous amount of work must have been got through ere the arrangements for voting could have been turned out, like a famous sewing machine, so simple in form that a child of six could understand it. The Deputy Commissioner who took up his share of the work while the arrangements were still being made, has certainly done his very best by the scheme, which as you have said somewhere, was anything but a simple one in its first conception — a defect that the next elections may remedy. Mr Parker, who, besides being Judicial Assistant Commissioner, Registrar of the University, and Vice President of the Municipal Council, seems to do everything in Lahore except preaching in the Pro-cathedral, has, of course, been worked like a horse, and to the Secretary of the outgoing Municipality who will, no doubt, act on the next Committee, there must have fallen a large portion of the work, apart from the unenviable morning task of registering votes. The fact is that the local authorities had to do everything but tell the voters who to vote for. This they were even expected to do, and men would come to Mr Clarke and Mr Parker, loud in their professions of readiness to vote for any or every candidate His Lordship might be pleased to name. Intelligent burgesses of this kind were sent away with the intimation that, under the circumstances, they had best not vote at all.

There is a delightful simplicity and *naivete* in the forebodings of the organ of the educated natives as to the future of 'Lokil sluff' which is quite too good to be confined to its own narrow circle of readers. We are told that the new committee will be a *fiasco*. The old committee was kept straight by the 'moral influence of the Deputy Commissioner which prevented petty jealousies and intrigues, and kept the shady side of the committee men's characters from showing themselves'. But have we not often been assured by the incorruptible *Tribune*, that the influence of the official Briton was a sort of withering upas tree, and that a really popular system of representation was wanted? Such a system is provided, and, as I have shewn above, the people have taken to it as ducks to water. Only, the educated native is 'not in it'. His claims to the chief seats have been ignored by a public which has a blind faith in such grocerly qualities as wealth, reputation and social influence. So he writes: — 'This scheme is ultra radical. It refuses to give a proper recognition to education, merit and position. The people are ignorant and apathetic, wholly unaccustomed to act for themselves, and the whole thing is an egregious blunder.' So it was not a popular system of representation that was wanted after all? Not in the least. The aspiration of those who have most clamorously hailed Lord Ripon's *'Boon'*, was for a transfer of power from the white *Hakim* to the dusky *Vakil* and, since the people have shown that they prefer another class of persons to the eloquent and educated native, who has his brains merely for his patrimony, and his interest in litigation for his stake in the country, he cries out, 'Oh! this isn't my notion of local Self-Government at all! I was going to take the D.C's place and have a company of argumentative educated natives to support me. If this is your boasted new jurisdiction I prefer the old arrangement with the D.C. as *Deus ex machina* as before.' And he is indignant, in a loftily aristocratic manner, that poor electors should emerge from their 'normal position in society' to 'strut in factitious importance'. Where in this wail of conceited snobbishness, helpless in its discomfiture, is there any trace of the notions of liberality of thought, equality of mankind and all the brand new gospels that were to usher in a new Era? There is food for reflection in all this, and especially for those who fondly fancied that a system of popular representation 'broad based upon the people's will' was likely to content young India who, after all, has claims deserving of more notice than they are likely to meet with at the people's hands. Make him Deputy Commissioner and the whole business of local self-government may go to Jericho. And why should he *not* be Deputy Commissioner and all the rest of it? This is the real question to which he awaits an answer. When his time comes you may be quite sure that his aristocratic instincts will tolerate no fooling round with electioneering papers.

# Music for the Middle-Aged

*Civil and Military Gazette, 21 June 1884*

**Attribution: Sussex Scrapbooks 28/1, p. 1**

This article is an overflow from Kipling's work on the collection of verse parodies called *Echoes*, written in collaboration with his sister Trix and published in August 1884. Like the parlour songs in 'Music for the Middle-Aged' the verses in *Echoes* adapt familiar English and American poets to Indian conditions. The last verses in this article — 'I Had a Little Husband' — in fact appear in *Echoes* among the 'Nursery Rhymes for Little Anglo-Indians'.

The 'recent protest' against drawing room music referred to in the first sentence is an article (perhaps by RK?) in the *CMG* of 17 June 1884.

(To the Editor)

Sir,

Your recent protest against the drawing-room music of the present should be writ large to my thinking, over every drawing-room from Peshawur to Cape Comorin. There is neither wit, wisdom, nor appositeness in the post-prandial *hurlements* of Anglo-India as at present inflicted. We, who have been burnt with the fervour of an Indian sun, and sodden with a score of rainy seasons, till Love has departed with our livers, and cynicism, hand in hand with sickness, invaded our systems, must, perforce, sing and be sung to of sentimentalities which had their growth primarily among the daisies and clover of English fields, but which the land of *ferashes* and fever refuses to recognise. We have, ostrich-like, buried our heads in the mud of '*Twickenham Ferry*', we have crossed and recrossed the '*Bridge of Midnight*', dragging with us at each passage a band of patiently applausive friends; we have called poor '*Maud*' a thousand times into the dusty desolation of an Indian compound, woefully (I had almost written wilfully) ignorant, that Ferry, Bridge, and Maiden were grotesquely out of place here. In the name of common sense, let the mothers of our families — they are, as you say, the greatest offenders — sing songs that may be 'understanded of the people', ditties dealing with the conditions under which we of the East live and work. Here is my scheme, imperfect as yet, for the regeneration of after-dinner music.

I purpose to publish, by subscription, a series of Songs entitled '*Music for the Middle-aged*', to be followed if life permits by '*Songs of the Sixties*'. I would not, at first, turn out mature warblers too suddenly from the beaten paths wherein they are wont to travel. The Form of their songs shall be respected, but the Spirit altered, and I flatter myself improved in the altering, to perfect harmony with our every-day life.

Take for instance Tennyson's '*Maud*' referred to above. Give
her the true local colour, and behold the result: —

> Come under the Punkah, Maud,
>     For the air is devoid of ozone,
> And the scent of the brick-kilns is wafted abroad,
>     And the germs of infection are blown,
> Are daily dispersed o'er our bed and our board,
>     From the huts that our *nauker-log* own.

Here is something which we can all understand and appreciate. '*Twickenham Ferry*' again, adapted to Eastern exigencies,
would obviously run: —

> *Juldee Ao! Juldee Ao!* To the Simla dak gharri,
>     The fever's about, and the glass going up
> So send in for leave, and no longer we'll tarry,
>     And by eight in the even at Simla we'll sup.
> *Juldee Ao!* (*ad lib.*)

No one will be prepared to deny that the open vowels of this
refrain are infinitely preferable to the senseless 'Yo-ho-o' of the
original, inasmuch as they convey a meaning patent to any
griffin who has been in the country twenty minutes.

Once more, I submit that all the pathos of parting, as experienced by the oldest members of the community, is compressed
into the following lines: —

> In the spring time, Oh my husband,
>     When the heat is rising fast,
> When the coolie softly pulling
>     Puddles but a burning blast,
> When the skies are lurid yellow,
>     When our rooms are 'ninety-three',
> It were best to leave you, ducky, —
>     Rough on you, but best for me.

When the world comes to admit — as it will — the excellence
of my system, I make no doubt that there will arise a race of
virile poets, owning no allegiance to, drawing no inspiration
from, Western thought, who will weave for the drawing-room of

the future, songs as distinctly *sui generis* as an overland trunk or a *solah topee* and breathing in every word the luxuriant imagery and abundant wealth of expression peculiar to the East.

To ensure this, however, our children must be trained from their cradles to discard the nursery rhymes of an effete civilization — thus only can they grasp the tremendous potentialities which lie before them. I for one, hope to hear the nursing mothers of Anglo-India instructing their babes in infantine lispings such as these: —

> I had a little husband
> Who gave me all his pay.
> I left him for Mussoorie
> A hundred miles away.
> I dragged my little husband's name
> Through heaps of social mire,
> And joined him in November
> As good as you'd desire.

The words are relatively of little importance, so long as the spirit of the poesy is national and unfettered.

Jacob Cavendish, M.A.

# The Tragedy of Crusoe, C.S.

*Civil and Military Gazette, 13 September 1884*

**Attribution: Kipling to Edith Macdonald, 17 September 1884**

The immediate inspiration for 'The Tragedy of Crusoe' was the fact that Kipling himself had just returned from his annual visit to the Hills. He had been at Dalhousie with his family in August but returned alone to Lahore in September to endure the end of his second season of Indian hot weather. Wheeler, his editor, was then absent, and Kipling had the paper to himself; that probably explains how it is that this, the first extended piece of imaginative prose that he is known to have published in India, got into the pages of the *CMG*. At the same time, Kipling expected soon to be called away from the *CMG* to the *Pioneer*, and he meant therefore to 'have a final flare up on the old rag' (to Edith Macdonald, 17 September 1884).

(From a Correspondent)

*Monday.* — Reacht the island — I would say the station — this morn, Mrs Crusoe being, at my own desire, left, it may be for a month or twain in the cooler air of the hills. Now, since we were first wed (and I shall not, even in my own diary, write down how long ago that was) I have never been a day parted from Mrs Crusoe; which I take it is not altogether becoming to a man of my spirit. Howbeit, yesterday, when I hinted, very gently, at this much to Mrs Crusoe — for though she is mine own dear wife, yet I dare not speak *all* my mind to her — she seemed in no way offended, but only laughed a good deal; saying that 'men's insides were made so comical, God help them', and if I had *that* fancy in my brain I had best go to the island and there live as I might for two months, till she saw fit to join me. Though I was a little taken aback, and, to tell the truth not over well pleased, at her ready agreement in my plan, yet I made shift to look vastly content, and left the mountains in so great a haste, that both sherry flask and sandwiches were left behind. This, I hold, was the fault of my wife, who should have given them both to me.

When I reacht the ship — I should say of course my house — I found that it had leakt greatly fore and aft, through the late heavy rains; spoiling my wife's new spinet, and, what is of far greater importance, many of my newly bound volumes that had but lately come out from England. I spent a dreary day soothing their swelled and blistered backs as well as might be, and thus forgot my tiffin. At dusk I went forth to explore the island, on mine old horse, whom I dare swear that the *sais* hath not exercised any time these two months. By him (the horse, not the *sais*) I was fought with for two miles, and runned away with for another two; the beast only stopping for want of breath. I find the island, as far as I can see, to be wholly uninhabited, except by the natives. Nor am I altogether sorry for this, since I cut but an indifferent good figure, this even, laid, for the most part, astride of my horse's head, and swearing, Lord help me, in a manner that I hoped I had long ago forgotten. Home, exceeding sore and disposed to be very wrath with all about me. I was made none the sweeter when my man Friday told me that there was no whisky in the house. Says I, 'How then did Friday manage to get so beastly drunk?' Friday takes me up short at this, and says he is not more drunk than I, but he has been rejoicing at once more meeting his old friend. At this he sits down very quick, and says that I am his Father and Mother and goes fast asleep. I cannot find it in my heart to be very angry with Friday, but rather envy one who can be so merry — though it is true he has no library to be ruined by roof leakage. For form's sake I have admonished him with a new leathern punkah rope, its end; and so grimly to dinner at the Club.

There I fell in with Jones (Cadwallader — He that I quarrelled with last July, because of a horse he sold me) and we dined together alone. He is the only inhabitant of the island; Mrs Jones, like Mrs Crusoe, being in the cooler hills. I see that I was a fool ever to fall out with thus pleasant a fellow, and withal one that can talk so well. Moreover, I will at once write to Mrs Crusoe and tell her that she must call on Mrs Jones. We two then smoked each other's cheroots in great friendship till close upon midnight, when I returned home; and finding no lights in my house but all in Friday's, I did again fall to with a punkah rope for five good minutes. To bed shortly after, where I lay awake till Friday had howled himself asleep.

*Tuesday.* — A woful day. This morning came Friday to me, smiling for all the world as though no words had passed between us overnight — whereat I suspected mischief but said nothing. Presently, while I was taking stock of my sodden library, he says: — '*Kerritch hogya*' but I made shift to escape into the garden and there examine the roses. Yet no man can avoid his fate, or, for the matter of that, Friday, when he is bent on being heard. So, at breakfast, I, being in a white-hot heat to get away betimes to work, my man bows himself double and says several times very loud: — '*Kerritch hogya*'. Then I thought how Mrs Crusoe, she that is now at the Hills, would have dealt with him at once, and that with no inconvenience to myself. For, though I can speak Thibetan, Nagri, Malay, and the Lord knows how many other tongues, the barbarous and hybrid speech wherein the affairs of a household are wont to be ordered is a

great stumbling-block to me. Friday, methinks knows this, for
which I hate him the more. I clutcht my hair (what is left of
it that is) three several times, and prayed inwardly that Friday
might not see the great depths of my ignorance. Then says I,
with my finest air: — '*Kitna che?*' '*Sahib*,' says he '*Sarce che*
worshster, *tael che, nia kunker estubble kiwasti, rye che,
marubber che*' ['How many?' 'Sahib,' says he, 'worcestershire
sauce, oil, new gravel for the stable, ? , pickels'] — and if I had
not taken him up short there, I believe he would have continued
till now. As soon as I had stoppt him he goes off again, like a
crazy clock, telling me that Mrs Crusoe had dismist her dhobie
ere she went hillward, and askt me to get another; that there
were three kinds of meat, all good, in the *bazar*, and I was to
chuse what I liked best — that I was to say what I would have to
eat not only for this week, day by day, but the next and the
next. Also he askt whether I should retain the old cook, whose
face I had never seen, or whether I should be fed by contract;
and a thousand other things that till now I fancied came in the
course of nature — as do *tiffin* and dinner. I have sent him away
for a while to fill me a pipe while I try to make ready against
his return. Oh that my wife were here!

*11 of the clock.* — Even though I know that none will read this
foolish diary save I, yet I dare not, for very shame, write down
all that I have done and suffered within the two hours past.
How Friday saw that I, Civil and Sessions Judge and a ruler
among men, was helpless as a little babe when there was any
talk of *degchies*, storerooms, and the like; how I floundered
from one blunder to another (for I hold that housekeeping is in
no way man's work) trying all the while to keep up my sorely
shrunken dignity; how Friday led me on, little by little, as men
coax an unwilling dog into the sea, until he had gauged the sum
total of my ignorance; how I sweated and turned hot and cold
under his words, as I have often seen prisoners sweat and change
colour under mine. All this, I say, I dare not set down. Let it
suffice for my humiliation, that, at the end of my torment,
Friday had roughly, and after his own fashion (which I take it
was not of the best), shewn how I was to manage my own
house in the matter of jam, clean sheets, and two daily meals,
and in the doing of it had so trampled on and crushed my
spirit, that I could but sign all he wished (and the papers were

not few) in hope of being released from his tyranny. But Lord! Lord! how many things be necessary to a man's sustenance whereof I have scarcely even heard the names till today —much less smelt and handled of them. Moreover, I see now what a strange and terrible car of Juggernaut it is that Mrs Crusoe, my never enough to be valued spouse, controls. I, who have rashly taken its guidance into my hands, am laid spent and prostrate among the wheels whereon I have ridden so smoothly before. All day I have done nothing at all save wonder how Mrs Crusoe can receive me with so smiling a face each evening, when she is on the island, if this be the kind of torture that falls to her lot. But it may be that she has some management to overcome it, for I have never, now I think, seen signs of it in her face, and this day has gone far to age and sour me, who am still, thank Heaven, a young man for my years.

To the Club again in the evening where I met Cadwallader Jones; but for shame, lest he should laugh at me, durst not enquire how he fared when his wife was away. To bed at midnight, wondering which of all the dainties I had so plenteously provided in the morning would be given me for my next day's meal. Surely it is not too warm for Mrs Crusoe to visit the island now.

*Wednesday.* — I am sorry that I ever smote Friday with a punkah rope, for I see that he is minded to poison me. This morn, in my big silver dish, set forth with many flowers and on a fair white cloth, came three sodden fragments of flesh which seemed as though they had been but newly torn from the inside of some dead beast. There was rice also, but I have never eaten small shot, so I put it all aside, and for two rupees of my own money Friday got me certain sardines in tin, and a very little oil. With these I must stay my stomach as best I can. They taste wondrous fishy, and the tea is smoakt and of a new flavour. Mrs Crusoe never gave me anything like it.

I had naught in the middle of the day at my office — neither meat nor drink — and returned home through the mire in a conveyance hired from a native. (*Nota Bene.* — It was girded about with ropes, like Paul's ship, and I held both doors shut with my own hands till I was mired to the elbow.) When I askt Friday what he means by sending neither tiffin nor carriage, he says that I gave no order, which was true enough, but I fancied that tiffin was eaten at least once every day by most men. I am very sick and tired and dare not abuse Friday as he deserves, or he will leave me altogether and I shall starve. Was too ill to go to the Club, so gave Friday two annas to get me a cup of tea. It tastes sadly of Friday his hookah. To bed wondering whether starving outright is better than being slowly poisoned, and also what became of the stores I had ordered yesterday. Dreamt that Friday had boiled sardines in tea for my breakfast, and that Mrs Crusoe stood by with a basket of tripe and laught. A very terrible dream.

*Thursday.* — Friday hath a new turban with two broad gold stripes and a pink one in the middle, and walks not over steadily. He asks me at nine in the morning what I would eat. Said that I was too sick to attend to work, and desired a savoury omelette. At ten 'twas ready, but there was neither tea, milk, bread, or anything else, saving two forks that were not of the same set, and a plate. Friday says I made no *bundobust*, and my head aches too sorely to reply. Made shift to eat the omelette which, methinks, was of bad eggs mainly; and lay down for the rest of the day, never a soul coming nigh me. In truth I am wrong here. Friday's children did harry an old turkey-cock in the verandah, which was close to my head, for two hours; and I thank Providence that made me a Civil and Sessions Judge and gave me Mrs Crusoe, for the fever that rackt me till I could stir neither hand nor foot — else I should have assuredly killed them all. In the evening my distemper went from me a little, but am still too weak to eat. Friday hath gone to the bazar and hath forgotten to bring me iced water. To bed, where I dreamt that I smothered Friday and all his children under an omelette of turkey cock's eggs. I have never been wont to dream in this fashion before.

*Friday.* — The fever left me in the night. Found this morning that I had but one clean shirt, and that frayed and chafed at the wristbands. Now I know I had twelve when I left my wife, so askt of Friday — who walks as though ground was air under him — what had become of all my gear. At this he wept for ten minutes (over mine only towel) and prayed me to send him to prison since I had blackt his face thus far. At this I was very wrath and said that no one had called him thief, but that I wanted my shirts again. Thereat he wept more than before, till I kickt him out of the room and shut the door. When next I opened it after smoking a pipe to consider how I should do, I found seven of my shirts — three that had been worn and four that were new — lying in a heap on the threshold. They smelt terribly of cocoanut oil and bad tobacco, and were marked and stained with all manner of stuffs. But Friday knew nothing of them at all, save that I was his father and mother and had suspected him of robbery. He wept all day by fits and starts, and I gave him four annas to quiet him. But this did not amend the quality of my meals. Dined again at the Club where Cadwallader Jones (who, methinks still, cheated me in the matter of that horse) called me a 'sick dove' and clapt me on the back with his hand. Mrs Jones returns to the island shortly. I would I were Jones, or at least that Mrs Crusoe was here. To bed thinking sorrowfully how I have done no work at all this week by reason of the pestilent Friday, who was more in my mind than anything else. Lord! Lord! and I had a thousand and one matters to finish and furbish up ere the Courts opened! Yet I will give him one day more of grace, and then — it is surely cool enough for Mrs Crusoe. Stoppt the punkah to see if this were so, and went off in a strong sweating till dawn.

*Saturday.* — Friday is again drunk nor was there any sign at all of breakfast. I eat sparingly of my sardines, with a cheese scoop; the rest of the table gear being all filthy with the remains of some feast. I found them in the pantry and judge that Friday hath been entertaining his friends. I have telegrapht for Mrs Crusoe, and till she come must make shift to live on sardines.

Jacob Cavendish, M.A.

# The Amritsar Fair [I]

*Civil and Military Gazette, 22 October 1884*

**Attribution: Sussex Scrapbooks 28/1, p. 72**

Amritsar, the holy city of the Sikhs, lies thirty-three miles east of Lahore. Its religious shrine, the golden temple or Darbar Sahib, stands in the midst of a great tank, or artificial lake. The city holds two annual fairs on the date of religious festivals; the second, on the festival of Diwali, is that described by Kipling in the two-part article that follows.

Living as he did in a society where nearly everyone either rode, or drove, or played polo, or all three, Kipling was quick to pick up the horsey talk of Anglo-India: he writes very knowingly here of the points of the 'Indian horse'. After the brief excitement of owning his own horse in his first year in India, Kipling himself rode very little, preferring to drive. When the motor car became practicable, Kipling was one of the earliest to have one, and thereafter he never troubled about horses again.

### (From our own Correspondent)

Amritsar, Oct. 19

An orderly, good-tempered crowd, restrained only by one policeman and slight lattice fence from overwhelming the platform, was waiting at every station between Lahore and Amritsar on Friday night. The mail-train had left Lahore so crammed and double crammed, that even the compressible native passengers were compelled to admit there was no more room anywhere. But their faith in the traffic arrangements was simple and undisturbed. Other trains, they had been assured, would arrive ere long; so, after a little deferential jesting with the policeman at the wicket, these expectant congregations sat down to roost quietly under their blankets, till it should please Providence and the authorities to send them an 'especial'. An English crowd would have trampled through the rotten fence, bonnetted the policeman, and swooped down on the comparatively empty first-class carriages, rather than have been delayed an hour on their trip.

Close upon the heavily-laden train came an equally crowded one conveying a detachment of the South Lancashire Regiment from Mian Mir to Allahabad, *en route* for Aden. Nearly three hundred perspiring khaki-clad men were set free on the platform for half an hour. During this time it was resolved, *nemine centradicente*, that the beer was abominable; that to travel ten in a compartment was equally so, and that Aden was infinitely superior to India 'cause it was nearer 'ome'. Then the mass of boisterous humanity was suddenly blown back, as it were, into

the reeking carriages, by a bugle call, and sailed out into the
darkness, amid a shower of barrack-room *badinage*, on its way
to the sun-scorched rocks 'nearer 'ome'. The rest of the night
was occupied with 'alarums and excursions' — at least this was
one wearied traveller's view of it. Crowded specials seemed to
arrive every half hour; and the passengers therein held strident
converse from opposite ends of the platform for the next thirty
minutes. Horses too were coming in by twos and threes along
the road all night, and were picketed temporarily on the outskirts of the plain, where fifteen hundred beasts were already in
possession. Expostulatory squeals from the new comers, and the
thud of the wooden picketing mallets, enlivened the small hours
of the morning. As soon as it was light enough to read the
notice-boards, owners transferred their charges to the regularly
laid out lines in the centre of the great *maidan* under Fort
Govindghur. With this move the day's noise and confusion
began. Two-year-olds, savage at the loss of their night's rest, and
maddened with the pain of rowelled bits, were scarcely likely
to respect the feelings of their seniors. The three-year-old lines
were rudely awakened by a batch of light heeled youngsters,
who were being personally conducted to their places, and, from
thence, the clamour spread to the outskirts of the gathering.
The scene, so far unobscured by dust, was curious. Twenty or
thirty rows, each several hundred yards long, of tethered horses
are dozing before sunrise. To these enter some half a dozen
prancing, squealing shadows, and, before you shall have time to
mark who began it, the whole equine camp is in an uproar. As
the gaily embroidered cloths were turned back from each
animal's withers, the keen morning air wakened him to renewed
exertions, and the day dawned on a very Pandemonium of horse
flesh. One of the last joined had, thanks to a lazy *syce*, been
insecurely tethered, and, breaking loose, warmed his young
blood with a gallop across the open. A disgraceful capture, and
a pair of chain hobbles, were the end of this outburst; and the
rebel was ultimately bought by a remount officer for the Punjab Cavalry. There were, by the way, no less than eleven of
these gentlemen on the spot and, as far as can be known, they
'bulled' the prices as usual — to the huge delight of the dealers.
A lone, lorn Englishman, with a limited purse, begins to wonder
whether the purchase of remounts might not be managed on
less expensive lines. The dealers are affable to him, very much

so; but his attempts at bargaining for any animal over polo height, are gently but firmly set aside. 'A remount officer' or more usually two or three remount officers 'coming to look at that horse Sahib. He not for sale.' An indifferent bay was bought for Rs. 350, and the dealer was of opinion that he might have done better. The average of prices was about a hundred rupees below this, and one officer purchased a string of fourteen for Rs. 212 per horse. Among the regiments represented, were the 1st Punjab Cavalry, Colonel Bird; the 2nd Punjab Cavalry, Colonels Lance and Grover; the 3rd Punjab Cavalry, Colonel Anderson; the Guides, Major Hammond; the 9th Bengal Cavalry, Major Robertson; the 14th Bengal Lancers, Colonel Pennington; the 15th Bengal Cavalry, Colonel Atkins; and the 18th Bengal Cavalry, Captain Money. One dealer, on whom fate has smiled, was weak enough to confess that there were more buyers than horses — a statement with a good deal of truth in it.

On the extreme right of the camp were ranged the polo ponies, and here, too, prices ruled high. A polo pony is easily manufactured. Take a fairly presentable sixty rupee tattoo; hog mane and tail; stand out for two hundred rupees and there you are. The sight of a remount officer bargaining for a few baggage animals told the tale. Baggage animals, of any stamina, there were practically none; but, a few yards away, you might come across the polo ponies; and these, in prehistoric times, would have been baggage tats. Five hundred rupees was the highest price obtained for any one of them, and a pair were bought for seven hundred. As a rule, the dealers asked three hundred for everything; and generally got something over two hundred. Decidedly, the Amritsar fair is not the place for cheap horse flesh. One powerful black galloway indeed was secured for a hundred and five rupees early in the day, and it would be scarcely too much to say that he was the only bargain of the fair. This statement is, of course, open to objection from every purchaser. They had all, by their own statement purchased a mount 'worth twice the money you know'. It is a cheerful creed and hurts no one. In point of quality, the yearling and two-year old lines (particularly the latter) were by far the best. The three-year olds, with a few exceptions, were indifferent; and there was very little worth notice among the seniors. It is only natural that this should be so in a recently established fair like the Amritsar one. *The* country-bred *par excellence* — that

IN TRAINING

roman-nosed, goor-fed bolster in which the Punjabi delights —
was, of course, very much to the fore. With his head reined in to
his bosom, and with quivering hind legs strained as far backward as possible, his lot must have been an unenviable one. A
dun-coloured monster, whose (un)natural charms had been
heightened by a liberal use of aniline dyes, was specially tor-
mented. The loin cloth had slipped over his tail; his *syce* was
asleep, the flies were numerous; and the tense head and heel
ropes allowed no change of position. Nearly all the horses were
far too tightly roped — their galled and scarred pasterns gave
significant proof of this. Badly formed weak hocks, ditto feet,
and a want of bone below the knee — the old established faults
of the Indian horse — were visible everywhere. The entire
process of producing the first imperfection could be studied
from one glance at the lines. First, the young animal is strained
and weakened by rigorous heel roping; then, when his hocks
are nearly bent the wrong way, the rough-rider's spiked bit
forces him to throw his whole weight on them for five minutes
at a time, while the native crowd applauds. The finished article
is fired and variously be-devilled. What careful breeding and
good tending can accomplish, was shown in the case of a
chestnut gelding by a Government stallion out of a country-
bred mare. The youngster, he was only seventeen months' old,
stood a little over fourteen hands, with an immense amount of
bone below the knee, and was nearly perfect in every other
respect. He has already gained his owner seventy-five rupees of
prizes at various shows, and has received a prize here. Any hint

at purchase was promptly repulsed. 'I have treated him like my *batcha*, and he shall go back to my village again, that my *izzat* may be increased therein. If you really want him I will sell for five hundred – not a pie less.' Some remount officer, in a year or two, will learn, to his cost, the merits of that colt, if the animal does not go down country. When his owner understood that no one was prepared with the amount he asked, he became confidential and even eloquent; relating at great length the history of the *batcha's* youthful ailments. How once he nearly died, but it was the will of God that he should recover and become the pride of his master's heart.

Other dealers were not so discursive, but, when they had a few minutes to spare on an unprofitable European, they too would talk, and talk well. One black bearded Cabuli appeared to be intimately acquainted with the leading social lights of Simla, and spoke with appalling flippancy of the *'Paniar kagaz* Ilhabad' ['Allahabad paper'.] From him it was possible to learn that all other dealers were rogues and blackguards; that such an one's horses were only kept alive by liberal doses of *massala*, that such another's polo ponies would all go lame in a week; and, finally, that 'Codlin was your friend not Short'. It would be ungenerous to doubt the word of so genial a host. His tent was a pleasant shelter at mid-day, from whence to watch the dusty, squealing pickets, and the superb horsemanship of the rough riders. From five in the morning till dusk, these men, clad in flowing white *pyjamas*, and armed with snaky whips wrestled hand to hand with the frivolities of equine youth, and the matured devilries of age. Kickers kicked, rearers reared, and the man-eater went about 'like a roaring lion seeking whom he might devour', till it seemed impossible that a man should enter the *melee* and live. Presently, out of the dust cloud, a bare-backed horse would be forced into the thirty-foot ride between the tethered lines, and, before he had time to realize his position, the yelling Cabuli on his back, had sent him flying along the turf to the shade of the trees on the main road. Here, a quick-witted beast would do his best to dislodge his rider – a performance abruptly concluded by the cutting whip, and another mad gallop down the rides.

By noon it was as well to escape these impromptu cavalry charges, and get away to the cattle fair. Though the pride of the Punjab may be in its horses, it is surely the patient *byle* that carries the prosperity of the province on its galled and blistered neck. Thirty thousand head of cattle — a scanty gathering as compared with other years — were to be found two miles down the Jullunder road. Apparently the whole province, each man with a buffalo or cow, was going thither. The roadway was choked with the slow-moving, good-tempered crowd, and, at a few yards distance, men, *ekkas* and camels melted away into a fog of white blinding dust. The two miles must be traversed for the most part at foot pace, for the cattle are by no means as complaisant as their owners, and all the yelling in the world will not force a drove of buffaloes one hands-breadth from their course. Nor is any advantage to be gained by attempting to press forward through the thick of the grimy herds. A small pony is at once sandwiched between two portly bullocks, and has, perforce, to accommodate his pace to theirs. Arrived at the main gate, the whole earth was covered, as far as one could see, with bellowing beasts and men. From one corner arose a chorus as of the groans of the damned. Some hundreds of camels were enjoying themselves after their own peculiar fashion, and their nasal *misereres* rose high above the deep hum of the fair all day long. Every portion of the ground was packed with buyers and sellers and onlookers; these last being in great force. When an Englishman made overtures to purchase a cow, the owner promptly went as near to a hundred rupees as he dared, and a dense crowd walled up the perspiring Briton lest he should be minded to escape. Under these circumstances the market was depressed. A striking feature of the gathering, to those who have any recollection of the humours of an English cattle fair, was the sobriety of men and animals alike. Once only in the course of a three hours' visit did a 'milky mother', irritated by an ungallant attempt to tell her age, exceed the bounds of beastly decorum. The result was ludicrous, for the dense crowd could neither fly nor give way; and the cow was wedged helplessly, head down amid a tumult of affrighted brown legs.

Towards evening the fair was gradually deserted in favour of the greater attraction in the city — the illumination of the Golden Temple, and once more the dusty road was choked with people hurrying northwards, hot, tired, but apparently very happy. Beyond a few cases of snatching ornaments from children there were no police offences during the day.

# The Amritsar Fair [II]

*Civil and Military Gazette, 23 October 1884*

**Attribution: Not in Sussex Scrapbooks but continuing the preceding article**

(From our own Correspondent)

Amritsar, Oct. 20

The illumination of the Durbar Sahib, and, incidentally, of the greater part of the city, began at six o'clock on Saturday evening. This showed, in a most favourable light, the amenableness of an Indian crowd to authority. As befitted their position, the police authorities were reticent about the nature and extent of their duties, so that it is impossible to estimate the amount of organization and forethought which they had expended on the arrangements of the evening. The result, however, was that, from the Municipal offices to the Clock-Tower, a carriage might be driven at full trot without a single hindrance. The white-robed crowd ranged themselves, like cheery ghosts, into orderly lines at a signal from the baton of authority — the blue and yellow policemen, stationed every ten yards or so, along the route. Even that evil-mouthed pest of all India, the pariah-dog, had been scared from his couch in mid-street; and the Englishman who had come to scoff at disorder and confusion remained, if not to pray, to pass thankfully on his unobstructed way with a feeling of personal gratitude to that much abused body, the Indian Police. The raised platform behind the Clock-Tower had been set aside for Europeans and the leading natives of the city. Here, too, came young Bengal, in long frock-coat and patent leather boots, to hold indignant speech with the police authorities, who would not admit him to the reserved seats. By dusk these were filled, and then, as the old nursery story goes, 'the fairy waved her wand, and the rats were turned to coach-horses, the frogs to powdered footmen, and the great yellow pumpkin to a beautiful golden coach'. In other words, the light of a million tiny *chirags* changed the squalid streets and uncouth crowds into strange and wonderful things. The great sunk square in which the Durbar Sahib stands, broke out into a hundred lines of fire; and Temple itself blazing, like a live coal, in the centre of them all. Then house after house followed suit; and it could be seen that each 'gemmed roof' was crowded with an assembly of brown goblins who, to-morrow, would revert to their everyday duties of buying and selling on the ground floors of these palaces — gem roofed no longer. A red light gave the signal for the fire-works, which were not good. It may be that the illuminated square spoilt their effect, for the rockets seemed pale and [in]effective; the Roman candles burnt dimly, as well as bluely, and the Catherine wheels were as so many bad fusees in comparison. The sea of many coloured turbans below was well pleased, however, and cried *wah! wah!* at each shower of golden sparks or flight of fire-balloons. The noise and smoke lasted for about half an hour, and, at their conclusion, the spectators departed. But the fairy city that had been so suddenly created did not disappear till some hours later. Little by little, the lines of fiery tracery became blurred and broken, the wonderful temple on the waters rotted away, and, amid a fearful stench of burnt wicks and bad oil, Amritsar was herself again.

On Sunday morning the horse lines were quieter. After all, it is impossible to squeal at your neighbour for more than twelve hours at a stretch; and even kicking, when you can hurt nobody, must lose its charm. The cattle fair too was less densely attended, and country cousins were more disposed to wander about the city, sight seeing, than to chaffer for bullocks. The great annual influx of visitors has, up till now, been allowed to come and go without the smallest effort being made towards its entertainment and, indirectly, its education in matters connected with its own pursuits. This year, thanks to Mr Nicholl, the Municipal secretary, a beginning has been made, in the shape of what, for convenience sake, may be called agricultural exhibit rooms. A large house close to the fair has been lent for the occasion, and here are gathered together samples of wheat from various districts; specimens of improved ploughs, sickles, pruning knives and the like, from a Calcutta firm; carpets and cottons, and a hundred and one other articles which might appeal to the country cousin's soul. How far the venture has been successful, may be judged from the fact, that over two thousand visitors pass through it daily. Some of their remarks on the articles exhibited were worth listening to. 'That a plough,' said one zemindar, pointing to a double-handed iron one from Calcutta. 'I could break that with my foot!' The light pole and tapering handles, compared with the robust tree which he and his fathers drove through the fields, moved him to a good deal of scornful merriment and it was only when a friend invited his attention to the size of share and the beauties of the clevis, that he would look at the plough seriously.

Others were more appreciative and fully alive to the merits of the *belaite* goods exposed for their inspection. They whetted the pruning knives on their palms, critically balanced the sickles and as critically tested the edges of the American axes. When it had been made perfectly clear to them that it was possible to buy exactly similar articles for the same price, they gave their orders; and a large number of implements were disposed of. A quantity of the largest size of brass garden syringes were at first regarded with suspicion. 'Surely the well and irrigation channel were the only legitimate means of watering the land; why, then purchase these strange inventions?' Presently, one brilliant genius murmured that they would be the very things for the next *holi*, and the idea took at once. The richer men (for garden squirts with India rubber piping are not cheap) have ordered several, and the next *holi* should be worth witnessing. The British manufacturer will be glad to learn that he has succeeded in adding additional *éclat* to one of the maddest and most riotous festivals of the East. A model by the Principal of the Lahore School of Art [Kipling's father] of men ploughing, moved the country cousins to child-like wonder and awe. A sturdy *jat* stood with outstretched forefinger and drooping jaw to stare at his very self, in clay, pressing down the rebellious share. In a corner of the field too, was his wife with her child on her hip. By all the gods in his Pantheon, this was *too* wonderful! Could the little men be alive? The question was answered with a roar of laughter, as someone pointed out where a chip in a bullock's ear showed the earth below. Native women attended in large numbers on Sunday, and stayed for long. The reason was not far to seek. Two large mirrors at the opposite side of the room, formed the attraction; and Eve from Taran-Taran or Jandiala must needs

AND THE PLOUGHMAN SETTLED THE SHARE MORE DEEP IN THE SUN-DRIED CLOD: THE WHEAT AND THE CATTLE ARE ALL MY CARE AND THE REST IS THE WILL OF GOD

Rudyard Kipling

IN A GOOD SEASON

see, at least a dozen times, how Adam's fairing — a new *chalder* and gay brass nose-ring — becomes her.

Nor is Adam one whit better. He takes no pains to conceal his satisfaction at the curl of moustaches and the sit of his turban, and shamelessly jostles Eve away from the wonderful glass. One old crone (could it have been the first time she had ever seen her own face thus?) lingered for at least ten minutes arranging an exceedingly filthy head cloth with every appearance of delight. The little comedy had to be watched in the glass, from the other side of the room, and, as soon as she was at liberty to study anything beyond her own beauty, she was aware of the reflection of a European in front of her. Back shot the veil at once, and the old lady moved ruefully away. These, however, were only the lighter humours of the show which was, seriously, a great success from an agricultural point of view. The venture is to be repeated on a larger scale next year, and should give the best results. There is already some talk of holding a similar exhibition at Jullunder before long. What would best satisfy the needs of the Province would be, to establish a permanent show of this kind in every large town — an expansion of the original idea which would not be very expensive. The entire cost of the Amritsar show came to something under fifty rupees. In this instance, various firms from Calcutta, Cawnpore and elsewhere, sent specimens of their manufactures, on the chance of their finding favour with the natives. It is as well to remember that the floweriest advertisements of agricultural implements fail in great measure to reach the classes for which they were intended. Let Ram-Singh, whenever he buys cattle or *ekka* ponies, have easy access to a few samples, and, even though it may somewhat damage them, let him be allowed to handle freely these samples. If he likes them, he will adopt them: and if he doesn't no one will be much the worse.

At dusk the show was closed and the country cousins went to bed. How the city can accommodate the crowds in it just now is a mystery. The inhabitants, however, complain of the poorness of the fair, and the consequent scanty attendance thereat. The outlying *tehsils*, say they, are a good deal troubled with fever, and the cattle disease has prevented a good many entries. If fever-struck *tehsils* and diseased herds are represented by to-night's crowd of men and bullocks, then Amritsar, at her best, must be a three days' block.

At four o'clock on Monday evening the prizes for horses and cattle were distributed, by the Deputy Commissioner, at the cattle fair. All the Europeans in the station, with a very few exceptions, had assembled there, under the shade of a large *shamiana*, the prize animals passing at the end of a lane of native officials, like pictures in the slide of a magic lantern. First a brown horse, seen for a minute or two through the dust, and then, as his hind legs disappeared, the head of a black horse would appear and so on. Four hundred and fifty rupees were given in prizes for the horses, and something like two thousand rupees for the cattle. The prizes for horses were for district-bred beasts only — brood mares in foal to Government stallions, ditto with foal at foot; mares in foal to country-bred stallions, ditto with foal at foot; geldings out of Governments, and c-b stallions, and mules. About a hundred brood mares were branded. These, for the most part, were aged and unlovely ladies. The cattle prizes were open to all. Amritsar secured first prize for bulls for improving the breed of draught cattle; for male buffaloes, and for district bred mules. The prizes for cows for improving the breed of milch cattle, for female buffaloes (so the entries ran) and for draught oxen, fell to Ferozepore. Ludhiana was represented by her loading camels, a loud-voiced brute of singularly unpleasing appearance. Kupurthalla won the prize for yearling calves; and Sialkote for bulls for improving the breed of draught cattle. Some of these latter were magnificent animals, and could only be adequately described by a Yorkshire dalesman. At the conclusion of the prize giving, the Government stallions and the stud donkeys were led by. Of the stallions two, called respectively the Amritsar Arab and the Taran-Taran Trotter, were the best. The latter fills the eye as much as his name does the mouth, and is altogether an animal to approach with fear, and to praise with fervour.

The stud donkeys were not sweet to look on, for it is only when the ass is patient and much enduring, as the story books assure us he is, that we regard him with favour. The four black-coated, shaggy-haired ruffians in question, were neither patient nor did they admit of any trifling with. To an ignorant observer they appeared ugly, not to say coarse and unrefined. The initiated, however, seemed delighted. After the prize-giving followed mule and camel racing, and various other sports. The camels either would not or could not race, and came home in couples, gurgling fearfully. The mule race was exciting.

An obstacle race through tubs was provided for the benefit of the rising generation, and the special delectation of the Clerk of the Course. This gentleman was besieged by clamorous youngsters, calling Heaven and Earth to witness that the prizes were unjustly awarded — a thing by no means impossible, seeing that one brown urchin is marvellously like another, and that nine-tenths of the runners avoided the obstacles altogether. The tent-pegging which succeeded was the most noteworthy feature of the evening, and attracted about a dozen competitors. The pegs had been constructed of new palm wood, and though more than once struck fairly in the centre, were too hard to yield.

At dusk the sports terminated, and, with them, the interest of the fair as far as Europeans are concerned. Our country cousins will not disperse for some time and it seems that Tues-

day and Wednesday will be the busiest days of all. This is difficult to believe. Except on the very outskirts of the *maidan*,
where knots of villagers are squabbling over broken-kneed *ekka*
ponies, the horse lines are almost deserted. Two or three of the
big dealers have 'folded their tents like the Arabs and silently
stolen away'. The remount officers have made their purchases
and are gone, and the crows are quartering the pickets in search
of a dinner. A veil of dust has hidden the Jullunder road, so that
it is impossible to say what is going on in that direction. Only
from time to time, like the sobs of the Mock-turtle, can be
heard the lowing of thirty thousand hungry cattle; and in every
nook and corner, where a man can stow himself, the country
cousins are settling down to sleep.

# A Week in Lahore

*Civil and Military Gazette, 6 January 1885*

### Attribution: Diary, 5 January 1885

Kipling's penchant for parody and his interest in American
poetry are combined in this item. He had been somewhat un-
usual among literary schoolboys in paying as much attention to
American as to English poets, and Emerson, Longfellow, Lowell
and Whitman were nearly as familiar to him as were Tennyson,
Browning and Arnold. It is interesting to note that the stock
figures of Anglo-India in 'Departmental Ditties', still a year in
the future, have already taken form here.

It is seldom that an American poet condescends to interest himself in so remote a land as India; and I am proportionately glad,
therefore, to be able to record this week a great kindness on the
part of no less distinguished a singer than Walt Whitman. Once
upon a time, indeed, the bard was styled — not by his admirers

— the 'Inspired Auctioneer of the Universe', but he has long outlived the reproach which the elaborate detail of his workmanship drew upon him; and the swing of his half rhythmic, half declamatory, wholly musical lines has now drawn round him a delighted and admiring school of followers. What the great poet's views of an Indian New Year are may be seen from the following reply to a modest request for 'something seasonable': —

'*Dekko*! Look here!'

From the pines of the Alleghanies I, Walt Whitman — colossal, pyramidal, immense — send salutation.

I project myself into your personality — I become an integral part of you.

I am the Junior Civilian horribly *dikked* by the Superior Being, and squabbling with a tactless, factious Municipal Committee; and I too pray for a happy new year.

I am also the Superior Being, Impassive, and waltzing on the toes of all within reach. I too pray, without prejudice for a happy new year.

I am the European loafer, drunk in the bazar on country spirits with blue lips and a green rat crawling down my neck. I too, out of the gutter pray for a happy new year.

I am the gay, the joyous subaltern, with six ponies in my stables and a shroff in the back ground. And I too pray for a happy new year.

I am the 'joy of wild asses' with my husband absent in the Soudan and a ten-strong following at my high silk heels. And I too pray for a happy new Year.

I am in Sirsa, Jhang, or Montgomery, separated from Dickie, Emmy or Baby, living in a tent with my husband who is seedy and overworked. I read the smudgy round-hand-home-letters, and I too pray for a happy new year.

Oh! Civilian, Superior Being, Loafer, Subaltern, Grass-Widow and Grass-Mother of many conflicting domesticities, I salute you.

In the name of our great ruler Humanity I too wish you all individually and collectively, some — how or anyhow — a Happy New Year.

# A Week in Lahore

*Civil and Military Gazette, 11 February 1885*

**Attribution: Diary, 10 February 1885**

A kind of follow-up of the story on the Lahore municipal
elections on 21 May 1884.

Kipling's brief experience of writing for the local paper in
Bideford during his school days evidently gave him some knowledge of municipal proceedings; 'gas and sewerage', as he wrote
at the time, were among his subjects (to Mrs Perry, 28 May
1882: MS, Huntington), and the conclusion of this article recalls
what he saw then.

One hears and sees so much about the Lahore Municipality — I
will not suggest that Municipal affairs appeal to other senses as
well — that I determined to find out for myself how our *patres
conscripti* transact their business. — Here is a brief record of the
last meeting: —

*Imprimis* their forum. A bleak many-windowed room with a
depressed and smoky fire hidden behind a table. A few benches
and chairs were ranged round the Vice President's seat and table
of office; the whole presenting in the cold morning air, a
ghastly resemblance to a public-school form-room. This resemblance was heightened by the display of three maps (of Lahore
city) and a T-square artistically disposed on one of the walls.
Six lamps, one clock, one almanack, one glass of water, and an
inkstand occupied a place of honour on the mantelpiece above
the depressed fire; and a representative of a native paper (who
by the way took notes in English) kept the fire warm. About
eight o'clock; then the members began to drop in by twos and
threes and discussed local news *sotto voce*, to wile away the
time. When about a dozen native members and four or five
Europeans had been collected the Secretary suggested that 'we
had better proceed to business'. The Vice President apparently

had no objection; and at a quarter past eight or thereabouts, business began. Every one sat down and salaamed to every one else two or three times over. When a late member entered he also had to salaam all round and decide whom he would sit next to. The sight of our worthy city fathers nodding and beckoning from bench to bench and chair to chair after the fashion of Sunday School Children was impressive and took time withal. At the end of the ceremony, the Secretary briefly introduced the first question on the list. This concerned the appointment of an European Sanitary Inspector to Lahore city, and was stated in the vernacular. When the Secretary stopped talking, the members broke off as it were into knots; some discussing the matter among themselves, others addressing the Secretary, and, in general, all talking at once. Any detailed report was of course impossible. The Secretary answered objections as fast as they came up; and argued with a Mohammedan member in a Cashmere dressing-gown, in a lively and fluent vernacular studded with strange exotic terms such as 'budget ke estimate', 'Sanitary Sub-Committee munzar', 'salary establishment March kivaste' and the like. At the end of ten minutes or so of this work, a European member remarked cheerfully — 'Then we'll appoint MacEwen at once'. A private and confidential confab all down the line, broken only by the deep bass voice of a Sikh gentleman who seemed to be addressing the world at large on the merits or demerits of MacEwen Sahib. Fresh argument advanced suddenly by the gentleman in the dressing-gown, squashed by the Secretary; and after some further discussion the European Sanitary Inspector was appointed. Time, 25 minutes.

The second question for consideration is the contract for the Municipal printing work. It seems doubtful whether a contract can be given to a member of the Municipal Committee. One of them is quite ready to undertake the job — a matter of perhaps Rs 2,000 per annum. A European member suggests that the 'work should go to the best man'. Fresh epidemic of arguments down the line. Business temporarily suspended, until a late member who makes his appearance at this point is salaamed into a seat and has salaamed all round in turn. Conversation between two European members and the Honorary Secretary as to contracts. This lapse into the English tongue cut short by three men, including the member in the dressing-gown, all speaking at once. Vice President throws in a word occasionally and the other members plunge head-long into the argument; declaiming like a Greek semi-chorus. Member who expects the contract smiles engagingly, until a rival appears on the scene, *videlicet* a gentleman in black continuations, and a poshteen. Stranger has no connection with the Municipality, but has strolled in casually to explain to Municipality that he will undertake work 5 per cent cheaper. Attention of the meeting devoted to the daring interloper, who smiles even more engagingly than the other contractor. European member proposes that SubCommittee should be appointed to consider question of contract. Private and confidential discussion springs up between the gentleman in the dressing-gown and two friends. Every one speaks at once. Member of Municipality who hopes for the contract leans forward with his hands on the table and orates. Conversation taken out of his hands and drifts up to Vice's table, where the voice of a European member is heard protesting that 'what we want is economy'. Another European member proposes that the contract should be given to the lowest tenders for one year. Hands go up for and against amid great excitement. Votes are equal and Vice President has to give the casting vote. Voice of the European member encouragingly: — 'Now then Rai Sahib!' Rai Sahib gives vote in favour of the motion, Member in the dressing-gown jumps to his feet and says something. European member declares that the motion is carried. Rai Sahib nods affirmatively; and the gentleman in black continuations who has just made the lowest tender retires to side-table and is effusively congratulated by the representative of the native newspaper. Time 20 minutes.

General distribution of plans on tracing paper proclaims that business has advanced one stage, and the Lahore Tramways Bill is up for signature. Partial occultation of members behind the papers and subdued conversation all round. All that is necessary is to sign the agreement between the grantees and the Municipality. The bill itself will be introduced into the Legislative Council at Calcutta on the 16th of this month. The Secretary (to drop into the past tense once more) disappeared behind a stiff fence of crackling documents, accompanied by the Vice. When he next emerged the agreement had been signed; the member in the dressing-gown was deep in conversation with a friend and it was after nine o'clock. There were thirteen matters for consideration that morning of which three had been discussed. According to Cocker the other ten would take three hours and twenty minutes to settle. As a matter of fact they did not take that time; but at nine o'clock the meeting had warmed up and was settled down into its stride, and at this point the visitor left it.

The above, as far as an Englishman *not* conversant with the vernacular could judge, is a fairly accurate account of one hour's work at a Municipal meeting. In the space of sixty minutes they had decided three important questions of private and public interest — and these without undue heat or recrimination. An English vestry, where men wage war to the knife over an additional sewage-cart or a scavenger's badge could not have done more.

# Typhoid at Home

*Civil and Military Gazette, 14 February 1885*

**Attribution: Sussex Scrapbooks 28/1, p. 2. Diary, 8—10 February 1885**

In *Something of Myself* Kipling recalls that he was once given a 'really filthy job' as a reporter in Lahore, 'an inquiry into the percentage of lepers among the butchers who supplied beef and mutton to the European community of Lahore'. If he actually wrote such a thing, it has not been found. But, as this article sufficiently shows, he did have 'really filthy jobs' to do.

**(From a Correspondent)**

If you would eat your dinner, it has been wisely said, keep out of the kitchen. If you would enjoy *chota hazree* or afternoon tea with an untroubled mind, avoid any inquiry into the milk-supply. For this reason it will be as well not to read what is written below — the record of one morning's exploration of the cow-byres in Lahore city and Anarkullee.

In the first place, the inspection was, for certain pressing reasons, a short one. It occupied in all two hours, and with two exceptions, was limited to one division of Lahore city — that which lies nearest to the Delhi Gate. A casual policeman volunteered to show the *sahib* to such places as would be most likely to contain what he wanted. 'Cows, Protector of the Poor, are usually bought at fairs, and there are few of the city cow-keepers willing to part with their beasts. But, without doubt, the *Sahib's hookum* shall be obeyed.' An Englishman parading the bye-ways of a native town, in company with a policeman, is an object of the liveliest curiosity, not to say suspicion. Either he has come to hunt up a thief, or there is a 'takkus' in process of incubation. If, however, his avowed object be to purchase a cow, he will be welcomed, and above all, referred to neighbouring *gowallas* and byres without end. The yellow-breeked guardian of the public peace plunged into a bye-way leading from the main street to the right side of the city, as you come into it through the Delhi Gate. This passage was fully three paces wide. Down the centre of it struggled a stream of bluish ooze, gay atop with the rain-bow hues of putrescence. Here and there, side drains from the neighbouring houses added to the sluggish currents, or spread themselves aimlessly over the interstices of the worn and broken brick pavement. Presently, and after many turns and windings, the roadway narrowed from three paces to two; and the blue stream became wider and swifter. Obviously, the policeman was tracking it to the fountain head; as a traveller might track a river to its source. He hurried on over the uneven ground through the still narrowing gully, past closed and shuttered windows; past small doors in blank walls, giving access to dark courtyards even more uncleanly than the region through which he was making his way; beyond the reach of the sunlight, into high walled clefts (it is impossible to call them lanes) where it seemed that, last summer's sultry breath still lingered; and eventually halted in a *cul-de-sac*. Here lay the first, and comparatively the cleanest byre. Within a space, twelve paces long by four broad, six cows and seven buffaloes, were standing side by side. This expression must be taken in its literal sense, for they touched shoulder to shoulder and hip to hip. Their hind feet were immersed in the blue stream above referred to; their fore feet were buried nearly to the knee in accumulations of filth. They were mired, caked and coated with the same filth from the withers downwards.

Within three feet of the rank was located a *hulwaie's* shop, and the proprietor thereof, wrapped up in his *rezai*, sat upon the shop-board waiting the morning supply of milk which the *gowalla* was even then drawing. How the latter had contrived to jam himself between the wretched beasts was a mystery; and his sublime indifference to the horrors in which he knelt, a wonder. One brass *lotah*, already full, was in the *hulwaie's* possession; a second, empty, lay within a few inches of the blue stream, and a third was being filled by the *gowalla*. Add to this picture some calves and a collection of pariah dogs disporting themselves after the manner of dogs all the world over; a knot of natives in the gully for their morning toilet; throw in a few strong smells, and there you have the first byre complete. The details have been sketched as lightly as possible; but any one who knows the manners and customs of the Punjabi will be able to fill them in *á discretion*. I have said advisedly, that this was the cleanest byre of any in the division, inasmuch as the filth was merely ordinary farm-yard muck, accumulated in some places to the depth of eight inches or more. Other byres, as will be seen later on, were not so satisfactory, 'The milk of these cows,' explained the *gowalla*, in answer to my question, 'is given to the *hulwaies*.' 'But the *Sahib* wants to buy a cow. Have you one to sell?' (This from the policeman). 'These, protector of the poor, are very good cows, and give milk often to the *Sahib-logues*.' The *gowalla* was accommodating in his statements; and there is no special reason for discrediting the later one. The *hulwaie* who happened to be nearest bought the milk; but if there was any over it was doubtless passed on to European customers.

(For the sake of brevity, I may state that the two queries in the order named, were asked at every byre in the division, and almost exactly similar answers were returned. The milk was bought, by the *hulwaies* and was also sold to the *Sahib-logue*. It never for a moment seemed to cross the *Gowallas'* minds that a *Sahib* had called to see how inconceivably foul were their surroundings; and in justice to them, it must be said, that they were uniformly kind and courteous. But this is a digression.)

From the first byre the policeman and his companion were referred to the second. Another hurried tramp through more narrow gullies, open sewers and the like, led to an *ooplah*-plastered wall, opening into an irregular shaped courtyard fifteen paces long by seven wide at the broadest part. Here five buffaloes and seven cows were accommodated; and excepting only the foot-deep deposit of filth, seemed comfortable enough. Two charpoys, three men, two dogs and a puppy shared the courtyard with the kine; and the temperature was somewhat higher than that of the outside gully, which again was much warmer than the open street. Two tattered chicks hung over two doors at the right of the courtyard, and hid two detachments of 'milky mothers'. One lot resented vigorously any attempt to break the seclusion that shrouds the *'purdah nashin'*, but a glimpse into the darkened chamber showed a frowzy charpoy and a heap of tattered garments mixed up generally with the cows and calves. The second room — stall, stable, or cess-pit — was pitch dark, and the unwary explorer sank over ankle deep into the foul compost that lay thick on the floor, and was nearly suffocated by the fetid stench inside. Evidently the place was full of animals, but it was at first hard to estimate the exact number. The *Gowalla* stated that six cows who had lately calved were shut up there for a few days; and when the eye became more accustomed to the gloom, it was seen that his statement was perfectly correct. Six cows, and five calves were massed together in a room, nine paces long by about three broad, and the heat of this Black Hole was almost unendurable. All these cows will in a short time be in regular use as milkers. The 'unutterable aroma' from their byre made me suspect that one of the new-born calves had died, and was rotting inside. This the *Gowalla* denied at once. It was unfortunately too dark to make a lengthened exploration; even if the temper of the inmates had admitted of it. As it was, they objected strongly to an Englishman pacing out their lying-in chamber.

From this byre, the policeman crossed the main street of the city and passed to the left of the Delhi gate. It would be hopeless to attempt to describe the narrow gullies through which he led his 'charge', or the extreme filthiness of some of the interiors which that 'charge' saw. These bye-lanes were comparatively deserted, for a frosty February morning has not charms for an under-fed, under-clothed Punjabi. But the dead walls, the barred and grated windows, and the high storeyed houses, were throbbing and humming with human life, as you may hear a hive of bees hum ere they go forth to their day's work. Voices of children singing their lessons at school; sounds of feet on stone steps, or wooden balconies over-head; voices raised in argument, or conversation, sounded dead and muffled as though they came through wool; and it seemed as if, at any moment, the tide of unclean humanity might burst through its dam of rotten brickwork and filth-smeared wood, blockading the passages below. Nor was this impression removed when we turned out of the gully into a third courtyard surrounded by a mass of ruinous houses, thus taking the pent up army on the flank, as it were. Wherever a *charpoy* might be laid, a man or woman was sitting on one, and children were crawling underneath. By unclean corners of walls; on each step of ruinous staircases; on the roofs of low out-houses; by window, and housetop, or stretched amid garbage unutterable, this section of Lahore was awaking to another day's life. Twelve cows and five buffaloes, besides an apparently unlimited number of calves and goats were found here. These were being milked for the morning's market. They stood, as was the case in all the other byres, nearly up to their knees in filth; but the refuse was blue and rotten below the surface, and smelt beyond all description. As they were moved to and fro for the convenience of the milkers, their legs sank in nearly to the hock, and came out with a reluctant 'sob'. Semi-circular depressions showed where the cows had been lying all night, and the blue black-veined slime was, of course, plastered liberally over udders, stomach and breast. The *gowalla* and his family were not much cleaner than the cows. They were just awake; and came out of their huts wrapped in all manner of foul garments. One woman had on a specially unclean *chudder*, which, in the course of milking, flapped and dangled into the *lotahs*. Her children, when they saw the chance, dipped their fingers into the warm milk and licked them afterward. These fingers were smeared with three distinct, albeit nameless, abominations. The brass *lotahs* themselves were externally comparatively clean — that is to say, they were merely marked with greasy fingers and daubs of cow-dung. The buffaloes chewed some polluted *bhoosa* which lay on the ground. The cows I did not see fed at all. Now even if that particular byre had been floored with marble, and drained

according to the latest scientific principles, it would still be a
public danger. Three men in that courtyard were deeply scarred
and pitted with small pox. There is no reason for believing that
cases of this disease are rare in gullies pullulating with frowsy,
fetid humanity, or that milk does not convey infection more
surely and readily than even water itself. The cleanest cowshed
in the world would be deadly under the circumstances I have
described; and the one that actually existed there could, of its
own power, spread any amount of disease. I have, of course,
omitted two or three of the more disgusting details with reference to children and dogs. The reader, as I have said before,
may fill them up as he pleases.

The fourth byre, which lay about a hundred and fifty yards
from the third, was reached by a broken and slimy flight of
steps, which gave into a small courtyard on the second floor.
This was most difficult of access. The very bulk of the animals
inside, made it almost impossible to open the door, and once
inside, there was barely standing room for one man. Three
cows and three buffaloes were herded here. It was out of the
question to attempt to pace the yard. Indeed, all observations
had to be taken squeezed between the sides of two buffaloes
who rather resented the intrusion. A stick thrust into the ground
went in without opposition, to the depth of ten inches. Here
too, as much of the refuse as could be seen, was blue and putrid,
and there appeared to be no drain from the raised courtyard.
How the heavy buffaloes could have ever climbed the steps
which led to this byre is a mystery. The brass *lotahs* were lying
on the ground below, at the foot of the steps, and the offal of
the calving-shed was placed beneath them. *Ooplahs*, of course,
covered the neighbouring walls, but these, when properly made,
are perfectly cleanly. In reply to a question as to how the
*lotahs* were cleaned, the *gowalla* obligingly took up one of these
*ooplahs*, made a small fire with it, and held the *lotah*, mouth
downwards, over the intensely acrid smoke. The cows' food was
composed of wet and sodden *bhoosa*, water, and rotten gram
stirred in very sparingly. This concluded the list of byres in that
division of the city. I had visited eight in all; but have only
described four typical ones. The others were equally filthy in
every possible respect, and nothing that I have written can convey any idea of the utter loathsomeness of these establishments;
the absolute disregard of every law of decency and cleanliness in

OOPLA (COW-DUNG FUEL)

their management, or their pestilential surroundings.

My guide now offered to lead me to a spot where the cows intended *solely* for the use of the *sahib logue* were kept. Not far from the Mayo Hospital, he walked *through* a mud hut, and ushered me into a spacious courtyard, where I counted sixty-seven kine and buffaloes herded together. At a distance, the place looked respectable enough.

Closer inspection showed that only in the matter of space was this byre in any way superior to the ones which I had already visited. Accumulations of filth were piled in mounds from three to five feet high. I counted nine of them. The blue, rotten compost lay deeper here than in any other byre, and the buffaloes had worked themselves holes nearly two feet deep therein. It was necessary to pick one's way across the slough of unutterable abominations under the guidance of one of the *gowallas.* The cows were starved, and literally plastered with filth; the buffaloes who browsed among the refuse heaps were fat. Brass *lotahs* lay about wherever they happened to be put down. Four of them were placed mouth downwards on a layer of *ooplahs* preparatory to being smoked. Filthy children and women were scrubbing the outside of others; and glimpses into the mud huts that were scattered irregularly over the yard showed more *lotahs* thrown on *charpoys* and bundles of bedding. In the middle of the sewage-logged ground, was sunk a brick well; and when I arrived a *bhisti* was drawing water for the general use from its depths. That water naturally stank.

My readers will be good enough to recollect that I went purposely in the early morning to ascertain how far human convenience was subordinated to a regard for public health. I am extremely sorry that I should have credited the native with any feelings higher than those of swine. The whole yard was one reeking latrine — unblushingly used as such. The *gowalla* I asked, declared that the cows here gave good milk which went to the *sahib logue,* and that, if anything went wrong, the *Sircar* would shut up the yard. Not one single cowkeeper seemed to have any idea that the beasts or byres were anything but what they should be. This concluded the morning's investigations. At an outside estimate, I had seen perhaps one tenth of the cow-byres in the City under their most favourable circumstances, that is to say, when the chill of a winter morning killed any positively unattackable stench. What these places must be in the heat of summer I dare not guess.

If any one should consider what has been written exaggerated or overcoloured, an hour's investigation will enable him to judge for himself of the conditions under which the milk supply of this Station is managed. But there is not the faintest hope of arousing popular interest on so unsavoury a matter. Some years ago, an investigation into the state of the cow-sheds in Bombay brought to light facts very much like those which are written above — and little, if anything, was done to remedy them. It rests with the public of Lahore to bestir themselves in this matter, and to demand that every byre within and without the City walls shall be at once removed to some spot where it is

A BOMBAY MILK
WOMAN

possible to exercise efficient and intelligent control over it. But there is small likelihood of their doing even as much as this. Those who already keep cows of their own, will thank Providence that they are sure of unpolluted milk. Those who are too poor or reckless to do so, will remain as they are, on the principle that, as no ill-consequences have happened to them they may still escape scot-free. And the result will be — exactly what we see around us at present — preventable disease leading to death.

# To Meet the Ameer

*Civil and Military Gazette, 31 March 1885*

**Attribution: Sussex Scrapbooks 28/1, p. 11. Diary, 27 March 1885**

Late in March of 1885 Kipling was sent to Rawalpindi, on the northwestern frontier, to be the *CMG's* special correspondent at the meeting between Lord Dufferin, the Viceroy, and Abdur Rahman, Amir of Afghanistan. The British purpose in the affair was to secure the support the Amir against the Russians, whose manoeuvrings in central Asia were then and for long afterwards a thorn in the side of the Empire. The Rawalpindi assignment was the most important 'special' work that Kipling had yet done and was a good test of his enterprise in finding stories and in filling space under difficult conditions. His father wrote in March of 1885 that 'Ruddy goes to Pindi as a special. He has started his pony and tum-tum [dog cart] thither, and although a little nervous about his first big thing, I think he will do well. He has done some capital special correspondence' (to Edith Plowden, 16 March 1885: MS, Sussex).

Despite miserable conditions — the rain came nearly every day and the Amir delayed to come day after day — Kipling doggedly supplied his paper with copy: thirteen articles, on the order of 30,000 words all told, came from his pen and were duly published between 24 March and 14 April. After sending his first article from Rawalpindi, Kipling moved on to Peshawar, closer to the Khyber Pass, through which the Amir was making his provokingly slow way. After several days at Peshawar he ventured even further, to the mouth of the Pass at Jumrood (it was here that he maintained, in later years, that he had been shot at by an overzealous skirmisher in the Pass). He then went back to Peshawar, and, the Amir having at last crossed out of his territory into India, Kipling returned in the wake of the Amir's train to the *durbar* at Rawalpindi.

The article that follows is the fourth of the series.

**(From our Special Correspondent)**

Peshawar, March 27

[. . . .] At last the comedy seems to be approaching its end. Touched, doubtless, by the thought of Colonel Waterfield waiting in the rain at Lundi Kotal, our only Ameer has consented or condescended to put in an appearance at Peshawur on Monday next — the 30th instant. Add to this a couple of days' stay here, and our excellent Viceroy will only be detained for the better part of a week, amid the dust and confusion at Rawal Pindi. One of the Ameer's many intentions was to stop at Dhakka for a day, and to go on directly to Ali Musjid. Accordingly, he halted for four and twenty hours at Gardi Sharkhani. He will spend the 28th, to-morrow, at Ali Musjid; the 29th at Jumrood; and arrives here the next day. This has endeared him to all concerned.

Two of his Sirdars arrived in camp this morning, and are at present enjoying their mid-day meal. Neither Kazi Kootb-ud-din nor Aga Hyder-Shah were pleasant to look upon, as they squatted on their charpoys and asked all manner of questions regarding the arrangements of the camp. The Aga was clad in a camel's hair garment adorned with gold stripes, and his lower limbs were encased in what looked remarkably like European trousers. He was short, thickset and of a florid countenance, laughing and talking a good deal. The Kazi, who lounged about picturesquely in a corduroy waistcoat with brass buttons and a pair of snowy white pyjamas, was meagre, red-haired, and much lined and seamed with exposure. Both wore the Tartar cap of black Astrakhan fur, and both talked loudly and quickly. It is difficult to interview Kizilbashes satisfactorily, but, with the help of an interpreter, something — not much it is true — was extracted from Codlin and Short. A complimentary allusion to their silver mounted swords and belts — magnificent pieces of workmanship — was 'cornered' promptly by the remark, that in *their* part of the world 'arms were the ornament of a man. Nevertheless Peshawur was a great city'. This somewhat inapposite codicil was thrown in, possibly to soothe the feelings of the degenerate white man who walks about with a cane. Did they know when the Ameer was coming? 'The Amer was a *Badshah* and could come in when he liked.' And with this significant answer, the conversation, as a novelist would put it, became general. Kazi and Aga plunged into the gulfs of their own strange speech, and the interview, if one may so style it, was at an end. The question as to the Ameer's arrival had been asked, I believe, previously by one of the officials in charge of the camp; and the answer then given had been almost identical with mine. Decidedly Abdur Rahman will come down imbued with a proper idea of his own importance.

The details of his Court, by the way, are rather interesting. I give below the list of his personal friends, councillors, attendants and the like, who will be most with him during his stay in Peshawur: — Mahomed Nahin; Nazir Safed Mahomed; Sirdar

Nur Mahomed Khan; Mahomed Omar Khan; Mahomed Jan; Mir Mahomed Husein, ex-Mustafi; Jan Mahomed Khan, brother of the present Governor of Jellalabad; Kazi Shahb-ud-din, brother of Kazi Kootb-ud-din, at present in camp; Mahomed Khan, Chessplayer to His Highness, and a prophet of considerable honour in his own country; Dilawer Khan; Shere, Afghan Khan; Kurban Ali Khan, whose duty it is to attend to [the] Ameer's Samovar among other things; Syed Ahmed Khan; Jamma Khan; Mahomed Akbar Khan, water bearer (perhaps the only equivalent in the English language to this is the title of Groom of the Chamber) Mahomed Sirwa Khan, Chamberlain; Mahomed Alum Khan, door keeper; Golam Hyder, Commander-in-Chief; Mahomed Azim — the deaf and dumb painter of the Ameer's court; Ahmed Jan Khan, Councillor; Mirza Abdul Raschid, Doctor; Jan Mahomed Khan, Court tailor; Faizulla Khan, personal servant; and Mahomed Nubbi Khan, writer to the Ameer.

These the Ameer had with him at Dhakka; and unless he has made some sudden and unexpected change there, these will accompany him to this station. Everything, as I have already told you, is prepared for his reception, down to a cretonne bordered teapoy in the drawing room of the bungalow — and we can henceforward only possess our souls in patience, until the worthy gentleman actually arrives. Lieutenant Leigh, of the 60th Rifles, has gone on to Lundi Kotal with the Government carrier pigeons; but these useful birds have so far brought us no certain news about anything in particular. When Abdul Rahman has actually set foot within the limits of Peshawur, we may be certain of his arrival. Till then anything that may be written, rumoured or telegraphed, is of less than no value.

The unsettled state of the weather — among other things — is supposed to have delayed our illustrious visitor. For the past four days the sky has been gloomy and overcast, with heavy thunder and rain at night. At three this afternoon, a hailstorm broke, which would have stripped the trees of Peshawur had it lasted. Luckily it was all over in five minutes, after having whitened the ground with hailstones of from half an inch to one and a half inch in diameter. Some took more than ten minutes to melt.

# The City of Evil Countenances

*Civil and Military Gazette, 1 April 1885*

**Attribution: Sussex Scrapbooks 28/1, p. 17. Diary, 28 March 1885**

'The City of Evil Countenances' was written at the end of Kipling's first sojourn in Peshawar, as a personal response to the experiences more formally treated in the special reports that he was sending to Lahore. In his diary for 28 March 1885 Kipling notes: 'Wrote the City of Evil Countenances and saw that it was good'.

Peshawar, March 28

Rolling thunder among the Khyber hills all day long; the day itself wasted in spiteful attempts to rain, varied by a shower of hail which clears the crowded streets as a mitrailleuse would do. Evening seems to have brought down the rain in earnest. A steady drizzling downpour blanketing the Fort, and the crops beyond, filling the roads with glutinous mire and the heart of man with despair. A downpour that shows little signs of ceasing throughout the night, neither the charms of an annotated Greek testament with strictly secular remarks written in the margin; or an odd number of the Calcutta Review with every other page torn out; or even Eugene Sue's fantastic *Le Morne-au-Diable* (which must surely have crept into the dak bungalow by mistake) can counteract the depressing effect of the evening. In the Amir's camp — swept and garnished for his reception — the *soorkee* of the paths has been converted into red gruel, and is discolouring the newly laid sods, the fountain basin overflowed a couple of hours ago and is now adding its share to the general slop. From the supply godown a puff of the evening breeze brings the scent of fruits and spices — or rotten pummeloes and curry powder, as romance or reality are uppermost in one's mind — and the mute eloquence of over-ripe bananas, tells us that the days are long and the life of Bombay fruit short. The last *mohurrir* has shaken the rain from his garments, and save for bottles of sherbet and certain gigantic *Samovars*, the go-downs are deserted. The two Khans, fore-runners of the Ameer's army of temporary occupation, have gone to bed like wise men; their horses protesting outside against the vileness of the weather. Nor does the police sentry on guard appreciate it one whit more; but luckier than the horses, he has consolations denied to brute beasts. As you watch him, standing shivering in the wet, the neck of his bayonet smokes furiously. Every now and then he takes the weapon between his teeth, and a few steps to leeward will tell you that native ingenuity has circumvented the *Sirkar's* ordinances against smoking on duty: and the regulation foot of cold steel is for the nonce acting as a *hookah*. The lower end of the socket has been deftly closed with a stone, above this has been jammed a pledget of fresh barley stalks, and over all the tobacco  The sentry applies his lips to the aperture by the locking ring. The cool stalks, in a manner, filter the smoke, and the *hookah* is in full blast. Should an inconvenient officer arrive on the scene, the smoker stands to attention; covering his improvised pipe with the palm of one horny hand, and detection, unless the officer be blessed with a specially keen nose, is almost impossible. A smoke under these circumstances would scarcely be appreciated by a European: but the sentry appears to enjoy his stolen whiffs immensely, and is quite ready to explain how it's done.

Meantime, the City of Evil Countenances has become shrouded from sight by the incessant rain, and a journey to the Edwardes Gate means a mile-long struggle through soft oozy slime — to be undertaken only as a counter-irritant against the growing gloom of the evening. The road to the city is thronged with foot and horse passengers of all kinds; all utterly heedless of the downpour, and all, so it seems, shouting to a friend half a mile away. Strings of shaggy-haired camels, nearly as repulsive as their masters, jostle mule carts, ekkas and restive horses fretting under the punishment of their spiked bits. These ships of the desert can make but little headway through the ooze, blundering and swaying from side to side like rudderless galleons. Their long hair throws off the water as completely as a mackintosh, but the loads of bhoosa and green barley soak up as much as they can to the discomfort of the dripping driver atop. A camel's *esprit de corps* is an all-pervading essence which rain intensifies. His arrival is heralded on the wings of the wind, and his presence remembered long after he has passed away. Indeed, so powerful is the rank stench, that those who know least of him, maintain that it is the most offensive in the world. To this slander the unwashed camel driver gives the lie direct, and the Afghan no less. The healing rain that makes the onion to sprout and (six weeks later on) the white ant to suicide himself in the lamp flame, has no charms for these men, but rather acts on them as the sun on the rose. This evening the city road is witness to the fact.

Under the shadow of the Edwardes Gate, the crowd thickens, and the continuous tide of humanity is broken up into eddies, bays and cross-currents. The waning light is darkened here by the houses, and though it is barely six o'clock they have begun to light the shop *chirags*. Then you shall see a scene worthy almost of a place in the *Inferno*, for the city is unlovely even beneath bright sunshine, and when set off with heavy slime under foot, dark skies and rolling thunder overhead, and driving scotch mist, everywhere repulsive to every sense.

Under the shop lights in front of the sweet-meat and *ghee* seller's booths, the press and din of words is thickest. Faces of dogs, swine, weazles and goats, all the more hideous for being set on human bodies, and lighted with human intelligence, gather in front of the ring of lamp-light, where they may be studied for half an hour at a stretch. Pathans, Afreedees, Logas, Kohistanis, Turkomans, and a hundred other varieties of the turbulent Afghan race, are gathered in the vast human menagerie between the Gate and the Ghor Khutri. As an Englishman passes, they will turn to scowl upon him, and in many cases to spit fluently on the ground after he has passed. One burly big-paunched ruffian, with a shaven head and a neck creased and dimpled with rolls of fat, is specially zealous in this religious rite — contenting himself with no perfunctory performance, but with a whole-souled expectoration, that must be as re-freshing to his comrades, as it is disgusting to the European, sir. As an unconscious compensation to the outraged Kafir, he poses himself magnificently on — degrading instance of civilization — a culvert, turning a very bull's head and throat to the light. Dirty *poshteen* melts into the back-ground of driving rain; neck, shoulders, and fiery red beard standing out in starting relief. But he is only one of twenty thousand. The main road teems with magnificent scoundrels and handsome ruffians; all giving the on-looker the impression of wild beasts held back from murder and violence, and chafing against the restraint. The impression *may* be wrong; and the Peshawari, the most innocent creature on earth, in spite of History's verdict against him; but not unless thin lips, scowling brows, deep set vulpine eyes and lineaments stamped with every brute passion known to man, go for nothing. Women of course are invisible in the streets, but here and there instead, some nameless and shameless boy in girl's clothes with long braided hair and jewellry — the centre of a crowd of admirers. As night draws on, the throng of ignoble heads becomes denser and the reek of unwashed humanity steaming under the rain, ranker and more insupportable. A free fight takes place in a side gully and terminates, after a little turban pulling and hair snatching, in a gale of guttural abuse and the presence of a policeman, not as an arbitrator in the fight, but merely a dignified spectator of the *rixe*. What might have happened in other and happier lands across the border it is impossible to say. Here the wild beasts seem to obey their keepers to admiration; and after all they are well looked after; the Sirkar's benevolence permitting none to die by sword, bullet or epidemic disease, if it can possibly be avoided. The ever circulating night patrols, and the ubiquitous policeman — (policemen are really ubiquitous in Peshawar) — bear witness to Government forethought in the first particular; the magnificent drain and water main which run through the main streets of the city, are equally eloquent as regards the second. A lakh and a few odd thousands of rupees have been spent — much to the Secretary of State's disgust on economical grounds — in order that the city of evil countenances might, if it willed, wash and be clean; or at least refrain from drawing cholera from the roadside and typhus from the standing pool. Reservoired, watered, drained and policed in the face of all opposition, and for the benefit of a proverbially thankless race, Peshawur as it now stands, is a city that could only have grown up under English care and English rule. Holy Russia would have tamed the wild beasts as effectually perhaps. They would have died largely under the process. France would have alternated barracks with cafes; lyceums of public instruction, and descents into the street of armed marauders. But it is easy to wax cheaply patriotic on this theme, as easy as it is to draw entirely erroneous conclusions from an evening stroll through one of the most wonderful cities on earth. The rancorous expectoration of our red-bearded friend — still on the culvert — as he performs his devoirs for the fourth time in the track of the on-going kafir may mean anything you please. A wanderer from the hills takes this opportunity of expressing his contempt for a whole nation — not even the long suffering missionary could credit him with influenza: or again neither security to life and goods, law, order, discipline, or the best blood of England wasted on their care, reconcile the calibans of the city of evil countenances to the white stranger within their gates. And to-morrow we do honour to the ruler of Afghanistan and its dependencies at Jumrood.

# To Meet the Ameer

*Civil and Military Gazette, 1 April 1885*

Attribution: Sussex Scrapbooks 28/1, p. 15. Diary, 29 March 1885

This is the sixth article of the series.

### (From our Special Correspondent)

Jamrud, March 29th *Day-break*

Circumstances over which the local officials seem to have no control, prevent a journey to Ali Musjid. A modest *ticca gharri*, however, will convey you as far as the historic walls of Jamrud, and from thence, to the mouth of the Khyber is but two or three miles. His Highness the Ameer of Afghanistan is due this morning — no one seems to know at what hour. Meantime, the top of fort Jamrud is an elevated and decidedly airy point of vantage. The Four Winds of Heaven are fighting it out between them on the bastions, and each gust brings with it a douche of fine rain. The Khattak and Swat hills are swathed in mist. Only towards the north west and the Khyber, is the air comparatively clear. Along the undulating Khyber road runs a scattered line of the Ameer's camp followers, who have been dropping in all night and through a great portion of the previous day. Interminable files of camels, yaboos, coolies, and loud-voiced donkeys and flocks of sheep, stretch from the camp to the south of Jamrud, into the very jaws of the Pass and in the grey light of dawn, these resemble nothing so much as lines of black ants on a foraging expedition. Three hundred horses of the 12th B[engal] C[avalry] are dozing in the enclosures below the walls of the fort.

Thursday's hail storm, by the way, was felt very severely at Jamrud, as long as it lasted; and, but for the fact of the beasts being picketed within brick walls, they would inevitably have stampeded over the face of the country. As it was, several of them broke loose under the stinging hail.

Half of the M.—3, R[oyal] H[orse] A[rtillery], lies under the northwest bastions, and as yet the only sign of life there, is the stamping of half awakened horses and an occasional squabble amid the drowsy syces. But it is impossible to slumber long in the teeth of the camp followers' chatter; and the babel of tongues that surges round the walls on every side.

*7 o'clock.* — The daylight has brought down the Scotch mist more densely than ever; and never did the Afghan hills look more rugged and forbidding than now. Jamrud has awakened the centre of a little city, the population of which is increasing minute by minute. Still no news of the Ameer. He has left Ali Musjid. He hasn't. The rain has delayed him. He will be here in the evening. He will be in in half an hour. Private Thomas Atkins, hard at work in the little pigeon box of a telegraph office, at the very top of the Fort, could probably tell us how much truth or fiction lies in these rumours, but his hands are fully occupied in the most literal sense of the word. There is only one decrepid 'ticker' in the Fort, and this has to bear the burden of the day's telegraphic intelligence. Sister Anne's employment in the time of Blue Beard had at least one advantage over this morning's waiting and watching. There is no reason to believe that her toes were numbed and her teeth chattering in the keen morning air. Otherwise, her vigil was exactly the same. 'Sister Anne, Sister Anne, do you see any one coming.' Only a flock of sheep, a rush of obstreperous yaboos or a phalanx of slow-paced camels, working their way across the stony road. The troop horses below are hard at work on their morning's meal; 'the wind is moaning in turret and tree', at least, it would, if there were a tree available, and the thin rain penetrates to one's marrow. A descent into the maelstrom of camp followers near the police barracks, keeps the blood from stagnation, and reveals incidentally some curiosities of character. Undoubtedly, our friends beyond the border, though their *pals* are as filthy as themselves, and their horses ungroomed since the day they were born, have a very good notion of camp pitching, and accomplish their work with not more than deafening clamour. Perhaps the rain has quenched them. A young Afreedee of thirteen is keeping watch and ward over a bunch of picketed yaboos. The lad's garments are filthy, but he smiles and swaggers affably; displaying at his belt a Colt's revolver. Subsequent investigation shows that it is loaded and as clean as oil and rag can make it. It belonged to his father who departed this life a year ago the embryo cateran does not say how, and the weapon was handed on to the son.

'Have you ever done anything with it?' The question is a somewhat brutal one, but the Afreedee regards it evidently in the light of a compliment. 'Not *yet*, Sahib, but please God, I shall some day,' he replies, with a cherubic smile, and swaggers over to his horses once more. A cheerful race these Afreedees.

*8 o'clock.* — Alarums and excursions. A dozen sowars and a European officer — all very wet — have come in from somewhere out of the mist and several bugles have sounded. The troop horses are being saddled, and the gloom is lifting a little. Tommy Atkins ticks away imperturbably in his dove cote, and the stream of camp followers thickens. More bugles; more camp followers and a gruelly streak of sunshine for an instant through the clouds. The hills riven into gorge and cavern, are chequered with light and shadow as though to do honour to the great man's arrival. But the great man makes no sign; and the clouds shut down gloomier than before. One by one the 12th Bengal Cavalry, prance out of the courtyard on to the maidan, and form in three Squadrons, bay, grey and chestnut, preparatory to moving out to meet the Ameer. All the men are shrouded

in top coats and there is no colour visible. The artillery on the
other side of the Fort, clatter out also into the open, and the
advance begins. First the bay squadron; then the three guns,
then the grey and chestnut horses. About 500 hundred yards
from the fort, on the Khyber road, they pause. Then the artillery takes up its position on the right of the road, a few hundred
yards away from it, and the cavalry lines the road on the same
side, two deep; then they halt, and the temporarily interupted
stream of followers sweeps on. These latter are now moving by
at their best pace. The Ameer must really be here before long.
The three guns are unlimbered in readiness for the salute, and
all Jumrood is a waiting. From the signalling tower — in spite
of the life and babble below — the impression is one of intense
loneliness and desolation. On every side the thriftless un-
friendly land sweeps away to the foot of the hills as bare as
the desert of Sahara. In the far distance, for the intervening
veil of mist puts them miles and miles away, lies the belt of
green crops that encircle Peshawar, and mark practically the
limits of British rule. The stony ground runs up to the limit
of the crops, and is dotted here and there with the ominous
heaps of stones, where a man has been done to death. Peshawur
is invisible, and the frowning hills bound the view on three
sides of the horizon. Only around Jumrood is there any sign
of life, and the gathering of men here marks more strongly
the silence of the hills and plains. The hour passes away,
Tommy Atkins is drenched and doubtless grumbling as he
waits by the guns; and once more the clouds lift. A solid column
of men appears over the crest of a rise close to the mouth of
the Pass. Without a doubt there are at last the Ameer's troops,
and the Ameer with them.

   *10 o'clock.* — The column has disappeared in a hollow, rises
again and approaches rapidly. There is a stir among the gunners,
and in a few moments a puff of white smoke tells the watchers
on the signalling tower of the fort, that their watching is nearly
at an end. One—two—three — twenty-one guns — the smoke
hanging heavily at the mouth of the cannon; and by the time
the last welcome is spoken, Abdur Rahman Khan, ruler of
Afghanistan and its dependencies, has fairly set foot on British
ground. For the past ten minutes the field glass has shown him
merely as a blot of blue on a small horse. A closer inspection
is necessary, and this involves a rush through some two hun-

dred Afghans, who are hastening forward to line the road. Colonel Waterfield and General Gordon are riding on the right of a handsome black-bearded man, in a blue *choga* embroidered with gold. The pace quickens as they near the camp, and the Ameer has passed. For those who are curious in such matters, it shall be recorded that he was smiling affably at the time, and looked about him on both sides of the way, with every appearance of interest. Behind him follow his cavalry, wild picturesque men on wild horses — to whose appearance it is impossible to do justice, while writing on the spot. No two sets of accoutrements are alike, *cela va sans dire*, if I except the regiment of Usbeg Lancers. These resemble Cossacks in every particular, down to the high-set saddle and the shaggy circular cap of hair. One or two of the officers carry the short-handled double thonged Tailor whips, and all, without exception, ride splendidly. To the Usbegs, succeeds a nondescript following of horsemen, some with grey felt jockey caps and string bridles, some with fur trimmed smoking caps and muzzle-loading carbines. Their horses are all small fiery little rats, and under the circumstances keep line remarkably well. The riders represent every shade of Turanian and Mongolian blood, high cheek bones, oblique eyes, shaggy hair, flat noses, cavernous mouths.

Their speech, of course, is utterly unintelligible, and they are all talking and staring about them. One or two have calmly pulled up their horses to look at the Englishman by the wayside. They point like children, and their remarks would, no doubt, be immensely amusing to listen to. The men are all cantering, and it is difficult to give any idea of their *outré* and ferocious experience [*sic*]. Somehow, the back ground of dark hills, the sullen sky and the rain seems to set them off to perfection.

The Ameer's infantry preceded him. There were two regiments of these, I fancy. As I write, they are taking up their position on the encamping ground, and look as cut-throat a crew as one would wish to see. One regiment is dressed in white duck trousers, European boots, and a tunic of blue with red trimmings. They look in the distance like engine drivers out of employment. All are armed with Martini-Henry rifles, and march in two Indian files, each the width of the road apart from the other. The second regiment (both by the way are Duranis and are composed of picked men) wears black 'understandings'; but in every other respect appears to be exactly like the first. Their notions of sentry-go are original and elastic; and many of them have their Martinis protected from the rain by dirty bits of cloth.

The screw-gun battery, six guns, which immediately preceded the Ameer, is the most workmanlike section of the force. It has already camped, set out the guns, quarter guard etc. *secundem artem*. The carriages are painted dull green, and the various parts of the limber and gear are carried by horses. Abdur Rahman, who limps slightly, now that he is off his horse, has just gone into his tent; a large blue and white striped *shamiana*, in the centre of the camp. Colonel Waterfield and General Gordon are doing the honours thereof, and Golam Hyder, Commander-in-Chief, is having his boots cleaned, preparatory to following them. Golam Hyder's uniform is a mass of gold braid — more gorgeous even than some Civilian uniforms — and he wears the Tartar cap of grey Astrakhan fur. His saddle cloth is a blaze of gold and velvet, with monograms and devices, *ad lib*, on its surface. The Ameer, it seems, has been suffering severely from gout — hence the delay in his arrival — and is still very lame. Usbegs, Duranis, tag rag and bobtail, are settling themselves as comfortably as they can in camp. The Ameer has been left to himself, and the scene closes amid more rain, a wild confusion of horses, tent ropes, camels, guns, and a far-reaching tumult of strange tongues. The following must be close upon three thousand.


                                   Later — March 29th, 6 o'clock.


No less than four contradictory telegrams from Jumrood, in the course of the afternoon. 'First he would, and then he wouldn't: then he said he really couldn't' — and to this view of the case Abdur Rahman has finally struck. If the spirit moves him, he may up-sticks and come into Peshawar in the middle of the night, but it is to be hoped that the blessed rain will keep him to some decent hour, and that he will arrive here to-morrow about seven. How long he will stay here is quite another matter.

# To Meet the Ameer

*Civil and Military Gazette, 2 April 1885*

**Attribution: Sussex Scrapbooks 28/1, p. 19. Diary, 30 and 31 March 1885**

The seventh article in the series.

Peshawar, March 30

[ ... ] Monday night, half past eight; pitch dark and the platform of the Peshawar station, covered with the Ameer's horses, which are at the present moment entraining for Pindi. Unless you are actually on the platform, in serious danger of your life from flying heels and panic stricken horses, you will not appreciate the beauty of the situation. His Highness really starts to-night at eleven o'clock, more or less exactly, and before that hour strikes, seven hundred and fifty horses are to be cleared away somehow. Four detachments have already gone off. This is the fifth and, I fancy, the last. The Assistant Commissioner is, apparently, the only man who can interpret the *Pushtu* of the yelling crowd to the natives around. Neither Cabulies nor horses have seen a train before; but the former are adapting themselves wonderfully to circumstances. In the first place they are absolutely fearless; plunging head first, into the squealing, kicking truck-loads of yaboos, without a moment's hesitation. Hyder Ali, Commander in Chief of the Ameer's army, has recognized the gravity of the situation and — think of it Cs. In C. all over creation — is working like a navvy in the midst of his men. Three horses are down in a wagon of eight, and from the appalling noise inside, seem to be kicking each other to pieces. Hyder Ali, guided by a single lantern, dives into the tumult, directs, superintends, harangues and — from the tone of his voice — swears till the wretched beasts are set right. If one restive grey stallion could speak, he might even tell us how the Commander-in-Chief backed him, protesting and snorting, up the slippery gangway and into his fellows once more.

What Mr Anderson's work through this dripping afternoon and evening have been, that unfortunate officer only knows. It is admitted, of course, that the Punjab Commission understands 'a little bit of everything'; but to turn one of that distinguished body, for the nonce, into a Trooper-cum-Traffic Superintendent-guard-cum-syce civilian, *does* seem rather hard. However, the horses *must* be got away, and the 9—20 mail train to Pindi, starts as near her proper time as may be.

In the centre of the platform stands a huge baggage cart drawn by two bullocks; and round this the tumult rages unceasingly.

'Duserah gorah lao.' 'Kubberdar!' ['Bring the other horse. Look out!'] 'What the deuce is this 'ere man a saying of sir?' seems to be the keynotes of the cats' concert: Pushtu gutterals, and a running accompaniment of kicks, all down the waggons, completing the chorus. The horses are all entrained, with their packs on; consequently when one falls down, the work of picking him up is rendered doubly difficult. Each Cabuli, too, carries a heavy load on his back and is as difficult to move as the horses themselves. Ammunition cases, in red wood, home-made Martini-Henri rifles; tent poles, furs, food, samovers, hookahs, saddles two feet high, and every other sort of odds and ends, lie about in wild confusion. Everything is wet and clammy to the touch, and in the black darkness one stumbles across men and horses at every step. If the scene could be reproduced on canvas, it would be ridiculed as wildly impossible. Usbeg lancers and locomotives cheek by jowl; tartars and telegraphs, jostling each other; western civilization and eastern savagery, blended in the maddest fashion, and on the just and unjust alike, the ceaseless pitiless rain. No words in my power could do justice to the tableau. After an hour and a half of hard work, the Commander-in-Chief retires; the Assistant Commissioner, soaked from head to foot, follows his example, in order to snatch a little rest before the Ameer's 'special' is taken in hand, and the waggons of horses and men steam off into the darkness; the thump, thump, thump, of their four-footed occupants, ringing in our ears as long as the tail lights of the train can be seen. It may be remarked here, that the ingenuous 'Yaboo' only showed his astonishment at the iron horse. The

Cabulis *may* have been surprised, but they took snuff and concealed their feelings.

The whole business — admirably as it was despatched — the mail train was not more than an hour or so behind time — was a huge mistake. Seeing that Abdur Rahman had been already so late in keeping his appointment, and that the mischief of this delay was beyond repair — a day extra would not have mattered. This would have given time for entraining the horses quietly, and possibly another four and twenty hours will mend the weather at Rawal Pindi, where, like Peshawur, it has been raining heavily.

Rawal Pindi, 31st March, 5—30 A.M.

That last sentence was a mistake altogether. The weather has not mended, and Rawal Pindi in the grey dawn is only Peshawur turned up side down. Here are the Yaboos and Cabulis coming out of the train instead of entering it. Here too are the sodden, rain-soaked followers; the gruelly mud under foot, and the heavy clouds overhead. Abdur Rahman left Peshawar last night at eleven for a wonder. I am unable to record the departure. It must have been a depressing function at the best, but he will be here in two hours and a half. Meantime, some drenched coolies are decorating the station, with mournful bunting and depressed laurel boughs, and sight seers, even at this unholy hour, are beginning to drop in. The red cloth is weighted with an unromantic brick, lest it should take unto itself wings.

*Later.* — The Guard of Honour — Royal Irish Fusiliers — has arrived and are being rained upon. Several big wigs, with plumed hats and restive horses, are being treated in the same manner. Also the K[ing's] D[ragoon] G[uards] in blue cloaks, and the 14th Bengal Lancers and 15th Bengal Cavalry and a battery of horse artillery. Lots of prancing and curvetting in the mud; more rain, gouts of mud everywhere — and a bevy of umbrellas on the station roof. The umbrellas are agitated, and a rush is made to the business side of the station. Up to the present we umbrellas, have been watching the troops below — and commenting on the appearance of the Punjab Volunteers. One company has yellow gaiters. Every one of the umbrellas is consumed with envy. The other companies have no gaiters. 'Aren't the fellows getting wet' say the umbrellas, and forthwith dismiss the volunteers from their minds. The Ameer has arrived, the Guard of Honour presents arms; the Band strikes up, and our respected Lieutenant Governor, Sir M. Biddulph, Mr Perkins, Commissioner, Colonel Henderson, and another cocked hat or two, emerge warily from the shelter of the waiting room verandah, and prepare to receive His Highness. His Highness is not in a hurry to come out, but finally descends — very lame — clad in a black surtout with gold trappings, and the invariable Tartar cap — and shakes hand all round. Desultory conversation in the rain, which the cocked hats appear to enjoy immensely, and then a rush for certain barouches, four in hands, landaus, etc., which have been waiting outside. Where were the elephants and the Judges of the Chief Court, the Commissioners, and Durbaies, who were to mount them; Forty two animals, swathed as to *Jhool* and *Howdah* with canvas and looking for all the world like huge dhobies' donkeys with the week's wash on their backs, have been swaying pensively in the midst for an hour past. These are now shuffled homeward riderless, and with the glories of gold embroidery and silk trappings hidden from view. Thus ended the elephant procession which was to be the greatest sight that Asia had ever seen. Man durbars but Jupiter Pluvius downpours, and the game is a losing one for thin-skinned mankind. The barouches are trotting away, and the K.D.G.'s, the 14th B.L., the 18th B.C. and the guns form the escort in front and behind them. Neither rain, nor mud can destroy the beauty of British Cavalry, or prevent their presence from impressing the bystander. In spite of mired horses, and soaked cloaks, the escort was an impressive sight and it is to be hoped that the Ameer looked at them as he passed. They have all gone away to the Commissioner's house — pro tem the Ameer's bungalow, the Guard of Honour playing 'for he might have been a Roosian' etc. Ribald, is it not? At the bungalow the third *ziafut* of Rs. 21,000 will be presented. As the umbrellas descend from the roof of the Station, the welcome news goes round that to-day is a *dies non*. There will be no durbar, and the review is postponed till Saturday. 'So home' as Mr Pepys said 'which pleased me mightily to change my filthy raiment, and thank heaven that the king comes not thus everie daye.'

# To Meet the Ameer

*Civil and Military Gazette, 7 April 1885*

**Attribution: Sussex Scrapbooks 28/1, p. 23. Diary, 5 April 1885**

The ninth article in the series.

**(From our Special Correspondent)**

Rawul Pindi, April 5

[. . .] Sunday has been devoted to discussing the chances of war, and since the one invariably entails the other, unlimited abuse of Mr Gladstone and all his works. Besides this there is nothing else to do. The weather, as a matter of interest, has been played out long ago, and we view it now with the calm despair born of quagmire tents and soaked garments. In the Viceroy's camp there reigns a holy peace, and as with us — melancholy resignation. Things are at a dead stop all round, and if Monday brings us rain once more — as from the appearance of the sky it most certainly will — we shall have to halt this funeral procession for another four and twenty hours at least. Tuesday's manoeuvres on Khanna plain have been eliminated from the programme, and the parade ground on which the review takes place to-morrow, will permit of very little room for extended movements. By the way, the programme has not yet been officially made public, and a good many people are still in the dark as to what takes place when and where it will be necessary to go. But the blackest ignorance of all reigns among those who ought to know better. Not a soul is posted up on the one absorbing question of the day: — 'When, o when, shall we get out of this?' 'It may be for years and it may be for ever. Love, I know not when or how' is the burden of our daily song.

'There is always something in the pleasures of our friends which profoundly disgusts us.' Every account received from the

Ameer's part of the station tells us that both Abdur Rahman and his following are having a delightful time, and are not in the least hurry to move on. Of the Ameer, I am unable to speak authoritatively: for the ruler of Afghanistan is as zealously guarded as a *pardahneshin*. A Sabbath day's journey to his camp, however, has convinced me that his troops at least are in clover. Their tents are pitched about a hundred yards to the right of the Commissioner's house, looking towards the station on a slight eminence with good drainage. This qualification of a camping ground is exceedingly necessary; for without any aspersion on their valour, I may say that the Ameer's troops must be about the dullest [*sic*: dirtiest?] that ever hammered tent peg into the ground. They are picturesque — immensely so. The Usbeg lancers, in their mustard-hued coats, shaggy caps and strange accoutrements, would make an artist's fortune. So would some of the interiors of the tents, where rich carpets, quaint Persian aftabas, turquoise-studded brow and breast bands, Russian Samovars, orange peel and slices of red raw mutton lie about in picturesque profusion; everything being toned down by dirt and use from its original brightness and purity.

The occupants of these tents are as frank and inquisitive as children; and air their few words of broken Hindustanee, or in rare cases, English, with a pride delightful to witness. What they want they ask for. For instance the apparition of an English visitor in a tent brought round him half a score of Usbegs chattering like daws. His boots seemed to excite the greatest admiration; then the texture of his clothes and finally his cheroot. One lancer watched this last article of attire — indispensable in *that* camp, and finally suggested that the Sahib should give it to him for a few minutes to smoke. The Sahib's caste prejudices against mutton fat and grime stood in his way here, whereupon the lancer promptly replied, 'Have you any more about you' and lest the questioner should be led into a lie, passed his hand rapidly over and into the sahib's breast pocket. Another worthy suggested an exchange of foot gear, and was considerably astonished on being refused. In their own country they must be beau ideals of ruffianly caterans. On their best behaviour in British territory they are simply amusing boisterous Fridays, and a Robinson Crusoe sort of tour through their tents is a novel and very amusing experience. In their manners towards each other they are loud, not to say impolite. Firewood lies stacked about the camp in large quantities and a heated argument concludes sometimes with an interchange of small logs and several screams. At least this happened twice in half an hour while I was there. Their horses are much cleaner than themselves, and are mostly short-legged, iron-grey Cabulis of demonstrative habits. The saddles, apparently, are but seldom taken off, and the horses are nobbled as well as heel roped. The officers mix freely with the men, and hold little levees of their own outside their tents; a group of from five to ten men lolling on the ground in front of each officer.

The lancers apparently do 'stables' in full review order, and whenever the spirit moves them. These things make the mustard-coloured coats dirty and the horses unkempt. The mutton carcases for the day's consumption are placed, tenderly, on a charpoy. Sometimes the charpoy is occupied by a man, more generally by a dog. One further peculiarity of these interesting savages is worth recording. They blush like girls; the blood showing plainly under the fair skin. Those anxious for a novel sensation, I would recommend to compliment as Usbeg on his martial appearance, and to stand by while the burly giant looks down on the ground; plays with his lance sling and becomes tricked into confusion.

# To Meet the Ameer

*Civil and Military Gazette, 8 April 1885*

Attribution: Sussex Scrapbooks 28/1, p. 825. Diary, 6 April 1885

The tenth article of the series. The review it describes was later the basis for 'Servants of the Queen' in *The Jungle Book*.

(From our Special Correspondent)

Rawalpindi, April 6

At last we seem to have started work in earnest and the gloomy forecasts of yesterday have been but partially fulfilled. To be sure the sky is as black as ink all round the horizon, but the clear patch of blue in the centre, and the restless winds, promise April showers at the utmost, and not the steady wet to which we dwellers in tents have become so painfully accustomed. In an hour or so, the grand Review of troops in camp will begin. Meantime, carriages and riders are already beginning to assemble by the three huge sheep pens which mark the spots whence the Viceroy, the Punjab Chiefs and the common folk, are to view the ceremony. Of decoration, beyond the naked pole of the saluting base, there is no sign — the army here gathered together is to march by with no scenic accessories, beyond those of gloomy skies, wind-shaken woods in the back ground and the shrill whistle of the iron horse in front. The King's Dragoon Guards' parade ground, lies to the right of the Jhelum road and to the left of the Rawal Pindi Fort, but looking in the same direction. It is situated, in the language of the guide books, on a slight eminence, overlooking a fold of low hills below the fort. The Jhelum road and the Punjab Northern Railway, bounds it on the left, and the fort on the right. As nearly as I can judge, the wooden sheep pens face due south, commanding a most un-Indian landscape. But for the white turbans and *puggris* studding the railway bridge, it might be a view at the foot of the Sussex Downs, anywhere a dozen miles inland from Lewes. The Review is to be merely a March Past, without manœuverings of any kind, and Abdur Rahman is to sit still by the Viceroy's side, and watch the living tide roll by. He should be weary of watching before the work is over. Pindi Fort is the better part of a mile away from here, and already the slope below the bastions is sown with little red specks, which shuffle and agglomerate themselves, until they finally assume the shape of two red bars, and moving on, are lost to view behind the trees on the Jhelum road. This is the first regiment getting ready for the March Past, and at least half a score of field glasses proclaim that it was the 33rd. The company, in every sort of vehicle, from the lordly 'fitton' to rattling ticca gharri, is assembling as fast as may be;

and whenever there is a lull in the rolling of wheels, the air becomes alive with the music of unseen bands of regiments moving into position along Jhelum road. Already half a dozen worthy gentlemen of mature years, mounted on fiery untamed steeds, and thickly covered with gold lace and red cloth, are caracoling from one end of the ground to another, and shouting multitudinous directions, apparently about nothing at all. Certainly, the Police who have been told to keep the crowd in order, pay not the least attention to their blandishments; certainly the regimental bands, which have taken up their position in front of the saluting base, are beyond their jurisdiction, and as yet no regiments have appeared. But their exercise appears to afford the wandering knights errant considerable satisfaction, and they are riding as if for life. First a hasty gallop from left to right of the parade ground, and a peremptory mandate, so it seems, to the rolling clouds in that direction. Then a tug at the curb, a flourish of horse tail and human spurs, and a fourteen-anna burst in the opposite direction. And so *de capo ad lib*, and with as much martial expression thrown into the business as a pulling horse and an insecure helmet will allow. These vagaries always foretell a good review — as much as the flight of the returning swallows, herald spring in England. Carriages and horses are arriving in shoals as I write, and the sombre skies greet, with a sharp shower of rain, an assemblage which includes half the best known men in India, and a fair sprinkling of the great ones of the earth. But the Viceroy and Ameer have not yet put in an appearance, and we have yet the excitement of the Viceregal salute to undergo. When three or four hundred vehicles are all jammed together in a space a few hundred yards long, the consequences of thirty-one guns just behind the horses are likely to be interesting.

11 o'clock or there abouts. The guns have fired, the horses have protested, and His Excellency, Earl Dufferin, Viceroy and Governor-General of India, and His Highness, Abdur Rahman Khan, ruler of Afghanistan and its dependencies, are riding side by side to the saluting point. The Viceroy is in plain clothes, with a star on his breast. The Ameer, like Alice Fell, is clad in duffel grey, with a gold embroidered black belt, long boots, and the tartar cap of grey Astrakhan fur. He is riding a small bay pony, and looks burlier and more thick set, than ever. With these two, ride a miscellaneous escort of English and Afghan officers,

all well-mounted, and ablaze with gold and silver trappings. They take up position to the right and left of the saluting point, and the show begins.

First the Commander-in-Chief and his staff, and Sir Michael Biddulph and his Staff, ride past to their post, opposite the Viceroy's, and draw up in line with the bands. Then, without a word or warning, the railway bridge to the left becomes alive with the glitter of steel, and the bevey of red coats, as the 33rd, the head of the first division, debouches into the open, at the double. And here I may point out the one disadvantage of the ground chosen. To get down from the Jhelum road to the open ground below, the troops have to walk down an embankment — which naturally threw them out of their step — dress and close up as best they can, and go straight on past the Viceroy. They have about three hundred yards wherein to recover themselves, and except to some ultra military eye, seem to go past perfectly. After the 33rd, come the Royal Irish — a strong regiment in every respect, and now we are fairly settled down to business. The bands in front of the saluting point, play the men through as they go. The unattached officers have ceased from galloping, and there is a great quiet over us all.

The 14th Sikhs, the 21st Punjab Native Infantry, the Rifle Brigade, the 4th and 5th Goorkhas, little men taking long strides, the Royal Irish, the 21st Punjab Native Infantry, the 1st Goorkhas and the Volunteers, have passed by. Red, khaki, green, buff, maroon, coats and facings — an infinity of booted feet coming down and taking up, with the exactness of a machine — thousands of pipe-clayed pouches swinging all in the same direction, and all with the same impetus, dazzle the eyes, and produce on the mind, the impression of some interminable night mare. Finally, one loses all idea that the living waves in front are composed of men. It has no will, no individuality — nothing, it seems, save the power of moving forward in a mathematically straight line to the end of time. It was a positive relief to cast one's eyes to the end of the parade ground, and watch the columns, ragged and extended, in their scramble down the side of the road. The procession still continues, and the Scotch regiments are appearing on the scene. The Highland Light Infantry, the 78th, followed by the Guides, the 19th Punjab Native Infantry, the Cheshire, with their riddled colours and the wreath atop, the 1st Punjab Native Infantry, the 3rd

Sikhs, the 2nd Manchester, the 24th and 25th Punjab Native
Infantry, and then, thank goodness, a pause for the Cavalry.
The Jhelum road, as far as the horizon, is covered with returning
troops, outlining the curves of the road, in red and dun colour.
Abdur Rahman Khan is not to be lightly spoken to, so that it
is impossible to say for certain what he thinks; but his hands
are dropped on his ponie's withers, and with head slightly bent
forward, he is watching the incoming and outgoing line. Even
an Englishman, accustomed as he is to talk of the degeneracy of
our armed forces in these days, has, for once, to let such idle
cavilling be, and content himself with wonder, pure and simple,
at the harvest of the dragon's teeth, which we garner within our
borders. Dublin and the Deccan, Paisley and the Punjab, Nepal
and Lancashire, one might continue the antitheses indefinitely,
have all contributed to the crop of armed men ready for war,
and it may be that the grey clad figure in the fur cap, is reading,
marking and inwardly digesting the lesson. But no muscle on
his face shows any signs of emotion, and the arrival of the Cavalry bands forces me to relinquish gush, in order to gaze on the
next scene of the pageant. This has at least more life and movement than the former, seeing that no regulations on earth will
keep horses' heads from nodding up and down in irregular time,
and there was something terrible in the utter immobility of the
foot soldiers. The 9th Lancers open the ball, and of these it can
only be said, as of all the others, that they are fine men on fine
horses — albeit the latter look a trifle drawn and tuckered up,
from marching and exposure to the rain. After the 9th come the
14th and 19th Bengal Lancers, the King's Dragoon Guards, the
3rd Bengal Cavalry, the 15th Bengal Cavalry, the Carabiniers, the
Guides and the 15th Bengal Cavalry [*sic*], in Squadrons, shaking
the earth as they pass. Are there any words to describe adequately the appearance of well-mounted, well-drilled cavalry? The
military world here contents itself with saying, that such and
such a regiment went by better than such another; that one
squadron kept its distance, whereas another did not, and so
on; but the absolute symmetry of the whole; the wonder of
it all, are taken as matters of course, grown familiar by long
usage.

Abdur Rahman Khan made no sign throughout this last revelation — for this it must be to him. But when the artillery makes
its appearance there is certainly something very like surprise

visible on his countenance. Three batteries of Royal Horse Artillery, four field batteries, the European screw gun batteries, and three native mountain batteries file by, all as neat as new pins. The Field and Horse batteries go past as one gun. A little thickened and blurred in the outlines, as if seen through a mist, but nevertheless one gun. How it's done, the civilian's mind cannot tell. To all appearance, the driver of the near wheeler lays the stock of his whip lightly on the withers of the off wheeler — and there you are, with about six inches between axle and axle, as level as though all six guns had been planed across the muzzles, jammed into a gauge and left there. This too, after guns and limber had to plunge down the enbankment, recover themselves, and reform in about three hundred yards. It may be said: — 'But this is only what we pay for, and all you have described, are but the incidents of an ordinary march past.' When twenty thousand men march past in a straight line for two hours, in the presence of the men who will have to make the history of the next four years, the occasion is of anything but ordinary importance; and it is only fair, therefore, to record how superbly the whole function went off. The one touch of the ludicrous, to relieve the almost oppressive gravity of the proceedings, comes in appropriately enough at the end, in the shape of the elephant battery. Left to himself, my Lord, the elephant, is an imposing beast; but there is something very comic in his appearance when he is harnessed, 'random' fashion, to a siege gun. The weighty piece of ordnance bundles after him like a child's toy, and all the ropes and chains and pads, wherewith his massive form is begirt, look like so many pieces of pack-thread. The Campbellpore behemoths bring up the rear of the Indian Army, at a sober and dignified pace; while behind them come the battery bullocks, and our old friend the Punjabi *bylewalla*, thinly disguised in a uniform, prodding them with a stick. So we drop from all the pomp and circumstance of glorious war, from patriotic enthusiasm and much gush, to the things of every day life again. But for a little while only. The Ameer has yet to see what manner of troops our feudatories could bring into the field, should occasion arise. Pattialia, Nabha, Jhind, Faridkot, Kapurthalla, Bahawalpore, have all contingents to show — and the sight must shock the Ameer exceedingly. When he was driving from the station on his arrival in Pindi, he asked several questions regarding the native contingents, and expressed the utmost surprise that the British Government dare to allow the dragon's teeth to be sown anywhere but in her own borders. But they took part in the last Afghan war, said the officer with him. 'Ah! and were killed off that way,' was the Ameer's reply. 'No, they kept our lines of communication open in the Kurram Valley.' 'Did they? I should have sent them where they might be thinned a little.' Evidently His Highness does not approve of armies within armies, and the close of the review must shock him exceedingly. Here are contingents of well-drilled, well-armed men in a conquered country, playing their bands, giving their words of command, and above all dragging their artillery, the deadly guns of the English, under the very noses of their rulers. And truly the native contingents are magnificent troops to look at. A little ragged in their dressing here and there, and below comparison with English batteries, as regards their artillery, but still magnificent men. I am unable to say which are which, for field glasses are of no avail here; a catholic taste in buttons preventing accuracy of observation.

They were all good, and would have been better as regards the cavalry, if so many of the horses had not been the pink nosed, mottled squealers that one is accustomed to associate with circuses, all the world over. About three thousand in all have gone by, and the guns are making ready to salute. Viceroy, Ameer and escort have swept round to the road, and are making haste to begone, as a sharp thunderstorm is doing its worst among us just now. But the abominable weather of the past week seems to have broken for good, and this is merely an April shower. The road to Khana plain is still full of troops, and the elephant battery is shuffling home hastily to tiffin. The great review of the Pindi Conference is over; and could scarcely have taken place under more favourable circumstances. There was no sun, which in April is distinctly a blessing; there was no dust, and the turf holds no mud, so that the troops have gone by speckless; and, so far as can be, after having been in review order for some four hours or so, untired. From beginning to end of the performance, there has not been one single hitch of any kind. Abdur Rahman has seen for himself the harvest of dragon's teeth as we grow it in this country, and doubtless has drawn his own conclusions. The sword is mightier than the pen by far to an Afghan; and each bayonet and field piece will carry more weight with our guest, than the courteous preambles of the Conference proper.

# Simla Notes

*Civil and Military Gazette, 24 June 1885*

**Attribution: Sussex Scrapbooks, 28/32, pp. 2–3. Only the first part is actually included in the Scrapbook.**

The article, under the dateline of 12 May, begins in the *CMG* of 16 June and is continued under the same dateline in the *CMG* of 24 June.

No comment is necessary on the first part of these notes. As for the politics in the second part, it is useful to know that Gladstone's government had been unexpectedly defeated in June, in part over a budget proposal to increase the duties on beer. Not long before, the government had withdrawn the troops marching to the relief of Khartoum in the Soudan, and at the same time was making on again-off again preparations for war with Russia over the Afghanistan question.

The prophecy is typical of the style of Kipling's later political utterances, on South Africa, and on Germany before the first world war, for example. The argument runs thus: the thing to be done is perfectly clear, but it is certain that no timely or thorough action will be taken; England, having missed its best chance, will then muddle through in costly fashion, only to be betrayed in the end by liberal politicians.

**(From our own Correspondent)**

Simla, May 12

At this point of the weekly narrative, a green monkey, with a pinky blue face, swings himself into the verandah, and suggests

YOUNG MONKEYS AT PLAY
(Copyright 1891, by J. Lockwood Kipling)

plantains and bread. He is the advance guard of a family nearly
twenty strong — hirsute fathers with short tempers and base
voices; unlovely mothers with babies not bigger than three
penny dutch dolls at their breasts; and irreverent hobbledehoys
who are always getting in some one's way and being bitten. The
hill side is alive with their clamour, and presently they assemble
in force on the lawn tennis court; despatching a deputation to
warn me that the babies are tired and want fruit. It is impossible

to explain to the deputation, that the sayings and doings of their descendants are of much greater importance than theirs. The leader of the gang has established himself on my dressing table, and investigates the brushes there. The flatsides would do splendidly to keep the babies in order. He tucks a brush under each arm, and strikes out for the open country, with a set of mother o'pearl shirt studs in his capacious pouch. Under these circumstances, I would ask all who know the ways of the monkey world, whether it is possible to continue writing? The deputation have fled down to the tennis court, leaving brushes and studs in the *verandah*. Virtue must be rewarded with bread crusts and over-ripe fruit. A tiny wizened dutch doll is one of the first to profit by my bounty; securing a large plantain skin, and essaying to nibble like its elders. The *bonne bouche* is unwieldy, and the dutch doll overbalances its little self. With a dolorous cry, mater-familias appropriates the dainty; catches the wailing monkeylet to her bosom, and feeds it by hand as she climbs along the top of the court fencing. The brush stealer, a 'strong masterless rogue' as the old statutes used to say, is deep in a packet of sugar. He scoops it up with human dexterity, and flings the paper away. A few crystals have dropped on the ground, and in the face of his sorrowing descendant, the brush stealer drops on his hands and knees, and licks them up like a dog. Darwin's theory must be faulty somewhere; for, behold, the manlike brush stealer has reverted to the beast, and a greedy beast at that. Yet a few more crystals are stuck in the fur of one sinewy leg. Clasping the knee with both hands, he swings a straight limb up to the level of his mouth, and mumbles it rapturously. Then he sits down to scratch and cuff an intrusive hobbledehoy across the back. Darwin's theory is correct after all. This is no monkey, but an irascible old gentleman with a short temper. He coughs consumptively and lies down for a nap, with his arm under his head. A few feet away, another dutch doll, the tiniest of the assembly, is swinging to and fro at the end of a supple pine branch, crooning some baby song to itself meanwhile. The brush-stealer rises stealthily from his lair, and with one gutteral oath, hurls the affrighted innocent down the *khud*, apparently sheer on to the Annandale race course. Then vengeance overtakes him, for the baby's mamma has witnessed the incident and grasps his ignoble old tail, and whirls him down the shaly slope with the rapidity of lightning. He returns, with the baby and a coat full of pine needles, intent on vengeance. The peace of the happy family is broken. Everyone is fighting with everyone else. The babies fly to their mother's arms, and in another moment the tennis court is empty. The pensioners of the Lakka bazaar are unpleasantly human; and unlike the mummy at the Egyptian banquets, remind one, not of death, but of our early births long since, when the 'heirs of all the ages in the foremost ranks of time' pelted each other with pine cones, and generation by generation shortened their prehensile tails. If the doctrines of transmigation and evolution be true, the brush stealer, in a few millions of years, may grace the Legislative Council of London on the Hill [Simla]. He is very, very solemn, and has broad and vigorous ideas on the subject of 'appropriation'.

But for the next century or two, the doings of men and not monkeys will interest us most; and I must return to the past week in Simla, with an apology for having devoted so much space to our country cousins. Reuter has informed us that Lord Salisbury has taken the helm of our blundering ship of State; and in a tepid sort or way we approve of the change. It is the just irony of fate, that our worthy ex-Premier should have been politically knocked on the head by a pint pot, and we are grateful to Providence for its mercy herein. It is also natural that on their accession to power, the Conservatives should straightway fall out among themselves. It is, best of all (I quote the military man's news) extremely probable that our new Premier will lead us rejoicing to immediate war with the 'Divine figure in the North'. Has he not called her a 'bankrupt swindler', and many other sweet names — all indicating his desire to come to conclusions at an early date? Is not the Right Hon'ble William Ewart Gladstone the only man who has mastered the art of eating his 'exuberant verbosity', and all the dirt which that oft repeated performance entails, by the shovel full; Lord Salisbury cannot and will not eat his words. Ergo, we shall fight. We shall blunder horribly at the outset; and throw away many army corps and much money in our laudable efforts to do things 'on the cheap'. Then the oriental mind, yet unused to our eccentric methods of doing battle, will turn against us, and we shall have our hands unpleasantly full for a time and times and half a time. Eventually, of course, we shall emerge from the conflict victors and triumphant, to float new loans for the depleted Russian treasury, and to give back gracefully her broken sword into her weakened right arm. Once committed to actual war, we shall fight as the 'mad Englishman' usually fights — with one hand tied behind his back, and the other ready to hoist up his enemy the moment he shows signs of having had 'enough of it'. Once that war is concluded, a Radical Cabinet, borne in on a flood of fair promises, will Soudanize Central Asia, leave it to 'stew in its own juice' and what not; and the merry merry game will begin afresh, to the greater glory of England and the greater comfort of the divine figure. Yet, many say that the war is to be a decisive one, and the 'smashing' of Russian pretensions final and irremediable. It is possible, of course, to 'smash' a power with 2,700,000 fighting men off the reel; but the operation is a long and expensive one. When a few hundred thousand great coats have been 'shooted at a bit', as the German strategist said at St. Privat, and when half a dozen British iron-clads have amiably rammed each other into old-iron in the Baltic, the British tax payer will rise up in his wrath, and England will sit down with a few hundred columns of special correspondents' gush over 'glorious victories': a few hundred miles of single line frontier railways, and an income tax which will impress her with the 'immorality of war' for the next decade. This is a noble and consoling forecast, and we can only pray that it may be utterly and absolutely false from beginning to end. [. . .]

# Simla Notes

*Civil and Military Gazette, 22 July 1885*

**Attribution: Continuous with the series of 'Simla Notes' of 15 July and 29 July in Sussex Scrapbooks 28/2, pp. 5–7; 42–4**

Major Wentworth King-Harman (1840–1919) whose lecture is here reported was later chief government inspector of small arms. The two names at the end of the report are those of General Thomas Fourness Wilson (1819–86), who entered the

Indian army in 1838 and was now a member of the Governor-
General's Council, and of Colonel Frederick Gustavus Burnaby
(1842–85), a soldier and adventurer killed in January 1885
in the Soudan.

(From our own Correspondent)

Simla, July 18

[. . . .] On Friday afternoon, those who were interested in such
things went down to the United Service Institute to hear Major
King-Harman lecture on the British officer and the weapons
(beyond those of loyalty, zeal and patriotism, and an immense
ignorance of the precise junction at which he ought to vacate
the ground in favour of the other side) — which he carries with
him into battle. It was a curious sight to watch forty or fifty
military men, from the grizzled General to the callow Subaltern,
listening attentively, while one of their service held forth on the
best means whereby a Ghazi might be stopped in mid rush with
revolver and sword, or a more civilized enemy neatly and effic-
iently despatched with either of the two weapons. The mystery
of death was not so uncommon a thing after all. Here was a
man, in a low, even monotone, showing how such a one had
warded it off with a strip of curb chain sewed on the jacket
from elbow to wrist; and how such another failed to enlighten
a flying Pathan upon the subject, because his sword was a regulation one and broke, after many downward cuts on the turbaned
pate. Then heads in various portions of the room nodded
acquiescingly, and an innocent, with pink and white cheeks,
murmured to his neighbour, how his sword, too, broke once
upon a time when he wanted it badly, and (the inevitable conclusion) it was an 'awfully near shave'. Then Major King-Harman,
to enforce his remarks, picked up from a side table certain
swords of various shapes, and bade the audience observe how,
with this skewer, a man might be run through the body ere he
had time to cleave you open; how with the 'Paget' blade, broad
curved and heavy backed — a degenerate service which preferred
cutting to thrusting, might make collops of their adversaries in a
deft and workmanlike manner. Furthermore, how he (Major

King-Harman) had had forged to his design a blade that should be good, both at cutting and thrusting; though he was doubtful about the wisdom of compromises. This blade he exhibited lovingly, and tenderly returned to its sheath. Then he poured scorn on the foil wherewith the subaltern was taught to fence, preparatory to using the heavy hilted regulation sword; and equal scorn on the 'lead-cutter', a shiny straight-bladed horror, related apparently to the Smithfield butcher's knife and the Japanese *Hari-Kari* instrument. Briefly, he held with thrusting not cutting, but if you must cut your adversary, use the Paget blade — and see that you get it.

Then the lecturer passed on to revolvers — the 'type of armed civilization with a life' (some say an erratic pellet) 'in each chamber'. He had specimens to exhibit of these pocket aids to glory, and demonstrated, *coram publico*, how the new Government ammunition did not fit the Government 'six shooter'; whereas the old did. But the old was obsolete. Therefore, it behoved you to find a suitable cartridge, while you were yet within reach of civilization, and not when you hastily rammed 'misfits' into too small a chamber at the last moment. He complained that the majority of revolver bullets were inefficient, and would not 'stop your man at thirty yards' (the soldier of all lands takes a tender and proprietary interest in the alien whom he wishes to slay. Hence the possessive, 'your man, your object, your prisoner',) unless you 'hit him in the eye'. Very few revolvers admitted of such painful accuracy. The Webby [*sic*: for Webley?] weapons carried a large enough pellet, and that was the best to buy. *Summa*. Buy the Webby revolver; see that your cartridges fit; practice often; and you may at some future time save your life, when you stand sadly in need of that article.

The lecturer thanked his audience for their kind attention; trusted that his words might do some good, and sat down near the swords and revolvers, as one who had been delivering some graceful little speech on geology, the easy question of river frontages in the Gangetic valley or the like. General Wilson, in moving the vote of thanks, described how he had entered the army at a date when Tommy Atkins marched to victory and continental hosts with a flintlock rifle, that dated from the year 1796, and was about as useful as a pea shooter at two hundred yards. On the occasion of his first engagement, said he, he was solemnly cautioned by his commanding officer in these words:

— 'Young man, whatever you do, don't draw that sword of yours. More than likely it's no good when it is drawn; and it is more than likely you'll do more harm than good with it.' (So jealously was swordmanship studied in the last days of the good old-fashioned duello.) 'Go into action with your double-barrelled gun loaded with buckshot, and may be you'll bring down your man at ten yards.' Armed in accordance with this counsel, did General, then Ensign Wilson, go into action; and we, of a later generation, who have heard of the Boers, and who hold the *jezail* to be effective at five hundred yards, wondered how on earth the veteran presiding at our meeting ever got out of his first engagement. General Wilson, very unkindly, refused to enlighten us about that double-barrelled shot gun, and the 'man at ten yards'. Even poor Burnaby had a breech-loader when he went on his last piece of knight-errantry, and the world was poorer by the loss of one of its bravest men. What did Ensign Wilson do when both barrels were discharged; and, with the archaic ramrod in his youthful hand, he paused on the field of strife to pour in the powder, the wad, and the wad above the shot; when he adjusted the percussion cap on the nipples of that fowling piece, and the 'man at ten yards' came up with a loaded gun or one of the swords that the Ensign was so particularly cautioned not to draw. But General Wilson had merely quoted the little incident to show how vastly the service had improved since the time that he joined it, how we might hope for further improvement, year by year, till — the speaker did not follow out the sequence — man shall no longer lift his hand against fellowman, because his doom would be sudden death, dealt by invisible engines in inaccessible positions at enormous ranges.

We moved the vote of thanks for suggestions how best to inflict sudden death on our enemies.

# Simla Notes

*Civil and Military Gazette, 29 July 1885*

**Attribution: Sussex Scrapbooks 28/2, pp. 42–4**

Kipling's Simla child is evidently the ancestor of the fictional

Tod and Wee Willie Winkie, both of whom are at ease with the native. In this description of him, the question that occupies Kipling in a number of his stories is quite clear: How can we manage so that the sympathy for and understanding of the natives shown by the child who has been brought up among them are carried over into the administrator who is to rule them?

### (From our own Correspondent)

Simla, July 25

[. . . .] At this point, it has dawned upon my stricken conscience that I have, for months past, omitted all reference to a large and *most* interesting section of society. To this section, namely to the Simla Baby, big, middling and little, I would tender, if there were any chance of this catching their eyes — my humblest apologies. After all, are the 'grown up' so very important? Their main duty in life is to buy ponies' panniers, bearers, dolls, ayahs and new garments for Little Knickerbocker or Miss Muffet. In many cases, if you will believe them, as all good children should believe their elders and betters, they only come up to Simla because Little Knickerbocker or his sister can't stand the heat of the plains from May to latter October. Let it be granted then, that the *raison d'etre* of the 'grown up' is The Baby and his wants. Let us, therefore, dismiss the 'grown up' from our minds, and turn to consider the Simla Baby in all its aspects. In the beginning it wears yards-long garments of 'braid and b'ue'. (Those two Scotch words may have a meaning of their own; but, until that meaning is found, will do excellently well to express the mysteries of Baby's Garments.) It is very pink, very soft and sleeps placidly in the glare of the mid-day sun, as an aztec on the stony soil of his thriftless mother country. It pullulates — that is to say, it ululates along the public roads, at the bandstand, on secluded bye-paths, and rustic *pugdundies*, whither its ayah and some dusky Romeo have retired to discuss '*anna*' and '*paisa*' over its innocent little head. It courts sudden death under your horse's feet, fast asleep in a perambulator. It babbles behind the curtains of a doolie, and clambers, if not thrust back like a leech, over the bars, essaying to drop head first on to the *kunkur*. Even in its most awful paroxysms of howling — and hill air opens the infant lungs to their tiniest extent — it is always adorable and, as yet, spoilt no more than its unprotected condition demands. Then the process — temporary — of deterioration sets in: Baby passes from long clothes into short ones, and is fearfully and wonderfully spoilt. There are about three hundred good reasons for spoiling Baby. I append a few. Firstly. — He goes home 'ere long, where the nemesis of a public school, wholly ignorant of 'bearers' and similar cattle, but desperately proficient in the use (illegitimate) of a towel and stump end yawns for him. Secondly. — His or Her Elder brother or sister went home last trooping season; and Baby misses them sorely. He must be comforted; and the Parental heart, while lavishing all its love on this last bird *in* of the nest, comforts itself also against the shadow of the great parting that destroys half the pleasure of our lives. Thirdly — the plains have made him 'fractious'. He cut teeth there, was plagued, far more direly than the Patient Patriarch, with blains, blisters and prickly heat. He is naturally high-tempered and sensitive, and must be humoured. Fourthly. — But Baby and Baby's Fortune are too sacred things to be touched on lightly here; and it may be that some tiny headstones in far away outstations tell, only too plainly, how Baby has come to be spoilt. Three-hundredthly and lastly. He is Baby, the Only Baby, and there never has been, is, or will be a Baby like unto him. While Peroo remains to carry him pick-a-back, or accompany him on his morning processions of state — *'Hathee per howdah: ghorah per zeen'* ['Howdah on elephant: saddle on horse'] as Peroo himself sings: as long as Assunta can tell him strange folk-tales by the hour when he is wearied of exercise, let Baby royally, devoutly and persistently be 'spoilt'. That nemesis of the brush back, the cricket net and the pitiless iron hard cricket ball, that takes a devilish pleasure in evading 'fag's' fingers will be his only too soon. And for Miss Muffet, delight of morning callers; despair of affable *saices*, coquettish beyond her half dozen years, and cunning as a changeling; are there not provided repressive Aunts; stern guardians who will insist on dragging the poor little innocent to Church twice weekly? (Miss Muffet's blue eyes cannot distinguish A from B, and her natural theology is composite and vague.) Also 'boarding schools for young ladies' — all six thousand weary, weary miles away? Miss Muffet sits her twelve hand hack like the little Amazon she is; climbs *khuds* that would turn an English child pale with horror, and has never yet had occasion to repeat her smallest command twice. Before she returns to take by storm, for the second time, her well-beloved Simla, she will have learnt many things.

Meantime – there is no blinking the unpleasant truth – she is a reckless, short tempered, hot tongued, golden-haired minx – amenable to no law save that of hunger. Two days ago, she escaped with elfin laughter from her *doolie*, and selecting the muddiest puddle, danced – actually danced – in it! Peroo protested feebly on the outskirts of the muddy tumult she was raising, (Assunta was chaffering for beetel round the corner, or it would never have happened). Why did he not pick Miss Muffet out of the mire? In reply to this, Peroo answered *'Miss Sahib ke hookum hai?'* ['Is it Miss Sahib's order!'] To his submissive soul, this set the question at rest conclusively, and Miss Muffet, still hard at work on her delectable *pas souillé*, asserted, radiant with delight, *'Han, hamara hookum hai. Jao tum'* ['Yes, that is my order. You go.'] The *'tum'* (when he isn't being treated in this way) is a gentleman in her Majesty's Bengal Civil Service, of some twenty odd years' standing, and a man of no small honour up here and down below. He went. He could not, for his garments' sake, snatch away the wilful little woman; and at the end of ten minutes, Miss Muffet, spotted like a camel-leopard, condescended to return to her doolie. A dozen years hence, Miss Muffet will deny that she ever did anything of the kind I have just described. She will have been at a seminary where young ladies don't dance in puddles as a rule.

Little Knickerbocker is several degrees worse than Miss Muffet: for, to childish wilfulness, he unites man's supreme contempt for all things feminine. His delight is in the legs of a horse, and he perils his sinful little soul hourly on the chance of investigating them. A special providence watches over his studies in natural science. Though ponies may wince and put back their ears, they never kick him. Yet if any person of less consequence – say a Member of Council, or a General Officer – were to follow his example, things would be greatly otherwise. Little Knickerbocker is hale-fellow-well-met with some six score *Jhampanies*, and they in turn almost worship him. Not long ago it was my exceeding good fortune to come across little Knickerbocker in all his glory. His Mamma had left him in her *ghari*, while she stepped into a milliner's shop. The visit was a protracted one, and several other ladies were shopping at the same time. That is to say, there were twenty *jhampanies* or so lounging in the road-way. Scarcely had Mrs Knickerbocker disappeared, than the *rickshaw* was taken with internal convulsions; and above the lap-cloth rim (he had dived below to investigate the structural peculiarities of rickshaws) emerged a tangled brown head, a disreputable sailor's hat, and the upper half of Little Knickerbocker. Then he held his *levee* of *jhampanies*, and I would defy even a Higher Standard, double pressure extra proficient to have done better; the conversation passed beyond his bystander's comprehension. It was flavoured with numberless jokes, for the coolies laughed like the children they are; and little Knickerbocker the loudest of all. It contained sound moral advice of some kind, for they sat on the ground and stared solemnly into his chubby little face. It enunciated grave truths of life and thought doubtless, for they shook their heads assentingly and said '*Je han*' '*Such hai!*' ['Yes sir. It's true!'] to the small philosopher. 'What was it all about?' At this question, the coolies straightway relapsed into stolid *netschies*, and retired to their respective charges. The spell was broken, and the levee dispersed; only Little Knickerbocker was equal to the occasion. He bent forward over lap-cloth with a grin — an unadulterated boy's grin — 'I was only talking to them about themselves.' Spirit of every ruler and administrator that India has known, has it been reserved for the Simla baby to talk to the people of the land 'about themselves' as Little Knickerbocker did; and to him and him only will the coolies speak unrestrainedly 'about themselves'? Here were twenty souls, who would have grovelled, cringed and lied with oriental fervour to any district officer who might address a word to them, chattering like daws 'about themselves' to seven year old Little Knickerbocker. To-day my respected Diplomat might make shift to rule India with some success; or at least with that much babbled of, seldom seen, 'touch with the people' — a shadow we chase through durbars, madressas, drains, universities and hospitals and — miss after all. But he will be neither ruler nor administrator — not he, a dozen years hence — after much intermediate hammering and being hammered — he will admonish his *syce* with the bar end of a stirrup leather and ask his seniors: — 'What on earth does the *soor* mean by all this infernal gibberish?' He too, will indignantly deny that he ever talked to 'those beastly *jhampanie* fellows' 'about themselves'. Is it only the children who know, and the men who are ignorant? Little Knickerbocker maintains that because 'you ride a real horse. Mine's only a baby one. And you can dance with mamma when I'm in bed. And you can eat anything without Assunta slappin' you' *therefore* you must know everything. He may be wrong; and the owner of the 'real live horse', the man without an ayah to slap him may feel something very like a pang of bitter envy as he watches the dispersion of Little Knickerbocker's levee, and departs with the child's courteous little explanation: – 'I'm only talking to them about themselves' ringing in his brain.

I started to prove that Little Knickerbocker was a ruffian and a pest, and my pen has betrayed me. He is a hardened, graceless scamp, saved daily from sudden death, and ungratefully pummelling the hand that jerks him from under horses' bellies and hurrying wheels. He is ever so much worse than Miss Muffet in his own impish way, and there must be hundreds of him in Simla.

And this brings me back to my starting point – a 'variety entertainment' at the Gaiety Theatre a few hours ago. In addition to the usual songs and recitations, a Magic Lantern display was provided for the entertainment of the children who made up the greater part of a somewhat limited audience. It had been showery all day, and my last remark must not be taken to imply a slur on the entertainment which was good enough of its kind, and a wild dream of delight from the child's point of view. To this point of view it is best to adhere. My cicerone was Little Knickerbocker (he is in sailor's trowsers really, but he doesn't read any papers save illustrated ones) and next to him sat a friend aged about seven. Between the two of them, these Travelled Tots had 'done' the greater portion of the Continent, having seen men and cities from London to Venice. To these gentlemen then it was safe to confide oneself. Travel had not developed in them a spurious taste for music. The overture began; and travelled Tot number one unburdened himself as follows: 'I wish they would finish with this rubbish, and go on to something nice. Where's the magic lantern?' Entertainments are impossible without overtures, but T.T. didn't know, if or he did, didn't care. He bore with the recitation benignly; tolerated some other items of the performance, and was betrayed into merriment by a banjo song and a corney-grain ditty with a hipping refrain. Comparatively speaking, he hybernated till the room was darkened and the magic lantern began. Then he smote his friend joyously in the ribs, and the two, in a high clear treble, commenced the divine labour of criticism, which only children understand aright. There were fifty one slides altogether — some comic, some representing places of interest in Europe. Both kinds were accepted and criticised impartially. Slide No. 3 showed the Tower of London. Travelled Tot number one had been there, and felt that it was his own. He enlightened travelled Tot number two to this effect; adding, in a voice that could be heard from footlights to ticket table, 'and I know every room in it too'. Number two was occulted for the moment, but bided his time till the Lake of Como turned up. He had been there, (the whole room was in possession of his secret) and he scored one. The Monument and the Houses of Parliament were claimed by Tot number one, calmly, clearly, and dispassionately; as also was Westminster Abbey. The Rigi, the glacier de Bossons, and the cascade of Terni fell to number two, whose divigations on the continent had been extensive. Paris he knew, and a Rhine view he identified as a walking place in his wanderings. St. Peters, I think, was number one's property, and the Thames below London Bridge. 'I've walked across it you know, and it takes a quarter of an hour to cross.' Then came for number two the crowning triumph of the evening. A view of Milan Cathedral slid on to the sheet. He studied it critically for an instant, and then announced, in an irresistibly comic drawl, 'Why, that isn't one *bit* like Mi-lan Cathedral'. Number one collapsed. He could identify old friends, but he was not prepared to disparage them. Neither child laid claim to the Falls of Niagara or Constantinople, but they took a lively interest in both. They gazed long and lovingly on some kaleidescope horror that twisted and untwisted like a vision in the early stage of brain-fever. This was 'nice' and 'ought to be done again'. Finally, they expressed themselves thoroughly satisfied with the entertainment and departed, comparing notes, in the same *rickshaw*. Modern scepticism had already poisoned their young minds; and, instead of being thankful for men with moveable legs and arms, they wanted to know 'how it was done'. Both passed over, as unworthy of notice, the really delightful descriptive music that was played as each picture appeared. It was too dark to see who the performer was; but (to drop the children's spectacles for a moment) it is only fair to say, that his or her delicacy of touch was only equalled by his or her knowledge of fifty-one separate tunes. This, like number one's criticism on the overture, is genuine though clumsy, and delivered, as his, in ignorance of the pianist.

Before finishing, (Is it necessary to apologize for filling a letter with the ways and words of the Simla baby? The Plains one is dear enough to us all) let me introduce another absolutely veracious story of travelled Tot number two. It serves as an awful warning not to handle babes too lightly in conversation. Travelled Tot number two was younger then. He was dining at a *table d'hôte* in Bombay. Anxious to set the child at his ease, a fellow traveller said kindly, 'Well, my little man, I suppose this is the first time you have dined at a *table d'hôte*.' To him the *blasé* Ulysses above his cup: — 'No. Frequently in Paris!'

# De Profundis

*Civil and Military Gazette, 7 August 1885*

**Attribution: Sussex Scrapbooks 28/2, p. 21**

Written in Simla, a month before Kipling returned to Lahore and renewed bouts of fever.

### (A Study in a Sick Room)

A brisk canter in May on a pulling horse; violent perspiration, followed by a twenty minutes' lounge at the public gardens, where the flooded tennis courts reek like so many witches' cauldrons, and the Enemy is upon you. Neither Mrs Lollipop's *banalities*, the maturer charms of the Colonel's wife, nor the fascinations of a gin and tonic at the peg table will keep him at bay. With the dreary foreknowledge, born of many previous experiences, you shall recognize that, for the next twelve hours at least, you are 'in for it'; and shall communicate the fact with a sickly smile to your friends. The instinct of the stricken wild beast for rest and retirement drives you to your bachelor quarters. Man's wisdom recommends quinine and an early retreat bedward. Your pony, finding that you sit much after the fashion of a sack of flour, and are to be dislodged at any moment, mercifully forbears putting his knowledge to practical use, and walks home in the twilight soberly. He is stepping, you can swear, on wool; the reins thickening and lengthening in the most marvellous manner throughout the journey. Finally four ponderous hawsers control a huge head twenty feet away, and there is no end to the white line of the mall. It runs straight as an arrow into the sunset, whence hot breezes, bearing on their wings the choking savour of a hundred brick kilns, fly out to meet and buffet you in the saddle. A grey backed, red bellied cloud closes the vista; and, as you gaze, you are conscious of a feeling of irritation. Somehow or other it has got into your head, and lies like a red-hot bar just below your hat-brim. Decidedly to-night's experiences will be lively.

The stifling breezes have turned to marrow-freezing blasts as the pony stops at your door. One last test remains — though you yourself know that it will only render your certainty more assured. If the gorge rises at a tea-ripened, vanilla-scented 'super', if the mind turn with loathing from a well loved consolation, then indeed lie down and wait with what patience you may for the morning. Alas! nerveless fingers drop the match ere it is well alight. One half — nay, one quarter puff, is sufficient to convert you, for the time being, to the views of King James of blessed memory. '*Bearer, Sherry sharab quinine ke botal lao! Khana ne chahseay.*' ['Bearer, a bottle of sherry and quinine. I don't want dinner.'] Kurim Buksh guessed as much from your face when you half tumbled, half slid off the pony three minutes ago, and has already communicated the joyful news to his familiars. The Sahib is *bokhar*, and there will be an evening party in the servants' quarters to-night. Meantime his countenance expresses nothing save dumb grief. He pours out the wineglassful of sherry, and departs with the decanter — to be seen no more. As you have not ordered the lamps, or given any express instructions about iced water being placed by your bedside, he has not thought fit to perform either of these offices himself. The fever has you bound hand and foot for the night; and your voice, even at its most powerful pitch, will be far too weak an hour hence to disturb the revellers in the *serai*. It's an ill wind that blows nobody any good!

The great red cloud has faded out behind the *ferashes*, the moon looks down through the dusty heat haze, and the circalas are hard at work outside. *Crick! crick! crick! crick!* in the silence of the evening; and some miserable ragamuffin returning from the bazaar joins his notes to theirs. Every howl, chuckle and quaver echoes and re-echoes in your head like whispers in the gallery of St. Paul's. Have patience, for, as you yourself well know, your torments are but beginning. When those thirty grains of quinine shall have effected a lodgment in the sick brain, and wrestle with the phantoms there, the play will be at its height. A present you are merely hot and cold by turns; the moods varying so rapidly that you dare not regulate the *punkah* by them. Scarcely has the *'zor se kencho'* ['pull hard'] left your lips, than the burning wave has rolled by, and your teeth are chattering like castenets. If you told the coolie to *'chor do'* ['let go'] now, he would probably curl up to slumber, and be beyond your reach before the cold fit had passed. By knocking the books off the table and appropriating the tablecloth for a wrapper, something may be done; but above all things it is advisable not to look at the *punkah*. It has an unpleasant knack of growing big and little with exasperating rapidity; of retiring anon to the beams on which it is slung, and thereafter descending till it sweeps the floor. Moreover, it is iridescent at the edges, as long as the half light lasts. When that has gone, you had best follow the sun's example, and sink to rest — though this is a brutal sarcasm — at once. Wait, if possible, till the cold fit has overtaken you, or the sheets will strike icily chill on first getting into bed. Thus you may snatch a little comfort out of the jaws of pain.

You were to have dined out to-night, and by this time should have been in your trap on the way to Mrs Lollipop's. But man proposes and the fever disposes. You have sailed far out of the reach of such mundane matters as dinners and flirtations, and are alone in that strange phantasmal world that lies open to us all in time of sickness — on the first stage of your journey towards the Purgatory of sizes and distances. Of this you are dimly conscious, for the racking pains in legs and trunk have given place to pains in the eyes and head only. The cold fits have passed away, and you have been burning steadily for the last ten minutes, preparatory to a final glissade down a rolling bank of black cloud and thick darkness, and out into the regions beyond. Here you are alone, utterly alone on the verge of a waste of moonlit sand, stretching away to the horizon. Hundreds and thousands of miles away lies a small silver pool, not bigger than a splash of rain water. A stone is dropped into its bosom, and, as the circles spread, the puddle widens into a devouring, placid sea, advancing in mathematically straight ridges across the sand. The silver lines broaden from east to west, and rush up with inconceivable rapidity to the level of your eyes. You shudder and attempt to fly. The innumerable lines retreat with a long drawn *'hesh-sh'* across the levels, and the terrible sea is contracted to the dimensions of a little puddle once more. A moment's breathing space, and the hideous advance and retreat recommences. The unstricken observer would tell you, if you cared to listen (which you do not, for you are deep in a struggle for life), that this phenomenon is simply the result of the quinine taken a few hours ago. But it is a very real Hell to you, for the advancing and receding tide gives place to all manner of strange dreams, wherein you are eternally progressing between infinite parallel straight lines, as eternally being driven back in terror by a something that advances and retreats at the further end of the passage, or overwhelmed by immense agitations of the solid earth, all directed against your poor Personality. Mountains are riven from top to bottom, that their fall may block up the ravine in which you are trapped. Rivers are diverted from their beds to pursue you across doabs of never-ending quicksands; and when you have shaken yourself free from these horrors, the round globe herself opens to let you down into the darkness of her central depths, or it may be to lap you in her central fires. You are alone on some way-side railway station, planted amid burning sands. A tropical sun is searing your brain as you pace up and down the platform waiting for the train that is to bear you away from your pain. At length it comes. Shewing first as a tiny speck on the polished burning metals, nearer, nearer, nearer, in a reverberating *crescendo*, till it halts hotter even than the mid-day sun, a monster of winking brasswork and roaring fires. From the foot-plate, where he had hidden himself till now, leaps off a royal Bengal tiger with yellow eye balls and opened jaws, and as he springs at your throat, the masterless train flies away out of your reach, and disappears as rapidly as it came. The sands bubble and heave with the under-pressure of some volcanic power and — you have a brief respite before entering on the second stage of your journey — the Purgatory of Faces. Your cheeks are deep purple, your eyes blood-shot, and your lips cracked and dry. Kurim Buksh has forgotten the iced-water, for the table by your bedside is empty; and if your life depended upon it, you could never raise your voice above a whisper. Nevertheless, you imagine that your shouts for *peene ka paney* [a drink of water] would raise the dead. As a matter of fact, they have not reached the punkah coolie outside. The thirst will pass off in a little — or at least you will have other things to do than to cry, as Dives did, for a little cold water to moisten your tongue. So far quinine has bred the visions you have seen. From midnight till about two o'clock you must deal with the delirium of fever by itself, and the second circle of your torment will be followed, as you well know, by a third and a worse.

Even now, the space of unadorned white-washed wall between the almirah and the gun cases at the end of the room is filling up with your visitors. Ladies and gentlemen, who call at unseasonable hours, and are not to be hastened but by the law of nature, which jealously watches the tension on the silver cord, and relaxes it when the strain becomes too severe. If your mind is an active one, and your habit of life — I will be considerate — tumultuous, I scarcely envy you what you will see. At the best, the Purgatory of Faces is a weary and profitless experience. At the worst, only those that have been driven through its lowest circles can testify what it is. The six square feet of whitewash at which you are staring so piteously, frames, it may be, a truthful but none the less unpleasant epitome of your past life. Phantasmagoria of the mind's magic lantern — each slide projecting its image clearly, thanks to the limelight of a brain that just now cannot lie even to itself. What they represent to you, it would surely be bitterly unfair of me to say — and would, moreover, impel you to denials unbefitting the character of an English gentleman. Your voice has recovered its volume, and your language, forgive me for saying so, is unparliamentary and even profane. As that queer frieze on the wall slides by, thickens, dissolves and reforms, you are giving away with both hands much that it would have been well to keep to yourself — if you could. But the delirium has opened your lips, so that you cannot close them, or even cloak your thoughts with the decent conventionalities that our respectable life here below demands. The recurrence of that one face, in spite of the jostling crowd behind it, is exceedingly annoying, but capable of explanation on the simplest psychological grounds. The punkah coolie, whom your ravings have attracted to the chick, argues that the sahib has, for the time being, gone *pagal*, and will consequently not notice whether the punkah is pulled or not. Once more it is an ill-wind that blows nobody any good. Peroo, Dalloo, or whatever his name is, has disposed himself for a nap, while you fight your way out of the purgatory, or lose consciousness of its horrors through sheer exhaustion. The time is not far off, and, if you only knew, your skin is beginning to show signs of moisture. Violent declamation, accompanied with fantastic gestures, leads, by a natural law, to violent perspiration — and it is now close upon two o'clock. That uncanny picture frame fills less quickly than it did, and it is dawning upon you that your visitants were nothing more than idle shadows, and not, as you first held, an avenging army of embodied sins. You have dropped your voice to something a little above a sigh, and are slowly coming to. The last face dies out on the wall, raging thirst has returned, and but one more purgatory remains, wherein the half awakened mind shall scourge you with irrational terrors, and you shall be broken in spirit as children are broken at the prospect of impending and inevitable punishment.

The Purgatory of Vain Imaginings has opened to receive you, and already you are deep in its labyrinths. You are working against time at some hopeless task, which, in spite of your exertions, unfolds itself before your wearied eyes like the endless paper reel of a telephone. Official displeasure, the contempt of your juniors, degradation, forfeiture of your pension, and beggary are staring you in the face; and the burden of your daily work rides you like the nightmare. In a glimmering sort of way you can reason and elaborate consequences. You have embezzled money, taken bribes, sold appointments, betrayed your friend, and the judgment for these acts is even now at hand. The past six hours have broken your self-control, and ludicrous and pitiable delusions force you to sob like a child whose sum *'won't* come right'. For a married man, terrors are reserved far more formidable than any that can assail the bachelor. His wife and children are starving, have disgraced themselves for ever; he is repudiated by those he held dearest, and so on till the inevitable climax is reached — hopeless despair and (the woman's refuge) tears. With these last, and the protracted mental strain, comes the end of the penance — in the prosaic form of a violent sweat till dawn, and the night's experiences are drowned in that first deep draught of iced water that Kurim Buksh — taught by experience — brings with *chota hazree*. What was it Byron said about hock and seltzer after a night's debauch? You will answer that the crisp tinkle of the ice against the glass, those three or four deep delicious gulps of cold water, when the sparrows in the rose bushes are beginning their day's quarrels and intrigues, are worth a thousand times all the liquors that ever human ingenuity brewed or compounded. Have you not just explored the three circles of your fiery inferno, and returned unscathed; or at the most, if your journey has been a long one, only so weak as a little child? Entitled by right of past sufferings to the delights of an unmitigated Europe morning and the protracted pleasures of an after breakfast cheroot — those six inch incense sticks which you may burn this morning with a clear conscience in honour of the Joss of Idleness, wondering how it was that they tasted so villainously last evening. By the time that the first honey coloured darling was burnt to the stump, you will be prepared to swear that I, your faithful historian, have, to put it gently, wilfully and falsely exaggerated. 'Of course I was a bit light in my head and all that. Every fellow with fever is. But all that stuff about infernos and pictures is awful bosh. Man's a l——'; and Mrs Lollipop, on whom fever once laid no gentle hand, will lispingly back you up in the assertion; for out of her mind too, as out of yours, has passed all recollection of the time when an evening's chill 'drove the de-lighted spirit' a wanderer through the caverns of that very Inferno whose existence is so impiously denied, and that with lips still blue and parched from the vehemence of its fires.

# My Christmas Caller, or the Prescription of Sieur Asmodeus

*Civil and Military Gazette, 25 December 1885*

**Attribution: Sussex Scrapbooks 28/1, p. 41**

*Le Diable Boiteux* — the limping devil — is from the romance of that name by Alain René Lesage, published in 1707. Named Asmodeus, he performs for the hero of the novel the same sort of services that he does for Kipling's narrator. 'The Land of Regrets' is the title and refrain of a poem by the Indian civil servant, Sir Alfred Lyall.

'I am strictly proper now' said a voice from behind the big almirah which forms the principal ornament of my bachelor dining-room.

Now it couldn't have been the Bearer, because in the first place he doesn't speak English; and in the second, if he did, even he dare not utter so huge a fib. This was on Christmas eve, yesterday — a day of all days in the year I detest because it makes me homesick, and morose and irritable. That's why I always keep within doors and reflect on all the unpleasant things I know — the disgusting ingratitude of the Punjab Government to an able and efficient officer among others.

'Strictly proper, and immensely improved since Le Sage's time' repeated the voice from behind the almirah. 'May I come in?'

'Come in' said I shortly, for my thoughts were not pleasant ones. As a rule, I dislike men dropping in uncalled for.

'Thanks many. Will you make room for me at the fire — your almirah's rather draughty.'

It was Le Diable Boiteux. I recognised him even before I read the card which he presented. As he said, he was wonderfully improved from Le Sage's inimitable but somewhat coarse original. A neat dress suit, studs, a rose in his button-hole, and a pair of immaculate pumps had converted him into a very pleasant gentleman of the nineteenth century, with a slight — a very slight — limp. He pulled an arm-chair up to the fire, and stretched out his feet to the blaze.

'Hope I haven't inconvenienced you in any way, Smallbones?' he said.

'Not in the least I assure you *mon ami*. I've had the pleasure of knowing you so long by name, that it's almost like meeting an old acquaintance.'

Le Diable Boiteux did not seem pleased: — 'You knew me at once then' he said. 'On my honour I shouldn't have thought it. I've changed so — improved I may fairly say — of late years.'

He adjusted the rose in his buttonhole with a look of ineffable complacency. 'Le Sage — old Alain René you know — evolved me in the first instance; and since then I've been marching in the van of progress. I *hope* you understand that my moral improvement is on a par with my physical. I'm a reformed character. One of these days I may even lose my tail!'

He must have tucked it into his inexpressibles, for never a sign of a tail could I see.

'You were much nicer as you were, I think' said I judicially. 'Reforms are bad things.'

'Don't generalize. In your department perhaps. In mine, never. Just conceive me if you can, knocking about the back streets of Madrid with a vagabond student! I wonder how I could ever have been so low. But I've used my opportunities well, haven't I?'

'I don't know. It seems to me you've spoilt, if you'll pardon my saying so, a really superior — ahem — Devil to make a very every-day English gentleman.'

'Spoilt!' retorted Le Diable Boiteux, 'I'll show you whether reform has curtailed *my* executive powers. By the head of the great God Mammon I can strip off a roof as neatly as ever! Would you like to see me do it?'

'I beg your pardon a thousand times' I said 'but I really thought from your appearance you had taken your place permanently with us.'

'Say no more about it' returned my guest courteously. 'I'm of an exciteable nature — easily roused, but over in a flash, you know. And it *was* hard to call my powers in question, just when I'm going to give you a sample of them — a first class *séance* in fact. I've toured all over India to see if there was a more discontented man than yourself in the country, and there isn't. Consequently — *me voici*. Can I take a cigarette?'

'By all means. But my dear Devil, it is hardly necessary to remind a man of the world — I may say of *both* worlds — like yourself, that to call your host discontented, after hiding in his almirah and toasting your shins over his fire is not good form.'

'True' said Le Diable Boiteux — 'but I've been attending a meeting of a Bombay Cotton Mills Company, and there's nothing so democratic as shareholders in bulk. Still the fact remains that you *are* the most discontented man in India, and I'm going to spend an evening with you for your benefit and my amusement.'

'One moment though, my dear Sir! If I'm to go careering about on your back through this frosty night all over the station, I must really put on my ulster.'

My guest sprang to his feet, and addressed me oratorically: — 'Hastings Macaulay Elphinstone Smallbones! I ask you as a sane and sober man, *do* you think that I, a self-respecting gentleman, so advanced that I've almost forgotten the use of my wings, shall deliberately expose myself to rheumatism and bronchitis by flapping from roof to roof of this particularly chilly station with you on my back? Why you must ride nearly fourteen stone!'

'Thirteen-seven to be strictly accurate, Devil. How *am* I to guess how you are going to manage your *séance*, except after the approved fashion of Le Sage? You really ought to stick to it, you know.'

'What a fine old crusted Conservative it is! Besides I'm not a devil any longer. I've been promoted to the place of a benevolent imp, first class, third grade, *sub. pro tem.* In time I shall be a graded Goblin, entitled to draw the pay and allowances of a Robin Goodfellow. Ha! Ha! Le Sage never contemplated *that*! Conduct my *séances* after his bungling manner — not I! Science has done wonders since his death; and I avail myself gratefully of her aid. Come my friend let us begin!'

'I don't quite know what you're going to do; but give me your word there's nothing wrong about the business — no writing in blood or any lunacy of that kind.'

Le Diable Boiteux laughed merrily: — 'Blood and parchments and sulphur are relics of an effete and outworn generation.

They served their purpose in life; and in death you use 'em for the Christmas magazines. I dropped them — let me see — a hundred and forty years ago or thereabouts. No, my methods would make old Le Sage stand aghast with horror. Look here.'

He lifted delicately between his finger and thumb a pair of *pince-nez*, that had till then been reposing unobserved on the ample contours of his waistcoat, slung from his neck by a cord.

'Ever used a telephone?' said Le Diable Boiteux airily. 'Sometimes' I answered; the telephone in my office being the bane of my daily life. 'That's all right' said Le Diable Boiteux. 'You will see when you put them on, that this pair of glasses is to the eye exactly what the telephone is to the ear. One hundred and fourteen years hence similar instruments will be invented by your kind, when you shall have brought electro-magnetism to a higher pitch of perfection. Let me slip the cord over your head and adjust the nippers on your nose. It's an improvement on roof-lifting. What do you want to see?'

I reflected for an instant. Le Diable Boiteux nudged me in the ribs.

'I know what you are thinking of *mon ami*. What you are pleased to call home. Be it so. You shall see it.'

Even as he spoke, I found myself staring at the bustle and confusion outside the Criterion. The fog hung heavy over Piccadilly, and there came to my nose, or seemed to come, that delightful composite odour of gas, orange peel and hot asphalte so characteristic of Babylon the mighty. I am a Cockney by birth and education, and both sight and smell were inexpressibly delightful to me.

'Oh for a glimpse of my own people!' I sighed aloud.

The scene shifted in a flash, and I was staring at my two brothers, my sisters and a host of relations gathered round a mid-day dinner in the old brown house in West Brompton.

'Hideous notion, eating a heavy meal in the middle of the day' murmured Le Diable Boiteux in my ear. 'It would kill me in a week. Your people seem to be enjoying themselves though: listen a bit and see how much you are in their thoughts.'

I listened attentively for about ten minutes, before it dawned upon me that Le Diable Boiteux was speaking sarcastically. I heard much — the babble of fifteen tongues over turkey and beef and ham and all manner of dainties; but for any reference to myself I might have been dead and buried a century back.

Stay, though, when the dinner was at end, and everyone was toasting every one else, a small, curly-locked boy brought down his pudgy fist on the table with a bang, and gravely swallowing a wine glass full of water cried: — 'Uncle Djimmy! He gived me my bwicks.' So my health was drunk in water by a baby unnoticed in the general uproar.

'What *can* you expect?' said Le Diable Boiteux soothingly. 'You never "gived" the others "bwicks" my dear fellow. Just face the fact that the best and kindest of one's own people drop you out of their lives as much as you drop out of theirs. Unpleasant notion I admit; but it is so. You haven't been home for eight years, and that youngster's "bwicks" only came a month ago. However, try some more, and see if any one re-members. The nippers will work as fast as you can think.'

I tested their powers exhaustively, and found that Le Diable Boiteux had spoken the truth in both instances. They en-abled me to see and hear as quickly as I could think, and also to understand that Hastings Macaulay Elphinstone Smallbones had disappeared from the thoughts of all the great family of Smallbones as well as from the minds of his friends. Eight years' absence is a long time, I am willing to allow; but still I expected that I should have heard my name mentioned at the Christmas gatherings of our clan.

'Human nature all the world over' murmured Le Diable Boiteux once more. 'Didn't old Alain René make me show Don Cleofas something of the same kind? You know his works better than I.'

Le Sage was the last person in my mind as the visions flashed past. I was penetrated with a deep sense of my personal in-significance — a wholesome but unpleasant experience which some men go through life and miss. I made no answer, but continued to gaze steadfastly through the magic *pince-nez*. Sisters, cousins, aunts — I have two — old and once dear friends at home, had all alike forgotten me in their Christmas feastings. And here had I been nursing my *heimweh* over my solitary fire, and hungering for the sight of their faces — aye even for a glimpse of the surliest and least loveable among them!

Le Diable Boiteux broke in once more upon the current of my thoughts and his pictures.

'Haven't you seen enough yet?' he enquired. 'Take my word for it — in the multitude of their occupations and interests and desires they have naturally enough forgotten you. What else would you have? See! Your elder sister has six, and your younger four children — ten good and substantial reasons for forgetfulness. Blisworth is gone to Australia; Billiter is engaged; Von Downiski gone to the dogs, Pawson of your college going, if my old insight is what it used to be; and Teague so superbly successful in the things of your penny-farthing world, that he'd cut you if you spoke to him.'

'But — but — these were all my oldest friends!' stammered I, still glaring at the pictures as they fled past.

'I know it — ' returned Le Diable Boiteux composedly. '(Can I have another cigarette. Thanks.) That's why it does you good to look at 'em. Old Alain René himself couldn't have improved on the notion!'

(Le Diable Boiteux seemed to relish referring to his creator in this flippant way — just as a shopboy might snatch a fearful joy from calling his employer by his surname unadorned.) He gently tweaked the *pince-nez* off my nose, and patted me familiarly on the shoulder.

'It's unpleasant, but it is also necessary. The memory of you isn't so indispensably necessary to the comfort of your extensive family circle as you would like to believe. You have all gone your own ways in the world, and you naturally lose touch. Do you mean to say that you've been eating your heart out all these eight years through sheer home-sickness and dislike of your surroundings?'

'I'm afraid so,' I murmured.

'Skittles!' retorted Le Diable Boiteux scornfully, flicking the ash off his cigarette. 'It's your morbid vanity. You don't see a maravedi's worth of good — I mean a *pice* worth of good in the whole of this country, do you?'

'I'm — blessed, if I do' I responded fervently. 'Don't swear' said Le Diable Boiteux. 'It's not good form. Only Doré's imps do it with us, and they are reckoned very low in the social scale. His anatomy always *was* most queer you know. Well, as I was saying, it's your morbid vanity that makes you a dull, discontented, commonplace, unsocial man. Why *can't* you accept the conditions of your life?'

'You are rude Asmodeus,' I retorted, calling him by his (un)Christian name.

'How often am I to tell you that I'm no more related to the

genuine Asmodeus than you are? Old Alain René gave me that name, but I'm only one of his creations all the same – just like Guzman D'Alfarasche and the rest. Homilies aren't much in my line, or I'd read you one as long as my ta – hum, as long as my arm. There's a deal of good in this "Land of Regrets" as one o' your fools of songsters called it. An enormous amount of good. Just look here!' He slipped the *pince-nez* on my nose, and stood behind me like a lecturer before a magic lantern.

'Here's old Battlesby of the Commission. You know him and hate him, don't you? Screw, cold blooded old reptile and all the rest of it? He's in his *duftar* now, spending Christmas Eve in a way that would startle you. Look over his shoulder!'

I peeped, and saw, to my unutterable surprise, that old Battlesby was writing cheques, and no meagre ones either, in favour of five or six charities I'd never heard of. I hate charities – specially for whitey brown little boys who snivel and wear magenta comforters and sing hymns on state occasions in tuneless falsetto. Battlesby, however, seemed to appreciate them as much as he did soldiers' children, drunken mariners, widows, or hospitals. The way that grey headed old skinflint squandered his cash in the ten minutes that I looked over his shoulder was sinful!

'Bad going over the Chedputter race course, Smallbones, when you were stationed there I fancy?' said the Devil. 'But there's a first class thing in the way of Christmas dinners for loafers to come out of it. Pity Battlesby didn't subscribe, isn't it?'

'Go on to the next picture Devil' I said sharply. 'Ha! Ha!' chuckled Le Diable Boiteux. 'You didn't know him, wouldn't come out of your shell to know him; believed the worst you heard – and lost a good friend. Bravo Smallbones! Let me introduce Mrs McStinger – another person you don't love.'

'Tongue set on edge by the fires of' – 'Hush!' interrupted Le Diable Boiteux. 'Not in *my* presence. She's a tongue of her own I admit, but here she is in camp.'

Mrs McStinger was seated in a double-poled tent with McStinger by her side, addressing Christmas cards – some fifty at least. 'What a wicked waste of time and money' I growled.

'Not in the least' said Le Diable Boiteux. 'She uses the ones she receives to send on, being a thrifty soul; but there isn't a man in the Commission who knows her, who doesn't worship

her. Look at young Sapless, he's sent her a ten-rupee card fit
for a girl of eighteen. Who pulled Sapless through his go of
typhoid by sheer nursing? Who lent Crane her own shawl-wrap
when the boy was coughing himself dead on a frosty night after
a Cinderella? Who looked in on the quiverful of kids when their
governess was down with diptheria? I've the whole world to
see after, and you've only got about three hundred people to
know and like; and *yet* I know more about the McStinger than
you do. That's another case where you wouldn't take the
trouble to know; *would* take the trouble to dislike — with the
usual result. Come, I haven't half done yet. Shut your eyes a
minute, while I see if I can work a panorama of the province
on this size of lens. The instrument's as good as they make 'em;
but it mayn't stand the strain.'

I closed my eyes obediently, while he whipped off the *pince-
nez*, did something to them, and resettled them upon my nose.
There then appeared a perfect miniature picture of the province
in which I have the honour to serve, from Peshawur to Delhi —
all as clear and as finished as if I had been merely looking down
from the top of the Ghor Kathri on to the city below. It was a
most curious sensation to watch this tiny struggling world,
and to catch the clamour that came up from it.

As I looked, I saw that my brothers were filled — for a time
at least — with that peace and good will which for my part I do
not pretend to understand. I gazed and gazed and gazed again,
and saw and heard English men and women exchanging good
wishes and congratulations; saw the letters that bore these
flying north and south and east and west in the trains; heard
the arrangements for dinners, 'weeks', picnics, dances and all
the amusements that bring together our scattered bands from
Khaibar to the sea being canvassed and discussed; saw old
estrangements and misunderstandings, petty spites, small envies
and jealousies die away under my feet as the hoarfrost dies when
the sun shines; saw hand meet hand in friendly grasp, and in
one station — wild horses shall not induce me to say where —
lip meet lip behind the sheltering shade of a clump of bougain-
villea.

I chuckled audibly at this last. 'Never mind' said Le Diable
Boiteux cheerily, 'I've got my eye on 'em, and I think I shall
personally interest myself in seeing that that little business
runs smoothly. Now just take a look at yourself. Morbid vanity
is of use at times.'

I looked, and wherever I looked, I saw myself a figure of enormous proportions 'out of it'. There is no other way to describe the manner in which it was brought home to me that I had neither part nor lot in the general mirth around. No letters save of the most business-like nature were borne to me by the flying mail trains; for me no telegraph clerk clicked out a message of good cheer from some far off friend; in arrangements of balls and 'weeks' I stood outside all the arrangements, alone and unconsulted. The very subscription papers for these merry makings flew every way but mine; and gigantic and grotesque in the foreground loomed my dinner table laid with dinner *for one*, and decorated by my Khitmagar with a few frost-nipped roses.

'Cheerful sight isn't it?' said Le Diable Boiteux. 'By the way you're the only man in the province to-night who dines alone from choice and not from necessity. *One* bottle Bass, *one* tumbler, *one* chair and *one* lamp. Very pretty arrangement indeed!'

Le Diable Boiteux fell back a step, and contemplated the panorama in the *pince-nez* with an air of critical satisfaction. While I gazed on the huge presentment of myself, that stopped now like a cloud on the hills by Peshawur; anon stepped over the Indus at Attock; rested on the Dharmsala peaks and blocked out the view of the Simla range, I began to grow uneasy. *I was utterly alone in the province.*

'Devil' said I shuddering, 'I am frightened.'

'Oh it's all right. You're not so big in everybody's eyes you know.'

'It isn't that, Devil,' I replied. 'Can't you see that I am alone in the whole panorama? It's awful — Here roll it up or take the jugglery away.'

'Can't I see? Of course I can. But *you* might ha' seen it any time this eight years if you'd cared to look. Magnificently your chin comes out against the sunset by Mooltan, doesn't it? Yes, you are completely alone on this Christmas Eve in the year of grace 1885 — after eight years passed in the country. What do you think of it?'

'Devil, I don't like it at all. It's very horrible! Can you get it altered?'

'It rests with Monsieur alone as old Alain René would have said. Which life would you prefer? Eating out your heart after a life you can't get, and which wouldn't be the faintest pleasure to you when you'd got it: let alone the fact that it doesn't want you in the least; or coming out of your shell, taking some trouble to know the people you've cast in your lot with, and finding this 'Land of Regrets' (I should really like to pay the man who wrote that nonsense a visit), a country of charity, and kindly offices, and good will, and broad thought and honest human helpfulness and — Well, homilies aren't in my line, but you can fill in the rest from what you've seen.'

'There's no choice about the matter, Devil. My mind's made up. But how am I to set about it?'

'So bad as that, is it? Go round and mix with your fellows to begin with; though it's too late for any one to ask you to their Christmas dinner now. Where was I? Yes, mix with your fellows and — by the great Alain René himself — I had nearly forgotten the most important part of the prescription! Bend low and I'll whisper.'

'But that's nonsense Devil' I said. 'She'll never accept me!'

'Try and see! I can't say *I'm* fond of grumpy recluses of your kidney. But there's no accounting for tastes.'

He fell to reckoning up my table-gear as before while I laughed aloud out of sheer comfort of heart at the prospect he had opened to me.

'Well, I'm off. Goodnight, Smallbones' said Le Diable Boiteux settling himself into his ulster.

'Oh Devil, Devil!' I cried 'I'm afraid you're an awful imposter. Is *this* the end of your homily?'

'I wish you wouldn't call me Devil'' ' said Le Diable Boiteux, as he pushed the *chick* aside preparatory to stepping into the verandah. 'Don't you know my other name?'

'No, indeed!'

' "Le Dieu Cupidon: car les poetes m'ont donné ce joli nom et ces messieurs me peignent fort avantageusement" — Queer French perhaps, but old Alain René never wrote a truer word.'

He dropped the *chick* with a bang, and I woke up.

My Le Sage and Dickens had tumbled on to the floor from the reading table.

'Bearer!' quoth I, '*Mi aj rat nautch kojaiga Larens Hall men. Khana ki kupra thaiyar karo*' ['Tonight I will go to the dance at

the Lawrence Hall. Get my dinner clothes ready.']
There's nothing like taking a prescription on the spot.

H.M.E. SMALLBONES

## An Armoured Train

*Civil and Military Gazette, 5 January 1886*

**Attribution: Sussex Scrapbooks 28/1, p. 45**

Kipling's interests in weapons and in professionals at work combine in this account, laid out with great expository skill. The armoured train reappears in 'The Courting of Dinah Shadd', which opens on the scene of army manoeuvres:

[ .... ] mounted infantry skirmished up to the wheels of an armoured train which carried nothing more deadly than a twenty-five pounder Armstrong, two Nordenfelts, and a few score volunteers all cased in three-eighths-inch boiler-plate.

**(From a Correspondent)**

The armoured train should be ready for its duties at the Winter Manoeuvres about the 15th of this month; and should be at Delhi on or about the 18th for inspection by H.E. the Commander-in-Chief. Meantime, the guns which it carries have been mounted in their places, and on Friday forenoon a series of exhaustive firing experiments were carried out by Captain Moberley, R.A., under the supervision of Lieutenant-Colonel Wallace, R.E. Several important matters prevented the entire train and engine being run down to some secluded spot on the line for trial; so a range of 250 yards was chosen, not a quarter of a mile from the Railway workshops where the train had been put together; and a temporary line of rail was laid down. A large brick mound, slightly to the right of the Shalimar road level-crossing, afforded a splendid situation for a target and ensured safety in case a forty-pounder shell should take into its head to go astray. Captain Moberley, R.A., had charge of the trials and devoted himself more particularly to the big siege gun; and Lieutenant S. B. Von Donop, to the twelve-pounder Field Service gun. A five-barrel Nordenfeldt was in a third truck; the ten-barrel one being stripped for cleaning in the Railway workshops. A Nordenfeldt, as every one knows, is a fragile-looking little weapon, something between a sewing machine, a stocking-knitter and an organ in appearance — but of this later on.

In addition to Lieut.-Col. Wallace, R.E., Captain Moberley, R.A., and Lieut. Von Donop, R.A., there were also present on the ground Mr Sandford, Mr W.S. Bocquet and Mr Ticknor, all keenly interested in the success of the experiments. Seeing that these three gentlemen stood god-fathers, as it were, to the train and had cheerfully and ungrudgingly devoted much time, labour and thought to it, this was only natural.

As I have said before, a special siding had been made for the trucks to run on. This siding was a curve of about 278 feet radius with a dip of 1 in 75.

The target lay to the right of the center of the curve, so that the gun truck, on leaving the straight, would get one shot end on; a second by slewing the gun round to the right and thereafter as many more as were necessary until the truck came to the end of the siding, when the gun would be at right angles to the truck. (This extremely technical and scientific description requires thought.) The question at issue was simply whether the truck would be too much for the gun, or the gun get the better of the truck. And opinions were fairly divided. The Artillery officers, knowing the recoil of a forty-pounder Armstrong breech-loading rifled cannon in a confined space was no trifle, seemed inclined to prefer the guns; the officers of the North-Western Railway, bearing in mind the fashion in which wagons full of stone were shunted and knocked about on the line, fancied the trucks, and the result proved that they had good reason for their prophecy. About one point only did these gentlemen seem to have any misgiving. It was just possible that the truck springs might not stand the strains. Arrangements were made for recording the depression, and at about twenty minutes past eleven the forty-pounder was run into position for its first shot — with full service charge and plugged shell — at the target on the brick mound 250 yards away. The gun pointed dead ahead and, whatever might come after, could only drive the truck back. Seven inches of the gun's heavy wooden carriage-tail had been sawn off together with the hind wheels; and tackle running through eyebolts fitted into the bows of the truck, kept gun and carriage within bounds.

The charge was fired by lanyard from without the truck, in case of the unforeseen; and, as the shell dug itself a neat trench, nine feet long, three feet deep and four wide at the foot of the target, the great truck ran back and disappeared in a cloud of smoke. The gunners clambered into the the carriage while the officers of the railway investigated the truck, and Captain Moberley the recoil of the gun. Here is the result of their investigations: —

| | |
|---|---|
| Recoil of truck on line | . . 2 ft.  10 in. |
|     "   of gun in truck | . . 2 " 11 " |
| Average depression of springs (the suspected weak point above noted) | . . 3/8 in. |

Nothing could have been more satisfactory — especially as regards the mistrusted springs. Still no side shots had been fired; and the question which Colonel Wallace had set himself to find out — *videlicet* whether the gun would tilt the truck, or the truck retain the gun — remained unanswered. The carriage was run about a hundred and fifty feet further down the siding, and the gun slewed round twenty degrees to the right. Here of course things were against it, by reason of the 'super-elevation' (one must use a technical term now and then) of the right rail of the curve. Again the gunners adjusted the tackle (few things are finer than the way in which these big men handle big guns, especially in a confined space) and again the target disappeared under a cloud of dust as the truck ran back. After investigation of chalk marks within and without, these results were made known: —

| | |
|---|---|
| Recoil of truck | . . 3 ft.  10 in. |
|     "   of gun in truck | . . 2 " 0 " |
| Average depression of springs . . | 1/4 in. |

I should be afraid to say how far the springs go down when a ten-ton truck is loaded in the ordinary course of things; but it is safe to aver that the recoil of the Armstrong kept several inches on the safe side. The fourth and last shot was the crucial test. 'If this does nothing' remarked the designer of the armoured train, 'nothing will.' There were several things open to the choice of the forty-pounder.

Its heavy body lay 'thwart ships as the truck was brought to the extreme end of the siding. It might, therefore, quietly kick its way out behind if it broke the tackles; or, restrained by its heel-ropes, knock out the plates in front of it; or, failing this, jerk the truck over into a hole 'contagious' to the left of the line. While the gun was being got into position, the practical minds of the artillerists discovered that the side of the truck was a trifle too high; allowing no depression of the piece. Ordinarily of course a forty-pounder would not fire at two hundred and fifty yards range, but there might be occasions in actual warfare when a round of grape at even closer quarters would have a salutary effect on an attacking party attempting to 'rush' the train. Therefore it was decided that the armour was to be cut down an inch, or perhaps two. The incident was a slight one, but it showed in what a thorough spirit the armoured train is being built. After a little the gun was brought round, leaving twenty inches between the shortened carriage tail and the left side of the truck. Then the audience stood respectfully aside, and listened to the convincing agument of the forty-pounder as it hurled conviction into the bowels of the target. Naturally the truck did not run back, but it shook and — here an explanation is necessary. Between railway wheel flanges and the rail play is allowed to the extent of one inch and one quarter. The truck had been shifted leftward one inch; bringing the flanges of the left wheels up to the side of the rails. And that was all. No smashing of plates; no upheaval of the truck — nothing except that slight lateral shift leftward and a slightly higher average of spring depression, due to the pressure falling almost exclusively on the left fore and hind springs. The readings were as follows: —

Recoil of truck                  . . *Nil.*
Recoil of gun in truck           . . 1 ft.  8 in. (all
                                        it could get)
Average depression of springs . .  0    22/32

Depression of left forespring   ..   0    1 15/16
Depression of left hind      ..      1 0


The truck had vindicated itself against the gun. It only remained to fire the twelve-pounder service gun and see what happened there. The smaller piece, by reason of its wheels, can recoil in most lively fashion; but the results of the first discharge showed that neither recoil nor depression of springs [was] worth recording. The gun of course was tackled like its big brother; and thanks to its long bodied trail — the arsenals never having contemplated the fact that it might be hoisted into a cattle-truck — was not so easy to handle. This will, however, be remedied before the 15th, and in all likelihood both the forty and twelve-pounder will be enabled to command more than 90° of the horizon. The second shot of the twelve-pounder showed how the men would be protected from fire in actual warfare, and was witnessed by most of the party on the ground either in or on the truck itself. The effect produced by the recoil is merely as if the carriage were passing over points; the most unpleasant portion of the business being the dense smoke which fills the truck. Lieutenant Von Donop fired yet another shot with the gun as nearly at right angles as the trail would permit, and having proved satisfactorily that his protegé was 'sound and free from vice', turned his attention to the five-barrel Nordenfeldt in the third truck. For those interested in matters military, this last display was a very pretty ending to a most successful series of 'exhaustive experiments'. There is something specially and diabolically vindictive in a machine gun beyond all other engines of death. The five-barrel gun was cheerfully pronounced by the experts on the ground as 'obsolete — quite an obsolete pattern you know', and the unprofessional observer wondered what on earth the perfected articles might be like. Every one knows roughly the mechanism of the Nordenfeldt — how solid-drawn brass cartridges of Martini-Henri bore are put into a hopper; how a wrench of a lever drops five of them into place and the return of the same lever discharges them fast or slowly at the operator's will; but it is an impressive thing to see all this actually in practice. Most impressive of all to see the weapon feeling its way foot by foot to the required range, and marking each step with a little cloud of dust three hundred yards distant; finally settling upon the target with a volley of venemous precision.

But the Nordenfeldts are, after all, minor details. The problem was to determine by experiment to what extent a moveable railway truck detached from a train which could serve as a counterpoise, could be relied upon to furnish a platform for artillery fire; and the event showed that though made for a peaceful purpose, the ordinary goods-wagon can be converted into a battery all the more formidable from its perfect mobility; and so far as a mere outsider can judge, the results of the experiments should give complete satisfaction to the gentlemen who carried them out.

One other point — not exactly connected with the firing — remains to be noticed, and that is the fertility of resource, and what Mrs Malaprop calls 'artifice and ingenuity' with which the building of the train was marked. The conditions upon which it was armoured seem to have been that existing railway *materiel* only was to be utilized, and when done with was to be returned to stores as intact as possible. The Railway officials above mentioned entered into what must have been a wholly novel task with interest and enthusiasm; and fitted the train with 'notions' for the comfort and convenience of the firing party — by the Commander-in-Chief's sanction to be composed of Railway Volunteers — which must be seen to be properly appreciated.

If the Indian Government ever decide upon regularly building for offensive purposes, armoured trains, the Lahore workshops ought to be able to turn out the best possible specimens. Even with converted cattle-trucks, the present 'Armadillo' has no reason to fear the criticism which is inevitably awaiting it at Delhi a fortnight hence.

# A Week in Lahore

*Civil and Military Gazette, 11 January 1886*

**Attribution: Sussex Scrapbooks 28/1, p. 47**

The way in which Kipling's mind worked upon his experiences

is suggested by this brief item. Kipling was one of those writers who liked to take literary advantage of whatever came his way and could do so to surprising effect. Thinking on the puzzle of the stolen cricket ball may have led him to 'The Story of Muhammad Din', in which an equally useless polo ball is coveted by a child whose father obtains it for him. In the news story the ball is stolen; in the fiction it is a gift, but the question in both is, What good can it be? Kipling the journalist concludes that feeble-mindedness is the explanation; Kipling the writer of stories sees that a father's love and a child's desire are behind the mystery.

A virtuous bearer in the employ of Messrs Gillon and Co. has been convicted of stealing a cricket-ball, and sentenced to three months' imprisonment. What in the name of everything incongruous can a bearer want with a cricket-ball? He couldn't very well eat it. I am absolutely certain that the Lahore Cricket Club does not buy cricket-balls from bearers. The students who play on the Volunteer parade-ground, near Gillon's shop, seem to use cricket-balls of local manufacture. As a weapon, except in experienced hands, a cricket ball is useless, and there is not enough fuel in the whole of its composition to light a respectable hookah.

A *mochi* wouldn't buy it for the sake of its hide and sinews; and the most pushing of pawnbrokers wouldn't advance a *pie* upon it as an 'article of common use or wearing apparel'. The man who would peril three months of his liberty for the sake of the best cricket-ball in creation is obviously weak in the intellect, and should be treated as such.

# A Week in Lahore

*Civil and Military Gazette, 19 January 1886*

**Attribution: Sussex Scrapbooks 28/1, p. 49**

The Sultan Serai and Afzul reappear, transformed, as the Kashmir Serai and Mahbub Ali in *Kim*.

[ ... ] After all, it is the country cousin on a three weeks' visit
who gets to know more of London than his Cockney relative of
ten years' residence. And, in the same manner, it is the out-
station visitor who really understands the curiosities of Lahore.
Rumours of small-pox in the City deter him not, nor does the
fact of farcy having declared itself in the Serai, prevent him
from riding there and there spending a happy day — by preference
a Sunday. Decidedly, to know one's own station thoroughly,
one must always live elsewhere, or follow in the wake of some
enthusiastic excursionist — the man who 'wants to see y'see'
and 'know y'know'. Under his guidance it is possible to pene-
trate into the very heart of the country of the Houyhnhnms
which, as every body ought to know, is the property of the
Maharaja of Kashmir, and is kept in a disgraceful condition.
Not long ago there were six hundred Houyhnhnms tended by
about three hundred Yahoos — and the Pathan horse boy in
his frank brutality could almost give points to Swift's creation
— in and about the evil-smelling enclosures known collectively
as the Sultan Serai; and thither an Enthusiastic Excursionist
betook himself one day — before the present rain spoilt everything and converted the Maharajah's unsavoury possession into
a dank muck-heap. He did not want to buy a horse — albeit
few dealers believed him when he said so — but his soul yearned
for information of a vague and general kind; and the inmates of
the Sultan Serai do not take kindly to interviewing. Even an
attempt to sketch one of the jetty-locked, red-cheeked, swaggering,
breezy, greasy blackguards was foiled by the sketchee dodging
behind the nearest picketed pony, or averting his rugged face
like a bashful child. They may be estimable men of course,
these hirsute outlanders, but *why* does each one of them look
so guiltily conscious of undigested murders? This was very nearly
the first question which the Enthusiastic Excursionist asked as
he entered the Serai; and he kept on putting it mentally to himself throughout the greater part of the visit. Those who know the
manners and customs of the keepers of the Houyhnhnms are
aware that the small fry of the dealers, swarm round an Englishman at once; while the bigger fish — there are three or four —
wait in the dignified seclusion of their own private serais until
they are interviewed. Staying only then to translate a telegram
to a huge Pathan (who handed the red envelope as if it had been
a bomb and required several assurances that no judgment would

IN A SERAI (REST-HOUSE)

overtake him for opening a 'tar' addressed to himself) the Enthusiastic Excursionist, threaded his way through roped horses, unroped camels, picturesque scraps of carpets, brazen samovars, woolly Turkomen sheep dogs, a Persian cat and much dirt to that secluded court, reached by a cool arched passage, where Afzul hides the pick of his purchases from the profane gaze.

(The question here raises itself, whether the selection of Afzul's name for the honour and dignity of print is not calculated to do that estimable Afghan a lot of harm. However he does not read English and has — sold so many horses to so many men, that he is in a measure a public character. His name shall be written therefore.) The Enthusiastic Excursionist was received affably. He did not wish to buy a horse (Afzul guessed as much by the look of his eye, but was far too polite to say so). He wanted to know about things generally; and in the meantime, till conversation flowed naturally, would like to inspect the six or seven beasts which were stalled in a side stable.

'All by Government stallions and zemindari mares' quoth Afzul pithily. 'Except the one in the corner; he is a Gulf Arab, and of him I have never before seen the like in this country. That is — bay, fourteen three a half; four; six hundred. That is — grey horse; fifteen a half; four; five hundred. That over there is — chestnut, four; fifteen; seven hundred; and that one next him is seven hundred also — fifteen one. All country-bred by Government stallion except the Gulf Arab. Ah! such an Arab (here Afzul raised his eyes piously to Heaven for a moment). I have never seen his like. I will ride him.' 'But Afzul,' interrupted the Enthusiastic Excursionist, 'I don't want to buy. I have come to see only.' 'It is well. You shall see — see how that Gulf Arab can go. Boy, bring a saddle.' In good truth so far as an extremely limited knowledge of horseflesh enabled one bystander to judge, the beast in question was a noble one. He was blessed with more bone below the knee than the generality of 'Gulfers'; his shoulder was a thing of beauty and his quarters a revelation. So was his price — eight hundred depreciated rupees. 'But who will give that *now*, Afzul? There is a new *takkus* abroad, and we are all poor.' 'What matter?' returned Afzul swinging himself into the saddle; 'I will take that horse — Ah! such a horse — to Simla and perhaps he may be sold to some lady there. Beyond doubt he will be sold. Such horses are not seen every day. Look here!'

The grey shot out under the archway in a hurry; was dextrously directed through lines of his picketed friends: safely steered between two broken-down dog carts, over an affrighted hen or so and a few hundred yards of drain-channelled uneven soil; brought round with a jerk; sent flying full tilt back again at the dark archway — turned again and, simply to show his handiness, wheeled in and out at a gallop between the trees that stud the outskirts of the further Serai. 'Ah! such a horse!' ejaculated Afzul as he handed the grey over to the charge of a small boy whom it attempted to dance upon. 'That is a grand horse. You did not want to buy. But I wanted to show you. One does not see horses like that every day. And now we will talk — How many horses have I! About one fifty, all for cavalry remounts just now. Country-breds, except the Gulf Arab and another. They average over 14.2. Perhaps two thousand horses of all kinds come into the Serai in one year and are sold. All are sold or nearly all; and one with the other they bring about Rs. 200 each. Yes! Even with the polo ponies for which the young *sahibs* pay so much. There are many bad ones of course — very many cheap and bad ones.'

'And have you regular customers?' 'The Calcutta Tramway Company buys perhaps three hundred horses in the year — Badakshani horses — from out of the Serai. The Bombay Tramways Company also took a good many not long ago — *pucca* horses not ponies you understand. They know about horses the Bombay Company.'

(Here followed a digression on the many merits of the Company and the exceeding wisdom and acuteness of its agents; coupled with the information that it was not possible to train inferior horses to Bombay.)

'And where do these two thousand beasts come from?' 'My horses?' 'No, you egoist, all the horses that are *not* bred south of Peshawar.' 'Oh those! Those come from Turkistan.' 'Can't you tell where? Turkistan is a big word.' 'Eastern Turkistan — over there.'

(Afzul knows more of horseflesh than he does of geography. He was certain they came from all over Turkistan — Balkh — and elsewhere. They were collected by agents in those mysterious regions and brought down south by 'these men', — the population in the Serai who for the greater part are Suleman Khels and from the neighbourhood of Ghuzni.)

'I don't go with the horses myself. I am always in India,' continued Afzul. 'The horses are collected in Turkestan and *then* the loot begins. Alum Sher, Cabuli, will be able to tell you. He goes with the horses.' He was not much over six foot high — wore a jet black beard, clean *postheen*; fancifully embroidered Bokhara belt and pouches; looked like a hero of medieval romance, and was a courteous Afghan horse-dealer. (I don't want to say in so many words that Alum Sher, Cabuli, was six feet six, because I am convinced that no one would believe me. Anyhow he was something near it.) He spoke an unknown tongue which Afzul translated and the gist of his speech was this: — It takes between twelve and fourteen days to bring the horses down from Cabul to Peshawar. Between Cabul and Peshawur His Highness Abdur Rahman, C.G.S.I., levies these trifling tolls per horse: —

|           |     | Rs. | A. |
|-----------|-----|-----|----|
| Cabul     | . . . . . . . . | 3 | 8 |
| Budkhak   | . . . . . . . . | 4 | 0 |
| Gundamak  | . . . . . . . . | 2 | 0 |
| Sarkhab   | . . . . . . . . | 0 | 8 |
| Jellalabad| . . . . . . . . | 4 | 0 |
| Bahool    | . . . . . . . . | 4 | 0 |
| Daka      | . . . . . . . . | 4 | 0 |
|           |     | 32 | 0 | [i.e. 22] |

Mares pay Rs. 7 less. This according to Alum Sher, Cabuli, is absolute fact. He objects to the payment; holds it excessive, but pays because it is impossible to avoid the octroi posts. In Turkistan itself is exacted an *ad valorem* duty on each beast of ————, but this, like Alum Sher's height, would never be believed. It is enough to say that the duty is not a light one. 'This is solemn truth and there is yet more loot,' said Alum Sher, 'the Amir's Naib in Turkistan takes the pick of the horses first — and at Cabul the Amir.' 'But he pays of course.' 'Oh, yes, he pays. He sees a fine horse and asks the price. We are poor men and afraid. What have we to do with the Amir? Can we ask the full price — no! If it is a four hundred rupee beast we say two hundred and so on. It is so with the Naib in Turkestan.' The tale of course is as old as the beginning of empire all the world over, but it did not become more hacknied as told by the hirsute Alum Sher, standing among the picketed horses in the Sultan Serai, in gruff, harsh gutturals. Later on, he told the Enthusiastic Excursionist of horses 'over there in Turkistan' that neither love nor money could buy. He had been in those regions and knew. So ended the interview.

# A Week in Lahore

*Civil and Military Gazette, 3 February 1886*

**Attribution: Sussex Scrapbooks 28/1, p. 55**

The inescapability of the memento mori in India impressed Kipling as it would any westerner. A passage in *Something of Myself* eloquently recalls the kind of experience more flippantly expressed in 'A Week in Lahore':

The dead of all times were about us — in the vast forgotten Moslem cemeteries round the Station, where one's horse's hoof of a morning might break through to the corpse below; skulls and bones tumbled out of our mud garden walls,

1. Rudyard Kipling c. 1882, at the beginning of his Indian career.
*By courtesy of the National Trust*

Our illustration is reproduced from an old sketch which has been sent to us by a correspondent who was in Lahore, at the time that Mr. Kipling was on the Civil and Military Gazette. Mr. Kipling is in the group. The block was drawn and made in England from a photograph taken in Lahore about 1885. Mr. Kipling is leaning against the pillar on the left.

A man named Wilson may be in the group. He had been a corporal in the 9th Lancers—a very smart fellow who was employed in the office as a draughtsman for maps, etc. He used to take R.K sometimes to a sergeants' mess, and this likely enough was the beginning of R.K's. earliest observations of life in the army."

2. The Office of the *Civil and Military Gazette*, Lahore, from the *Kipling Journal*, No. 16, December 1930.
*By courtesy of the Kipling Society*

# CIVIL AND MILITARY GAZETTE.

New Series: } No. 2,523 }

LAHORE, WEDNESDAY, FEBRUARY 11, 1885.

{ VOL. X.

## LIST OF CONTENTS.

## TELEGRAPHIC INTELLIGENCE.

[*Reuter's Telegrams.*]

### THE WAR IN THE SOUDAN.

### REINFORCEMENTS FOR EGYPT.

LONDON, Feb. 9.

The 3rd battalion, Grenadier Guards; the 1st battalion, Coldstream Guards, and the 2nd batta-

---

(*From our own Correspondent.*)

### THE FRANCO-CHINESE WAR.

COLOMBO, Feb. 9.

The *China Mail* of the 27th ultimo confirms the latest news of the French preparations for a strong advance on Tamsui. Further reinforcements have reached Kelung; bringing the number of the troops up to 3,500, besides 1,000 sailors and marines. Admiral Courbet states that, with this force, he will march to Tamsui. On January 15th, the French attacked the Chinese outpost adjoining the town, and met with a stout resistance. The enemy fought obstinately, and drove back 300 French regulars who lost 50 men. The accounts, which come through French sources, are unreliable. It is believed that the Chinese muster very strong along the road to Tamsui; and that the French met with a stubborn resistance during January. Large reinforcements, with arms and money, have been poured into Formosa.

The publication of the proclamation of neutrality at Hongkong, has incensed the French, who talk of reprisals, and say that they will search all British vessels. On the blockade of the Canton river, the Chinese fleet rendezvous at Shanghai, preparatory to breaking the blockade at Formosa. The ships and guns are effective, but the crews and officers are demoralised; as the sailors are being taught to drill by English words of command mixed with German words. Great efforts are being made to pour reinforce-

---

PRIVATE LETTERS FROM WADY HALFA, WHICH lie on the Nile just below the Second Cataract, state that there is an immense amount of sickness there—principally typhoid.

THE COMMAND OF THE 2ND BATTALION, WEST Riding (76th) Regiment, vacant on the 25th instant, goes to Lieutenant-Colonel T. T. Hodges; whilst the vacant lieutenant-coloneley will, in all probability, go to Major Titcomb, at present with the 1st battalion at Rawal Pindi.

THE SERVICES OF MAJOR A. GASELEE, 4TH Punjab Infantry, have been placed at the disposal of His Excellency the Commander-in-Chief, for employment on special duty in Beluchistan, in connection with Colonel Sandford's survey of the routes between Peshin and the Punjab.

A SEPOY OF THE 31ST PUNJAB NATIVE INFANTRY, at Rawal Pindi, shot a Lance-Havildar of the same regiment, on the morning of the 9th instant. Death was instantaneous, the bullet passing through the brain. Nothing is known concerning the motive for the deed. The murderer was immediately secured.

MAJOR-GENERAL CAMERON, WHO SUCCEEDS

---

material. There was a falling off in the importation of Government arms and ammunition, and stationery. Turning to exports, we find that the total for the first three quarters of .883 was over Rs. 60,37,00,000; whereas that for the nine months ending in December last, was less than Rs. 56,51,00,000. This decrease is largely accounted for by the falling off in the wheat trade. In the nine months, India exported less than Rs. 4,85,00,000 worth of wheat; against over Rs. 7,99,00,000 in the same months of 1883.

A LITTLE MORE THAN A YEAR AGO, THERE occurred in the small town of Bahadurgarh, in the Rohtak district, a robbery which is now famous, not only from the fact that it was accompanied with murder, but also because at least two of the perpetrators, Amir Khan and Mufti, were the prominent members of the most formidable class of criminals we have at present to deal with; namely, the Patian. Amir Khan was, in fact, the leader of a gang once numbering some twenty members, but happily now almost extinct. He combined in himself the qualities of great pluck, ferocity, and a very fertile

4. The Badshahi Mosque, Lahore—Ranjit Singh's Marble Pavilion is in the foreground.

*Douglas Dickens, FRPS*

5. Peshawur City from the Fort.
*BBC Hulton Picture Library*

6. Lahore, from Wazir Khan's Mosque, 1870, by S. Bourne.
By courtesy of the Trustees of the British Library (India Office)

7. The Church and main bazaar, Simla.
*BBC Hulton Picture Library*

Feb. 23/89

8. Rudyard Kipling, 23 February 1899; a sketch by John Lockwood Kipling made at Lahore two weeks before Rudyard Kipling left India for England.

and were turned up among the flowers by the Rains; and at every point were tombs of the dead (p. 42).

The verses that Kipling quotes he wrote sometime before July 1884, when they were used in an article for the *CMG* written by his mother.

But for the honour of the thing it might just as well be treacherous England. To bed on Saturday night in the certainty of a month of glorious sunshine; and to breakfast by lamplight on Sunday morning with the pleasing conviction that the rain has set in for the day. What *can* you expect from such a country and such weather? By all the laws of nature and Mr Blanford there ought to be a clear sky overhead and the *koil* should be thinking of rehearsing his summer operatic selections — instead of which: —

'The sky is an inkstand upside down
Splashing the world with gloom
The earth is full of skeleton bones,'

and the rain is forcing them into unpleasant publicity. Everybody knows that Lahore is a cemetery of half a dozen cities at the least and that To-day builds its mud walls from the dust of the men of Yesterday — or the Day Before — but one does not care to be reminded of the fact *every* time it rains.

Victor Hugo in his *Toilers of the Sea* introduces a diver to the abode of a monstrous 'poulpe'. The man is uneasily conscious that there is 'somebody smiling' at the further end of the dusky cavern. Investigation reveals a skeleton. Very horrible of course, but perfectly true. About a year ago much the same thing happened in Lahore. A house stood near a deep clay cutting, and as surely as ever the owner drove through the gateway in the dusk he was conscious, to use his own words, of 'some one grinning somewhere but for the life of me I couldn't tell where'. He was *not* an observant man and I don't think he had read Victor Hugo. For more than a week he was perplexed by this sensation of a smile somewhere. Eventually his eye fell on the cutting and there was the Cause of the grin looking out across the road and simpering at the passer by. It disappeared before the evening, and the grisly welcome ceased. This is a cheerful story and exactly matches the weather at the time of writing [ . . . .]

# A Popular Picnic

### *Civil and Military Gazette, 30 March 1886*

**Attribution: Sussex Scrapbooks 28/3, pp. 11–12**

The Chiragan festival, or festival of lamps, is held in honour of the Muslim Saint 'Abd al-Qadir Jilani. The Shalimar gardens, six miles east of Lahore, were laid out in 1641 by Shah Jehan.

The *mistri* beguiled me. He is a *flaneur* and a man about town when he isn't making office-boxes and charpoys. He said the Chiragan *Mela* would be an extremely fine *tamasha*, that he and all his friends were going. *Ekkas* were at a premium among the aristocracy of the City, and the *ticca-gharris* were bespoken. He made an appointment with me somewhere on the Shalimar road, but I think he must have forgotten it, for I saw him later on talking to a lady with purple-shot silk pyjamas, and very black hair, and a natural diffidence prevented me from accosting him. But after all the *chaprassi* did just as well. He accepted a lift to the *mela* on the roof of my *ticca*, and the *khitmatgar* climbed up too, till I was afraid that the roof would cave in. My friend the *chaprassi* is a man about town too, like the *mistri*, and he showed me all that there was to be seen. For the first half hour the view was disappointing. Somebody had published a statement in the newspaper to the effect that the Municipality had spent two hundred rupees on watering on the road. By the time that you had got opposite the new rifle-range on the other side of the railway line, you began to cough, and to realise what a wanton liar the man who made that statement was. The dust was inches deep; and one unbroken line of *ekkas*, bullock-carts, hackeries, *ticca-gharries*, dog-carts, and 'fittons' on the left hand side of the road, and another unbroken line on the right hand side of the road was ploughing it up the whole way from the railway-crossing to Shalimar and back again. When a breeze came you could see two *ekka* lengths ahead. When it dropped you could hear the driver yelling and the *ekkas* bumping into you like small boats round a big ship. No *ekka* held less than five persons — none at least of those I saw, and there was one long-necked cart with five and thirty people in it. Sixteen of them were children, but even then they had to pack close. When the dust allowed a clear view, you could see lanes of people closing in on Shalimar, through the green crops near Begumpora village and from the Mian Mir side too. Most of them were singing as they went along, and when they reached the main road, they chaffed the drivers of the *ekkas* and got in their way. One *ekka* lost a wheel and sat down like a hen in the middle of the traffic, while the fares rolled about in the dust and were nearly trodden on. This was considered a very superior joke. No one offered to help, but every one laughed a good deal — except the pony and *he* kicked till the driver beat him over the head with a bamboo. Then he went off to graze; and the last I could see of the business was the driver trying to collect passage-money from the spilt fares and nursing the loose wheel under one arm.

The real crush began about five hundred yards before you came to the gates of the gardens. My friend the *chaprassi* said that there were fewer people at the *mela* than last year; but that a lakh at least must be present. He speaks the truth generally, but I don't think he understands figures. A Police Inspector Sahib, who has seen nearly as many *melas* as there are inches in his waist-belt, said that he reckoned the gathering at between thirteen and fourteen thousand. Putting the two estimates together, and deducting the proper percentages, we get between twenty and twenty five thousand. This is quite high enough, if you add a thousand or so for children too small to count, and only big enough to fall over. It was the children's day out on Sunday. Perhaps there were twenty mothers of families. This is a very liberal estimate. The rest were children and men. I suppose it is not considered wholesome to let the womenfolk of the country enjoy themselves. It might over-excite them or lead to a revolution. A man mob isn't pretty to look at when you think of these things, and remember how for nearly every man enoying himself over the *kabab* stalls or the sweetmeat booths there's a woman at home out of it, and getting the place in order against his return. My friend the *chaprassi* had put a thin book-muslin wrapper over his office kit, and was really very well turned out all over; but he was very much shocked at the notion that his wife might possibly care to join in the fun. He said that *tamashas* like the Chiragan Fair were not for women, and then went away to stuff himself with thin cakes fried in *ghi* and three *kababs* and a bottle of muddy lemonade. The whole picnic cost him one anna and a half, but he explained that I couldn't have got as much for four annas. I believed him implicitly, and I know that I wouldn't have eaten the messes for a thousand rupees. *Kababs* are made in a horrible way; so are the cakes fried in ghi, and so is the lemonade. To show there is no deception — nothing but good honest dirt — they are all three manufactured in public, and they command a ready sale.

The first entertainment was a peep-show in a tent labelled 'House wonderful. Performances'. There were six holes in a board and the smells of six kerosine lamps. You looked through the holes, and if you strained your eyes you could see six things like labels on biscuit-boxes. The gentleman in charge of the show was very polite, and told me a good deal that I did not know before of a place called 'Lan'nin', and 'Yopra'. I knew what 'Lan'nin' was, because I had lived there once and it's the capital of England. 'Yopra' I took for a Hindu god at first. The peep-show didn't help a bit, and it was only just at the end that I found out it was a house in Paris where people play music. We call it the Opera House, but the peep-show man said it was a person. He said that all the *kala admis* were deeply interested in his show, and that English *sahibs* paid four and five rupees for a peep. I did not pay five rupees, but I gave him a perfectly new stock of 'patter' if he cares to use it, and a lot of novel information about 'Lun'nin' and 'Yopra'. He said that my words were true and I said he spoke the truth as honestly as I did. Which was true. My friend the *chaprassi* wanted to intro-duce me to a friend of his own after we had left the peep-show, so we wandered under the trees of the Shalimar Gardens, and nearly stamped on a baby. The ground was brown with babes — from fat little things just able to walk and quite naked, to miniature Mussalmans of eight, with enormous red and gold turbans and blue leather shoes. They were very nice babies, but they had a curious habit of settling down to sleep in the very spot where you were going to put your foot next. They never gave any warning, and their fathers left it to you to tread on them or not as you pleased. Everywhere, under the trees were spread little carpets, and to each carpet there were eight or ten men, a *hookah* and a fringe of babies. The *hookahs* had new *chillams* mostly; the men were in new clothes, the babies in every case were as well dressed as their fathers could afford. Some were in blue and gold; lilac and blue, saffron and vermillion, with gold and black velvet caps; one was red and gold from head to heel; another a delicate mustard colour, and scores of them were in pink and green. One baby, — the one I nearly stamped on, — had a pair of cretonne drawers. The pattern was intended for a curtain. It would have looked striking anywhere. On a baby it was amazing. He was very proud of those drawers. That was the reason I nearly stepped on him. You see, he *would* keep rolling over on his head every minute to show 'em off. He finished up by rolling into the middle of a carpet, upsetting the *hookah*, and breaking up the assembly in a Sodom and Gomorrah rain of red-hot tobacco. No one seemed to mind, and as it wasn't my carpet that was burnt into a sieve, I didn't feel called upon to interfere. One of the most striking things at a native *mela* is the way children are petted and spoilt. Perhaps they get the affection that isn't lavished on their mothers, besides their proper share. At any rate a native never seems to slap or scold a baby. He'll make one ill with sweetmeats or give it a mud doll to chew; but I've never seen him call one to order in English fashion.

A rupee makes you as rich as Croesus at Shalimar. You can buy up the better part of a toy seller's stock in trade with it, and for the rest of the afternoon small boys come up with their share of the loot to say 'Talaam Tahib' and run away shouting. If you care to beat down the man in charge to 'a reduction on taking a quantity' you can acquire nearly as much merit as a Buddhist priest by filling up a merry-go-round with small sinners, and making the man turn it till he can't turn any more. Of course a large portion of the brown innocents grow up into khitmatgars, who tell lies and steal money, or *ghariwans* who try to cheat, or members of Municipal Committees and cattle of that kind, but they are delightful while they are young, and their manners ought to make an English baby blush for his rude little self. The men, as I have said, seemed to come for the purpose of amusing the children. Their own share of the pleasure wasn't much. They wandered about, most of them, and shouted for lost friends in the crowd, but they never let go of the babies — except to let them bathe. The shallow tanks of the Shalimar gardens were full of brown babies of all kinds. They danced on the brink squealing till their fathers gave them leave to strip. Then they squealed shrilly all the time they shredded off their little wraps, and flopped into the water, as naked as original innocence, and squealed all the time they flopped. A baby of six with a shaved and scraped head can stay in the water for one hour and twenty minutes under a hot sun that forces an Englishman to wear a large pith hat. He doesn't duck his head more than once, and it reflects the sun like a mirror. Twenty thousand Englishmen couldn't spend four hours at the Crystal Palace without five hundred getting beastly drunk. A native crowd gives no trouble in that way or any other, except when the two creeds happen to get mixed, and some one starts a religious argument with a *lathi*. The Chiragan *mela* was purely a Mahommedan affair, and all the police who were out of eyeshot of any authority fraternized with the crowd. They slipped off their waistbelts, borrowed a *hookah*, held a baby by one hand and with the other, staked pice on the roulette-tables and tried to come to 'attention' when they saw an Englishman. Roulette-tables are demoralizing. My friend the *chaprassi* staked several pice and lost. So did some of the babies, and they went away and cried. The gambling instinct shows itself early in life. Never give an infant gambler pice. He doesn't spend it on sweets or merry go rounds. He goes on staking, poor innocent, and cries again.

My friend the *chaprassi* said that the Nats, who walk on slack ropes and balance themselves on bamboos, were the best part of the show. He was quite right. Their performances were very wonderful, and their tackle so insecure, that you expected a fall every minute from the rope to the stones below. On an average they collected two annas per performance, and they performed five times in three hours; but they never hurt themselves, which was what the crowds seemed to want.

This was about all that there was to be seen. The performing monkeys didn't draw, and went away early in the day with their red petticoats trailing mournfully in the dust. An exhibition of arts and manufactures was being held in the Dak Bungalow, but the crowd was more interesting. They didn't seem to have anything to amuse themselves with, and yet they were all laughing; they seemed to be very poor for the most part, and yet all the stalls and booths were beseiged; and last of all they didn't seem to know how to misbehave themselves. Even the boys in the tank who splashed the passers-by, did it in a half-hearted sort of way as if they were only pretending to be mischievous.

My friend the *chaprassi* did the honours of the fair in the finest fashion. The *Khitmatgar* had a carpet of his own, a *hookah*, several friends and lots of babies, and looked so dignified, that I was afraid of his cutting me in public, so I fetched a compass to avoid him. Of course there were plenty of *raises* and *zemindars* and upper class natives, but you can find these at Durbars any day in the week, and there's a certain respectable sameness about them. Nearly every body's *Khitmatgar* and bearer was there, but they had their foot on their native heather, and were gentlemen at large with clean clothes and money to spend. They were very courteous, but you felt the fact all the same, and it seemed to be rubbed into you that the people who make up our *nauker-log* have the manners and instincts of gentlemen away from their service and on their own ground. Humiliating thing to confess of course; but I fancy it's true. My friend the *chaprassi* will be 'O-chaprassi-iher ao' in another twelve hours, and my bondslave for rupees six per mensem as it is right and proper and just. But I saw another side of his character on the day when he piloted me through the packed tumult of the Chiragan fair of 1886. And it's very curious.

# Captain Hayes and the Horse

*Civil and Military Gazette, 14 April 1886*

**Attribution: Sussex Scrapbooks 28/3, p. 18**

Captain Matthew Horace Hayes (1842–1904), famous as a
trainer of horses, was now touring India to demonstrate his
methods. He was the author of such works as *A Guide to
Training and Horse Management in India,* 1875, and *Illustrated
Horse Breaking,* 1889. In his autobiography, *Among Men and
Horses,* 1894, Hayes remembered the meeting that Kipling
describes in this article:

> At Lahore I had the pleasure of meeting for the first time,
> Mr Rudyard Kipling, who was then a clever lad of about
> nineteen, and as yet unknown to fame. He was on the staff
> of the *Civil and Military Gazette,* and was doing much to
> brighten its hitherto somewhat staid columns. Although his
> tastes were wholly literary, he wrote for his paper a graphic
> and interesting account of my horsebreaking performances,
> which he witnessed, and which seem to have impressed him,
> if I may judge by his mention of my name in one of his
> *Plain Tales from the Hills.*

The reference that the Captain has in mind is in 'The Rescue of
Pluffles': 'I have seen Captain Hayes argue with a tough horse'.

### (From a Correspondent)

'The horse is a noble animal, but when irritated will not do so.'
Of his nobility opinions vary; of his unwillingness to do so no
one who has ever had the misfortune to own an irritable horse
can for a moment doubt. At this point — for Nature leaves none
of her works imperfect — steps in Captain Hayes. He makes the
horse 'do so', and instructs the owner how that horse may be
made to do so as long as he has a leg to stand on. Captain Hayes

is, therefore, the complement of the irritable horse; the one being incomplete without the other. As Saturn is ordained to spin round inside a ring of flame — even so is the young, lusty, and headstrong, or the old, angular and vicious horse ordained to spin round Captain Hayes until such time as it becomes a useful member of society. Everyone knows that the Captain's methods are 'occult, witheld, untrod'. He surrounds the stray-yard in which he teaches morality, obedience and order, with a line of *kanats*, and he objects to strangers looking on at his lessons. He objects also to his practices being revealed in print, but admits openly that the one and infallible way of teaching a horse anything is 'to take the starch out of him'. No horse will bolt, shy, kick, or otherwise misconduct himself from vice, if he has had the starch taken out of him, *more Hayesiatico*.

On Monday morning sixteen or seventeen gentlemen, and four ladies met at seven o'clock at the back of the Veterinary School, and after being duly sworn to secrecy, studied the taming of horses. There was a chestnut, a slim-built trapster belonging to Colonel Home. He had pronounced views on the subject of coming out of a cart after being unharnessed; quitting the shafts, it is said, as the Devil went through Athlone — 'in standing leps'. Otherwise he was absolutely quiet. Standing on the knee-deep straw of the enclosed yard, he seemed a thing for women to pet and men to pat — a country-bred in whom there was no guile. He allowed himself to be got ready for the 'un-starching' process with almost painful docility, Captain Hayes lecturing merrily meanwhile, and showing divers secrets con-nected with knots, hitches and halters, and the best method of catching horses by the hind-leg, etc. (His way, was a sound one, but a better method still is to send a *sais* to pick up legs or heads or tails or anything aggressive of that kind.) Then the manipulation began, and the chestnut trapster laid him down to his work as scientifically as the Captain and his Assistant. (By the way the Assistant's name is 'Ted', and his nationality is Australian. He is popularly supposed to be able to sit anything with four legs, and is as deathly silent over his work as a mute. In the middle of a most exciting struggle with the young idea — all hoofs and teeth — he may be observed to smile softly to himself as thinking of something that amused him a long time ago. Now and then he speaks but always in subdued tones; and he may sometimes be seen to sorrowfully provoke a beast to kick just to gauge the length of its hind leg. He seems absolutely without fear of any kind, and the sight of him waltzing a dumb *deux temps* with or round a horse is worth going some way to see.) But to return to the trapster. He fought well, not getting himself blown or lathered at the outset, and not showing the slightest degree of temper for more rounds than I should care to say. Ted and the Captain skirmished about him, and defeated him time upon time, but he came to the scratch for the two and twentieth time as composedly as though the game had just begun. All he wanted was his own way, and all that the Captain wanted was *his* own. In the intervals of the conflict — conducted with the greatest fairness and moderation on both sides — the Captain lectured, and showed how everything was done practically, and the male portion of the audience sat down on the straw and smoked attentively. It was delightful for every one except the trapster, for his own master had deserted him in his extremity, and was heartlessly speculating on the length of time necessary to unstarch him.

Round after round came and went; the sun became hotter, so did the horse, and Captain Hayes, cool, eloquent and masterful, placidly waited for the end. The trapster lost his temper and his belief in himself, and the first step of the process was at an end. A cart received him next, and herein, under the guidance of 'Ted' the silent, he behaved like a gentleman. Coming out of the shafts it is true that he stepped somewhat hastily; but this was accounted for by an overzealous *sais* making a mistake with one of the shafts, and hitting him behind. No horse worth his gram would stand still under these circumstances. Finally, he was taken away thankful, humbled and repentant. To him succeeded a small bay mare with her head in a muzzle, and a mild and cow-like expression in her eyes. She was only an inveterate man-eater, and was merely theorized over for a few minutes.

Some one admitted having a horse that let no European mount or saddle him. It was then close upon nine o'clock, but Captain Hayes expressed a willingness — even a yearning — to be introduced to that horse. 'Ted' smiled sorrowfully as one aware of the desperate wickedness of horseflesh and buttoned his jacket. A *sais* came up hanging on to the nose of a red, half Arab looking beast with the sign of the savage visibly impressed upon him, and the audience, after safely installing themselves behind the wooden bars of a shed, waited for the curtain to draw up. Under Captain Hayes' orders, saddle and bridle were stripped off, and the handsome creature was left alone in the centre of the straw yard. Then the fun began. A naked horse does not offer any obvious points to lay hold of, and this one lashed out in front, and behind; and filled in the pauses with trying to bite. Ted and the Captain waded out into the straw, and fished for him with a rod and a line. Anyone who doesn't know how it is done, may fish for horses to all eternity without getting anything more than a kick in the stomach. The horse suspected something wrong, and moved about quickly; then more quickly. Then he was hooked, and casting off the small remnant of decency that remained to him, he showed himself as vicious a devil as ever yet came under coercion. He bit his tongue; worried the ground; chewed his own knee in spleen; groaned; grunted; fought with his fore-legs against the anglements that beset him; reared, plunged, kicked, and if speech had been given him in that hour, would have sworn fearfully. It wasn't fright, because he attempted to rush his teachers; and it wasn't stupidity, because he had the clearest notion of the traps laid for him It was Original Sin, 14.2 in its shoes; and like Sir Galahad, blessed with the strength of ten. Victory crowned his efforts after some ten minutes savage fighting, and the red devil broke from its fetters and escaped quivering with indignation. 'Ted' smiled pensively, and retired up the stage to elaborate a fresh ruse; while the Captain, hot, panting, but still placid, continued his lecture. Once again the allied forces advanced to the attack, and so disposed their measures that the horse fell into their hands amid applause from the gallery, and fearful protestations on his own part. When a horse is really savage he grunts like a pig. This is very impressive. Also you never realise the full beauty of the contours of the body till you see a horse trying to stand on its head, or waving an indignant foreleg heavenward, or dancing a schottische round a man. Everything held this time, and except for one exciting minute, the horse never had a look in. He succumbed, grandly fighting to the last, about ten o'clock. Then the Captain moralized on the sinfulness of pride, and drank lemonade, being warm; while 'Ted' looked mournfully at the victim, as one who said: — 'I told you it was no good, and now I'm going to ride you.' Unfortunately the writer could not stay for what was doubtless the finest feature of the programme. He left at ten, and the last sight he saw was the horse that could not stand a European — the centre of an admiring crowd of Englishmen and ladies, a baffled beast, black with sweat, white with lather, and to all appearance cowed completely.

# [*Hobson-Jobson*]

*Civil and Military Gazette, 15 April 1886*

**Attribution: Sussex Scrapbooks 28/3, p. 18**

The full title of Sir Henry Yule and Arthur Burnell's *Hobson-Jobson* runs thus: *Hobson-Jobson: A Glossary of Colloquial Anglo-Indian Words and Phrases, and of Kindred Terms, Etymological, Historical, Geographical and Discursive*, London, John Murray, 1886. It contained 870 pages, was brought out in a revised edition in 1903, and remains the standard treatment of its subject today. In the revised edition Kipling himself is one of the authorities cited among the illustrations.

Colonel Yule's *Hobson-Jobson* is not a book to be lightly disposed of in one review. The difficulty in glancing over its eight hundred closely packed pages is where to begin; and having once begun, where to leave off. The idea of the book, we are told, sprang originally from a correspondence, fourteen years ago, between Colonel Yule and the late Mr Burnell of the Madras Civil Service. The two gentlemen conceived the notion of compiling an Anglo-Indian glossary; and the result of their labours is a fascinating volume, neither glossary, vocabulary, dictionary or anything else that may be described in one word, but simply — *Hobson-Jobson*: a glorified *olla podrida* of fact, fancy, note, sub-note, reference, cross-reference, and quotations innumerable, bearing on all things connected directly or indirectly with the East. Justly does Colonel Yule call it a 'portly, double-columned edifice'. It is a book which, unless we are much mistaken, will take its place among the standard works on the East; and will pass, gathering bulk as it goes, from decade to decade. Words, says Colonel Yule, are the jetsam which the tides of languages cast up on the beach of human thought — to be gathered together and placed in cabinets by the curious. When the author of *Hobson-Jobson* takes a word up, he deals with it lovingly, showing how it grew or fell away from its original purity by the corruption of time; also in what varying senses it has been used; concluding finally by three or four notes, or sometimes a page of quotations from all manner of strange and recondite sources, which shall throw a full or a side light on that word. Where his trove has no particular history, he tells, like the sages of old, a tale in a pleasantly discursive manner. *Bundobust,* for instance, has no pedigree; but its meaning is varied and its use extensive. Forty-three years ago an old khansamah informed the author that there must be a *bahut accha bundobust* in Belait, because the young and raw Sahib on his arrival at Calcutta was wont to say 'Thank you' to his servants when they brought him tea. Three months of the East, continued the khansamah, changed civility into abuse. This explanation is supplemented with a couple of lines from the ever-dear Ali Baba; and shows in some measure from what mixed sources Colonel Yule builds up his information. Of *bus,* Colonel Yule says justly, 'few Hindustani words stick closer by the returned Anglo-Indian'. Turning to Jinrickshaw, which Colonel Yule spells 'Jennyrickshaw', we find that its exact meaning is *'man-strength cart'*; and here those who may be ignorant of two most pleasant books are introduced, by the way of quotation, to Miss Bird's *'Japan'*, and Gill's *'River of Golden Sand'*. As a suggestive book, over and above all its other merits, *Hobson-Jobson* — pity it is that the title is so uncouth — stands alone. One of these days it may set the Government searching for a substitute for opium revenue when that drug ceases to be imported into China. The Chinese set a far higher value on the ginseng root than on opium, paying from six to four hundred dollars an ounce for it, and attributing to it miraculous virtues. An inferior sort of gin-seng comes to China from America; but there exists a very closely allied plant in our own Himalayas. Supposing that the genuine root could be grown in India, or the substitute educated up to its relative's powers, the possibility of an extensive and re-

munerative trade would seem to be assured; for gin-seng, apart
from the mythical attributes with which it has been invested,
has many of the good points of opium without its drawbacks.
On one point Colonel Yule errs slightly. He discredits the old
story that the fat-tailed sheep — the *doomba* — is ever provided
with a small cart to uphold its tail. Now there exists at the
present day in Lahore City, a fighting *doomba* full of years and
fatness. On state occasions his venerable *doomb* is packed on to
a wheeled platform which is profusely decorated with red
paper and tinsel. Thus adorned, he parades the streets fully
conscious of his merit. The tail is only honoured in the case of
a ram of unblemished courage. Every one in the East — the
book ranges from Constantinople to Japan — should possess
himself of *Hobson-Jobson* and once possessed of it should apply
himself diligently thereto. It will coerce him pleasantly to con-
sult other books and to explore fresh avenues of thought; and
may end in making him something that at a pinch might pass
for an oriental scholar. Further, it will interest him intensely
throughout.

# A Week in Lahore

*Civil and Military Gazette, 19 April 1886*

**Attribution: Sussex Scrapbooks 28/3, pp. 19–20**

Kipling's further remarks on the horse-training system of Captain
Hayes: see 'A Week in Lahore', 14 April.

What are Captain Hayes's notions of nerve? He says, verbally
and in print, that his system may be acquired by any one, even
if he has nothing more than ordinary coolness. 'Any one who
isn't afraid to go into the same yard as a horse, can do what I
can.' The Captain is a great man, and a clever, and exceedingly
wise; but surely he makes a mistake here. I admit that it does

not require superhuman bravery to go and look at — peradventure walk round — a loose horse, so long as that horse stands
still and thinks about his friends and family. But what are you
to do when he doesn't stand still? When he rises on end with a
joyous squeak, opens his mouth and comes down on you like a
wolf on the fold. You can't quell him with a glance of the
human eye divine, because he doesn't wait to look at you. You
can't hit him over the head, because his head is about eight feet
off the ground; and you can't whack him over the legs, because
that might spoil his value. Last of all, you can't very well stay
where you are, because he will hurt you. Will Captain Hayes
explain what is the best thing for 'taking the starch' out of a
horse who fears not God neither regards man — a confirmed
man-eater? I admit cheerfully — have not these eyes seen the
trick? — that Hayes himself *plus* 'Ted Kerr' can do anything he
pleases with any beast, but I do not think that it will be given
to five per cent of his pupils to successfully follow out his
instructions.

Even as those last lines were written, a letter came in con-
firmation of my doubt. A man has been Hayesifying a horse
and she — it was a lady — nearly Hayesified him. He seems to
have written the acount under the influence of extreme fear,
and I should like to know if it is all true: —
    'Dear ———. It was awfully easy to look at, and I had seen
Hayes go through the business twice, so I went home and had
the mare out of the cart to 'unstarch'. She is quiet as a lamb
in harness — only troubled with the slows; and as I wanted a
sober beast to try my 'prentice hand' on, I took her. I rigged
up a bamboo and string sort of enclosure; supplied myself with
punkah ropes and the long feather-headed bamboo that the
*mehter* uses for sweeping down cobwebs from room corners,
and set to work. The old mare thought I meant to give her
bread when I brought her in to the ring, and began nuzzling
my shoulder. I hit her on the nose, and she backed off looking
thoughtful and walked over to her *sais*. Then I sat down making
knots in a rope — same as Hayes does — and the *saises* said
*shabash*, and all the servants gathered round and applauded.
The mare stood in a corner dozing, and I began fishing for her —
same as Hayes does — though it would have been much easier
to have slipped a halter over her head, or even called her to me.

Something went wrong with the knots. I don't think I had the
the hang of them correctly — and the next that I remember
was the mare running back at an awful rate on a taut line, and
choking herself in a slip noose. She was grunting pretty freely
by the time the *sais* got the rope off; and she wouldn't let me
fish any more after that. She backed into a corner, and rolled
her eyes and snorted. Then I smiled, same as Hayes does — and
went out to talk to her, and she came out with her mouth open
to talk to me. Seemed that I'd shattered her feelings with that
slip-knot business. I stepped back quickly and got to the other
side of the bamboos. I tickled her in the face a bit with the
fluffy end of the broom  but that only made her worse. Then I
thought that the *sais* would be the best man to manage the rest
of the unstarching, so I lit a cheroot and gave him the necessary
directions as far as I remembered them. He said the mare was
perfectly *gureeb*, and would do anything he told her. I said he
was to do what I told him and he did — for about ten minutes;
apologizing abjectly to the mare for making a fool of her in her
old age. She put up with him for some time — though I could
see she didn't like it — until the smash came. Then she fought
for her own hand, and the *sais* ran; and the punkah rope snapped;
and there was a gaudy row. You take my word for it — a savage
horse may be bad, but a quiet beast, with her feelings hurt, and
her nose full of dust. and her coat studded with burrs is ten
times worse. I never saw any horse carry on like the old mare
did — not even the budmashes Hayes handles. The *sais* came to
me with tears in his eyes, while the old lady flopped about like
a newly hooked roach, to say it was a sin, and a shame to treat
a good horse so; and that she would never love him again. (The
*sais* is not a bit like Ted Kerr which disappointed me.) I lit
another cheroot and said he had to go through with the un-
starching. He tried some more; but the old lady unstarched him,
and she dragged him about two miles down the Ferozepore road
before I could understand how it was done. Now my advice
is this. First get another man's horse to unstarch; second see
that it's a bad beast that cannot be made worse; third see that
you go through with the business; and *fourth* see that you
understand what to do — specially the knot part. I fancy I
forgot one or two items of the schooling, and I know that the
*sais* forgot a good deal more. The long and the short of it is,
that I have about ruined the old mare. She won't let me ride

her; she won't go in a cart, and she will go for me if she gets a fair chance. It looked so blamed easy when Hayes did it, that I didn't think I could go wrong. May be if I hadn't started by trying to hang her, she wouldn't be so wrathy now when we meet.

'P.S. The worst of it is that the *sais* has told all his friends that I have gone *pagal* and try to kill my horses by pulling them in two with punkah ropes.'

How much stern fact there is in this sad tale I don't know; but true or not, it furnishes an awful warning to the gilded youth of the Punjab not to try their hand on horses because they have seen the Captain work wonders – once, or twice even or thrice. Pick up the knot and rope hints one by one, and then slowly and by degrees go the whole animal. [ ... ]

# The Queen's Highway

*Civil and Military Gazette, 13 July 1886*

**Attribution: Sussex Scrapbooks 28/3, pp. 22–3**

Kipling left Lahore for a month's leave in Simla on 3 July, and travelled through rain all the next day. This account is presumably only a little heightened. The Gugger (or Ghaggar) flows a few miles north of Umballa and must be crossed before reaching the foothills at Kalka and the start of the ascent to Simla.

#### (From a Correspondent)

There are milestones on the Simla road. This at first sight appears an unnecessary statement, but it is not so. The man entrusted with the erection of those milestones knew nothing whatever about distance or truth. Simla really is between seventy and one hundred and fifty miles from Kulka; the brazen fiction about 58 miles being invented and perpetuated for the benefit of ladies and invalids. This can be proved by going to Simla in the rains as a country-cousin has just done. But, to begin at the beginning — on a platform of the North-Western Railway high up Peshawur way. The rain had fallen, and there were enormous breaks on the line. It is astonishing what a fatherly solicitude one takes in the continuity of a State line when off on a month's leave. At last some one said that the break was on the other side of Umballa — after which interest slackened perceptibly. It would be annoying no doubt to the poor wretches coming north for coolness sake. Did any one know anything about the *Gugga*? That was the all important question. An affable guard said he had heard it was very high. Another fancied that it was not so bad; while a third said he hadn't heard anything about it at all — and didn't much care. All he wanted to know was how on earth was this (qualified) train to be got through to Delhi. Between Umritsar and Umballa the country was swamped, and at about three in the morning the train was threshing her way through water, and it was raining heavily. Dawn showed Umballa under water, inches under water, and the rain still falling steadily and sulkily. Every one was asking about the Gugga. A stranger, unacquainted with the land, might well have mistaken the knot of men under the station porch, for a band of pioneers setting forth into the wilderness, instead of a few travellers to the summer capital of India. A gentleman in a mackintosh, wet from head to heel, added to the depression of the little party by the cheery statement that 'he had, the previous evening, crossed on an elephant, and it was about as much as the elephant could do to get over'. Presently, for the dak babu was wet and sleepy, lumbered up the ticca gharris — with sodden cushions, reeking, steaming horses and dripping drivers. 'With the help of God' quoth the country cousin's coachman, 'the sahib will be able to reach Simla this evening. But it is not to be forgotten' added he consolingly, 'that even if the sahib is able to cross the Gugga, the Simla road may be broken — not once but many times. However I will beat my horses very much, and the sahib will assuredly give *bukshish*.'

Lying on those sodden cushions, hearing the ceaseless patter of the rain outside and rolling about uneasily with each motion of the cumbrous and all but springless carriage, the country cousin discovered that the dak gharri, rightly understood, is one of the many triumphs of Eastern Stupidity over Western Intelligence. The strong wheels, the powerful springs of the old English stage coach and of the American wagon might never have been invented. Far back in the twilight of Anglo-Indian history, a palki was put on a bullock cart, and it has remained there ever since, with such alleviations as Postmasters, who know nothing of the art of posting, have been able to devise. The smiths of some benignted *karkhana* at Aligarh weld its iron work with the barbaric belief, peculiar to Indian smiths, that weight is strength. An ordinarily skilful English wheel-wright would reduce the weight by a third, and yet turn out the whole machine of equal strength and greater capacity while, given fifty miles of such road as that ought to be between Amballa and Simla, a good American wagon builder would give you an easy running, strong and comfortable conveyance. Some reader who has been rocked and tumbled in an American stage, may be inclined to question this; and even in India there are to be found men whose recollection of stifling days, packed with their fellows as tightly as sardines in a Western stage, ploughing through alkali plains or rolling perilously down mountain roads, would lead them to prefer the dak gharri. But while in the West there are no roads to speak of, here they are better than the highways of American cities, and while there are to be found companies savagely intent on mere profit, here we have a Government and public cheerfully paying large sums for the best that is to be had. Do they get the best? Are the dak gharri and the tonga the best possible contrivances for the transit between Umballa and Simla? If it is pronounced that they are, then may we fear that civilisation *is* in truth a failure, and the Caucasian is played out. Then — he was very wet and clammy and jolted and uncomfortable by this time — the country cousin thought of the Gugga, and his little month's leave, and the chances of delay, and waxed public-spirited and virtuously indignant therefore. He imagined himself a stranger — a continental representative to the Camp of Exercise, a foreign Duke and all manner of other dignities; and pictured vividly the amazement and scorn that would overwhelm him were he to be pulled up shivering, houseless and hungry on his way to the capital of India — let us never forget that we are dealing with the capital of India — by a bridgeless, fordless torrent, or, worse still, were taken across in the rain, clinging to the back of an elephant, his luggage soaked and he himself numb and drenched. The more the country cousin jolted, and the wetter he got, the more did the absurdity — the utter ludicrousness of all the arrangements for that journey — impress itself upon him. He forgot he was a duke and a continental representative *pro tem* and, only remembering he was one of the crowd to whom two hours' delay meant a day's holiday lost, gave himself up to reflections of the bitterest kind on the merits of any one he had ever known or heard of directly or indirectly connected with the Government of India. This kept him warm, and prevented the chill of the sodden cushions striking too deeply. About half way through this commination service the gharri stopped. 'It is the Gugga by your honour's favour,' said the coachman. The country cousin leaped out, boiling over with indignation at the turbid and bridgeless torrent allowed through the crass short-sightedness etc. to obstruct, year after year, etc. The unfinished oath died on his lips, for there, behind the drowsy elephant, through a drizzle of rain, lay the Gugga, a mean dirty little trickle of two dispirited streams meandering through half a mile of wet sand. However, the principle remained the same if the Gugga didn't. The country cousin crawled into his carriage as they put the bullocks to, feeling that a burning grievance had been snatched from him at the last moment. The Gugga ought to have been in flood; and the country cousin's luck did not abolish the fact, that eighteen feet below the sand, through which the tail-twisted bullocks laboured heavily, lay sound blue clay ordained from the beginning for the foundations of a bridge which should carry trains and traffic comfortably. The sand and bullock business was bad enough in itself.

Later on, in this journey, was another river with an Irish bridge through it; and the bridge was composed of large stones levelled atop and sunk in concrete. Here came fresh bullocks, and a jolting to which the Gugga's performance was child's play. As the country cousin bounded like a parched pea on a grid-iron from side to side of his carriage, he imagined himself an invalid, weak and prostrated with fever; worn out with dysentery; broken down through overwork. Again he imagined himself a lady sent up to Simla for reasons which — but imagination failed him, as his head was thrown against the sliding-door hasp, and his toes rattled on the foot shelf. Revolving these things,

he came to Kalka — and the rain stopped with the carriage; and
the country cousin took heart about the roads 'up above'. All
that he said about the *dak gharri* and fifty percent more, might
with truth be said about the *tonga*.

In addition to the vices of the *dak gharri*, it has the violent
sifting motion of the winnower of a threshing machine. Imagine
a sick lady being violently shaken for eight hours with two
minute breaks at half hour intervals. This is the treatment she
must go through ere reaching Simla. We all know it, and we all
put up with it, because we are a slack, limp, go-as-you-please,
for-heaven's-sake-don't-make-a-fuss-about-it people; and it is
good for us to be told this again and again. The sun shone at
Kalka; there was dust at Dagshai; and glare and dust at Solon.
According to our notions — we are contented with little — the
journey had been a very successful one so far; and the country
cousin, in the baby jumper back seat of the tonga, congratulated himself on his luck. The driver was a clever man and a
bold, with no hesitation about sending his ponies spinning
round corners at a hand gallop, and putting them along the
level as fast as they could lay foot to the ground.

At the twentieth milestone a curious thing happened. The
tonga driver spun merrily round a corner into a thick drizzle
which ten minutes after turned to driving rain. Ten minutes
later the tonga met a stream coming down the road in a
hurry. This stream was broader than the tonga, and in depth
halfway to the wheel axle. Said the driver: 'It has been raining
much at Simla and Tara Devi. We will make haste.' From that
time the rain began to fall in earnest, and the country cousin
discovered the well known fact, that the only way in which
you can keep yourself moderately dry in a tonga is by half
sitting, half kneeling, half crouching on the back seat with your
legs tucked under you, and the cape of your waterproof thrown
over your right or windward cheek. You cannot open an um-
brella to ward the rain off if it blows in behind, because you
need both hands to hold on with. Hill rain has a trick of blowing
all ways in five minutes, and is very, very chilly. A tonga is
constructed to admit as much rain as possible.

Again the country cousin imagined himself an invalid and a
lady and his imaginings were not pleasant ones. Ladies cannot
well sit cross-legged in tongas, and they suffer a good deal from
chills nor does rain down the back of the neck improve their

health or temper. About the sixteenth milestone the country
cousin forgot about playing at imagination; and began to imagine
in earnest. The streams down the road side, the little torrents
from above that jumped half way out into the road, the chill
and damp and discomfort, did not so much matter; the worst
of it was that little rocks and handfuls of earth were beginning
to trickle gently down from the base of the cliffs. Wherever
one looked, a small handful of earth and a few stones were just
moving or had just finished rolling. It was disquieting to watch
this slither and slide all round — more disquieting in fact than
if one big slip had taken place just in front and blocked up the
road. At the twelfth milestone, the stones in the road were
bigger and harder to get over. A tonga need not turn out of the
way for a stone as big as a man's head; but the jolt and jar is
not pleasant. There was another tonga just behind the country
cousin's, and from time to time — four times in all — the leading
driver instructed the country cousin to tell the rear tonga to
hurry up, as a piece of cliff was going to fall. There are few
things more unpleasant then galloping in blinding rain under an
overhanging piece of rock or earth of doubtful reputation. So
the ride went on — the ponies ploughing mud knee-deep
through turbid yellow water, now running in-cliff where there
was rock and the imperfectly protected road seemed rotten at
the edge; now running outcliff where the hill was shaley and
great stones had slid into the middle of the road; now pulling
up invisible in clouds of steam to be succeeded by other ponies
— wet but willing little brutes who did all that lay in their
power; and were alternately abused and endeared by the driver.
And the tonga jolted and bumped over submerged stones in
the water, creaked and strained where there was mud instead
of clear washed road or running stream, while the tonga-bar
clinked and jingled merrily through it all and the bugle blared
huskily and the stones 'skipped like rams'. Presently there was a
soft crash — not a hard one — a wild lurch and a string of oaths
from the driver. Convinced that the end of all things was at
hand, the country cousin prepared to step forth into the ever-
lasting hills and die, like a gentleman, of starvation instead of
being pitched over-khud like rubbish. But the tonga righted
itself, and he was aware that it had, at a particularly sharp
and unpleasant turning, run over a dead camel — wet, shiny
and puffy in the rain. Luckily only two hind legs lay in the

direct route of traffic, or the consequences might have been almost as undignified as the country cousin feared. Then the ponies went on, and the rain fell, and the torrents spouted and once many big stones blocked the road completely, but a kindly hill coolie — who looked like a mountain gnome and made the ponies shy wildly — sprang from nowhere and removed the worst, and the tonga jolted forward and took no harm. Once, too, a string of camels, blundering down in the dusk on the wrong side of the road, gave trouble, and once again the Government Bullock train stopped the way; but the driver, like Thackeray's sailors, 'called upon the prophet and thought but little of it', and the tonga reached the last *chowki* but one, where a coolie announced that the road was *bund*. Without any exaggeration, it may be set down that the last six miles of road into Simla are, in the rains, nothing better than a stream bed; and the water channels them from six to eighteen inches deep. It seemed that the coolie's words might be only too true. 'Without doubt,' said the driver however, 'that man is a liar. We will go on and see.' So the tonga went forward, and the country cousin (a little reassured by the nonchalance of the driver) perceived that the real difficulty of the journey began at this point. The roads were diabolical and very steep, and there were many stones and heaps of slided earth. The dusk shut down about this time, and a cart stood across the road while the driver slept inside and was picked out at the end of a deftly applied whiplash. 'The coolie said truth. The road is *bund* — I do not think — but we will try.' There lay a strip of stones across the road — a bank about six foot high on the cliff and three foot high on the Khud side. He put the tonga back a few yards (luckily the ground was comparatively level) and went forward, but the ponies stayed in the middle of the trouble, and the *sais* ran forward and smote them under their bellies with a wet rope's end, and they pulled horsefully and the tonga came down on the further side with a soul-shattering bump, and in due course arrived in the thick dark at Simla; everyone except one small dog being drenched to the skin.

Now this is the true story of the Queen's Highway told by the country cousin, who went up it on the 4th of July 1886. The Simla dak service is worked at great loss to the Government, and there is much to be said in its favour. More may be said for a hill railway, and much more for the Umballa-Kalka line. In the meantime, one at least of the Members of the Council, two Commanders-in-Chief, the Lieutenant-Governor of the Punjab, and the wives of three of the most prominent officials in the land should be driven up and down the Simla-Kalka road daily in the rains in special express tongas at Rs. 40 per head. They might suggest a few improvements.

# Out of Society

*Pioneer, 14 August 1886*

**Attribution: Sussex Scrapbooks 28/1, p. 65**

Simla, 7,000 feet up in the lower Himalayas, the 'hills' of Kipling's *Plain Tales*, was the summer capital both of the government of India and of the government of the Punjab in Kipling's day. It had begun as a tiny local summer station for officers and their families in the early 1820s. The governor-general had spent a summer there in 1827, and thereafter it became the accepted residence of the government during the hot weather. In 1864 its *de facto* position as summer capital was made official. The cemetery Kipling describes long antedated the period of the town's imperial glamour.

A few score yards beyond the Khaibar Pass, just where the Chota Simla road turns downhill leaving the 'Barnes Court' offshoot on the left, is a trysting-place affected by ayahs and children and vagrant *jhampanis*. Also young people on ponies make appointments to meet there; and, if you sit long enough on the spic-and-span white railings, you may see all Simla pass by a-pleasuring. Next to the Bandstand there are few places more frequented than this little halting-place above the Chota Simla dip. Every one in Simla knows about it; but every one in Simla does not know that a few yards down the hill — a short tumble backwards, in fact, from the white railings — you come suddenly upon a relic of old Simla neglected and forgotten, as are most old things in India. There is an ancient wall — boarded atop and pierced in the middle for a door — which wall looks like the boundary of a long-neglected orchard. The door has rotted from its hinges, and the valves lie green and slimy on the grass within. There is no marked path to the place where the door has been; for long spotted snake-plants spring up merrily in the direct way, and there are ferns and club-mosses on the threshold. Pass over and you step at once, if you can keep foot-hold on the slippery soil, into Simla's first cemetery — the God's Acre taken up for the accommodation of the few residents who climbed hillward from the plains in the year of grace 1828.

It is hard to give any adequate idea of the utter desolation of the little plot the good people of those days fancied would be sufficient for their yearly needs. The frosts of fifty years have splintered and cracked the mortar of the tombs and bitten their outlines into rough and jagged shapes; ferns and grasses have taken root and flourish luxuriantly in the chinks and crevices; and one tomb, more weather-beaten than its fellows, has relapsed to a mere heap of road-metal. Many of the inscription slabs have fallen or have been picked out of the sides of the tombs, and green slime and fungus have covered deeply the rest. Perhaps the whole graveyard is fifty yards by thirty — but this is a liberal estimate. No attempt could ever have been made to level it; the ground being steeply sloping hill-side, terraced and stony. By reason of its confined space and the constant drippings of the pines overhead it is exceedingly damp, the water lying an inch or two deep at the lower end and leaving a green tide mark on the wall. No one seems to set foot in the place, for the grass grows thick and dank. There are delicate toadstools and ferns full in the way of passage, and, as I have already said, there is no marked path to the door. You can hear as you wander about among the graves the labouring breath of the rickshaw men bringing their rickshaws up the hill from Chota Simla, the least word of the babies and ayahs by the railings and the jests of the riders trotting past on the Mall above. Even in the midday sunshine the first cemetery is a dreary little place; but to thoroughly appreciate its loneliness and un-canniness you should go there on a dripping July afternoon in the middle of the rains and —always premising that you can stand firm on the slippery hillside — inspect the tombs.

It is written in the Simla Guide Book that the earliest grave is that of Margaret, daughter of a Dr Thompson, who died in 1829. The inscription slab must have fallen away or the tomb itself have disappeared, for Miss Thompson's grave cannot be found. One of the earliest legible inscriptions is on a small fluted column in the left centre of the graveyard recording the death of 'Thomas Edward Rees, son of the late M. Rees, Assistant Secretary, Office of the Revenue Department, who departed this life on the 14th of May 1830, aged 22 years, 10 months, and 12 days'. This tomb is in fairly good preservation, the white mortar having toned in process of years to a deep brown. There were indifferent stone-cutters in those days — natives who misspelt words and whose work must have been touched up by hands unskilled in the craft. On one slab, hidden away under a deep coating of green slime, came to light four verses of a hymn cut as prose, in which 'guardian' is spelt 'gaurdian' and the y's of all the 'thy's' in the devout lines have evidently been put in by an amateur, for they are scratchy and unsteady.

The very tombs are of a dead and gone shape (they look like huge cellarets), and it is seldom that the inscriptions vary. The dead 'depart this life' at 'Simlah' on such and such a date aged so many years, months, and days, and the crumbling grass-grown square of chunam-covered stones is 'sacred to their memory'. This very terseness seems to point to the difficulty our people in this far away corner of the land found, fifty years ago, in getting due and stately interment for their dead. As a nation we delight in lengthy legends on our tombs, and are willing to take any trouble to have them well and fairly graven. Evidently the stone-cutters of Simla had their *dustoor* from which they would not depart, taking as their unvarying model the inscription on the first English tomb their clumsy hands wrought.

However, it does not matter much now. In a few more years the remaining slabs will tumble from their setting, and the cracked and riven tombs will settle down into mounds of fern and fungus. The graveyard is as damp as a well, and all green things thrive aggressively.

Far down in one corner, where the yearly dropping of the pine needles and the summer rains have turned the ground into brown slush, is a squat little monument to the memory of Captain Matthew Ford, who died at Peshawur, aged 53, in the year 1841. He was an old captain, and must have seen service in his time, but nothing is given beyond his name, and the very brevity of the information sets one marvelling what manner of man Captain Ford of Peshawur was that his friends six hundred miles away should build him a memorial.

Children's graves are many and large. Alexander Duncan, infant son of Captain Parker, of the 10th Cavalry, died in 1834, aged eighteen months — poor little innocent — and rests under what must have been a sumptuous tomb — quite as big as the one a few yards off, sacred to the memory of Captain Henry Zouch Turton, 15th Regiment of Native Infantry, who died on the 29th of September 1835, aged 36, his little daughter, one year and eight months old, dying two months before her father. Charles Corbett, infant son of Henry Garstin, Captain in the 10th Light Cavalry, died in 1829, aged eight months and two days, so that, strictly speaking, he takes precedence of Thomas Edward Rees, and comes immediately after the Margaret Thompson to whom the Guide Book refers. His tomb is in the last state of ruin, and to decipher the inscription it is necessary to scrape away much slime and fungus from the slab.

In many cases, where the slabs have almost vanished under the coating of years, a little trouble brings out the long-forgotten names with startling distinctness — as incantations call up a spirit. The rims of the laboriously cut letters are as clear as on the day they were graven, for moss and lichen is a safeguard against change. It is only the strong-rooted ferns and the grasses that split the stones and deface the mortar permanently.

Major T. Elliott, of the 4th Light Dragoons, departed this life on the 5th of July 1837, when Her Majesty Queen Victoria had been a fortnight Queen of England. Major Elliott is set down Assistant Adjutant-General of the King's troops in India, for the news of William's death could not have reached Simla for months after the event. His tomb is in moderate good state, though the inscription had died out and cost some trouble to bring to light. The far end of the tiny cemetery — that stretch of tombs which lies directly under the tree-drip and holds the rainflow down hill — is the dampest and most utterly desolate of all. Most of the tombs are all but wiped out by time, and, where long ago some thoughful soul built a wooden shed over a specially dark grave, there remain only a few damp, rotten, spongy boards falling away from rust-eaten nails into the slime below.

A *pukka* shed with masonry walls and a wooden roof has
been erected over the finest tomb in the ground, but the rafters
have rotted and the rain comes in through a big hole in the roof,
while fragments of window sashes are stored in the shed itself.
Captain Codrington, of the 49th Native Infantry, raised the
memorial to his wife and three children in 1842: and the inscription and tablet came from Calcutta. Saving the ruined roof
of the shelter house, everything here is in perfect preservation.
The story told on the tablet is a thing to shudder at. Charles
Hay Acland, son of Captain Codrington, died on the 6th April
1841, aged four years; Lucy Elizabeth, aged three, died two
days later; the mother, Susan Elizabeth, died six weeks later,
and Katherine Mary, aged two, died eleven months later, on the
27th of May 1842. The Calcutta carvers did their work well, for
the inscription is as clear as on the day it was let into its place,
and below the inscription are two verses — pitiless Calvinist
verses — that come as a fit climax to the history of wretchedness
on the grave: —

> 'Lord, why is this,' she trembling cried,
>   'Wilt thou pursue a worm to death?'
> ''Tis in this way,' the Lord replied;
>   'I answer prayers for grace and faith.
> These sad bereavements I employ
>   From selfish pride to set thee free.
> To break thy schemes of earthly joy
>   That thou may'st seek thy all in me.'

He must have been a hard man this Captain Codrington —
reared in a hard faith and seeing in the wreck of his house the
hand of a jealous God. It is not well that this tomb of all others
should have been fenced about and protected so that the un-
compromising lines might live for forty years a record of trouble
and anguish more terrible than falls to the lot of one man in
ten thousand. The grasses and ferns should have laid hands on
the monument, and the lichens should have coated the verses
a score of years ago as they have coated and swathed and
gently hidden the tomb of George Crespigny, infant son of Colonel G. P. Wymer, who died on the 9th of May 1837, aged thirteen months.

In the middle of this moralizing, and a successful attempt to throw an unsightly basket beyond the limits of the forgotten graveyard, comes the sound of horses' feet from the Mall above, and a girl's voice, clear and incisive, saying to her cavalier: — 'Yes! it ought to be a delighful dance. By the way, what are you going as?' A pause. The cavalier evidently wishes to keep the secret of his fancy dress. Then eagerly: — 'Oh! do tell me. I'll be as silent as the grave about it. *Won't* you?'

Why of all possible comparisons that young lady should have chosen so ghastly a one I cannot tell. To make an effective ending to an ineffective description? It is possible.

# The Epics of India

*Civil and Military Gazette, 24 August 1886*

**Attribution: Sussex Scrapbooks 28/3, pp. 41–2**

The translation into English by Pratap Chandra Roy of *The Mahabharata* filled sixteen volumes published over the years from 1883 to 1896. Kipling had dutifully read the first instalments as they appeared, finding them increasingly tedious. Earlier in 1886 he had been provoked to discover William Morris citing *The Mahabharata* as among the 'hundred best books', and he wrote to express his annoyed skepticism to his old schoolmaster Cormell Price:

> I see by this week's P[all] M[all] Gazette that the worthy William Morris has been giving his opinion on the Hundred best books. Lord! Lord! What a lying world it is. He has gravely stuck down the Mahabarat and I will wager everything I have that he hasn't the ghost of a conception what he means when he advises the study of that monstrous midden . . . . I see every now and then at home some man who hasn't touched 'em lifting up his voice in praise of 'the golden mines of Oriental Literature' and I snort (18–27 February 1886: copy, the Kipling Society).

On the question of the value of Oriental wisdom literature Kipling sounds very much like Macaulay fifty years before, when asked to judge between those who wanted to make the traditional literature the basis of education in India and those who argued for western learning. Who, Macaulay asked, could seriously contemplate teaching 'medical doctrines which would disgrace an English farrier — Astronomy, which would move laughter in girls at an English boarding school — History, abounding with kings thirty feet high, and reigns thirty thousand years long — and Geography, made up of seas of treacle and seas of butter?' Who indeed? Kipling would have echoed; and, like Macaulay, he clinches the case against the epics of India by pointing out that 'Young India. . . avoids them altogether'.

The twenty-fifth portion of Babu Protap Chundra Roy's translation of the *Mahabharata* — excellently printed on fair paper — is now before the public. It includes nearly thirty additional sections of the interminable work. While it is impossible not to admire the unflagging zeal and industry of the author, it is equally impossible not to wonder whether they are being used to the best purpose. The *Indian Antiquary* thinks that 'it is almost impossible to say too much in support of an undertaking which, in addition to making the contents of this interesting epic available to students unacquainted with Sanscrit, is of the greatest practical use to Sanscrit scholars also'. Is it seriously contended that, by the vast majority of readers, the great epic will be regarded as a thing of interest, to be studied; Young India writes, and writes fluently, on the sin of 'neglecting the precious mines of Aryan literature which our ancestors bequeathed, etc.' Nevertheless it devotes its intellect exclusively to the acquirement of the marketable knowledge of the West; and if pressed on the subject, might be found almost as ignorant of the contents of the 'precious mines' aforesaid as the people it condemns so airily. In the case of Englishmen, whoso wishes to escape condemnation as an ignorant soul, must be prepared to admit in a general way, the excellence of the Indian Classics and the wealth of the treasures they contain. This is an article of faith, and therefore unverified by research. Monier Williams and Max Muller have told the world what to believe, and the world is content to take their assertions on trust; agreeing unhesitatingly in what they say.

Section after section of the 'interesting epic' has now been made plain to Western comprehension by the indefatigable translator; and section after section — with its monstrous array of nightmare-like incidents, where armies are slain, and worlds swallowed with monotonous frequency, its records of impossible combats, its lengthy catalogues of female charms, and its nebulous digressions on points of morality — gives but the scantiest return for the labour expended on its production. Here, for instance, is an extract taken at random from the account of Arjuna's slaughter of the troops of Duryodhana: —

And he soon covered the entire welkin with clusters of blood drinking arrows, and as the infinite rays of the powerful sun entering a small vessel are contracted within it for want of space, so the countless shafts of Arjuna could not find room for their expansion, even within the vast welkin. And the elephants crowding the field, their bodies pierced with blazing arrows, with small intervals between, looked like black crowds coruscated with solar rays. . . . And that hero of inconceivable energy, overwhelmed, by means of his celestial weapons, all the great bowmen of the enemy, although they were possessed of great prowess. And Arjuna then shot three and seventy arrows of sharp points at Drona, and ten at Dussaha, and eight at Drona's son and twelve at Duscasans, and three at Kripa the son of Karadwat. And that slayer of foes pierced Bhishma, the son of Cantanu with six arrows and King Duryodhana with a hundred.

Page upon page might be filled with extracts equally profitless; and appealing, exactly as much as this one, to the Western mind. The fantastic creations of the Hindu Mythology have as much reality in their composition and coherence in their action, as the wind-driven clouds of sunset. They are monstrous, painted in all the crude colours that a barbaric hand can apply; moved by machinery that would be colossal were it not absurd, and placed in all their doings beyond the remotest pale of human sympathy. The demi-god who is slain and disembowelled at dusk rises again whole and unharmed at dawn, to conduct a monstrous strife where mountains and thunder bolts are scattered broadcast over the plain; and the wearied reader, who has set forth on his journey of discovery, with the honest intent of exploring the precious mines of Oriental lore, finds his attention wandering and his commonsense revolting at the inanities put before him.

As with the *Mahabharata*, so with the *Ramayana*, which, we have Griffith's word for it, is 'more popular and more honoured by the people of the North-Western Provinces than the Bible is by the corresponding classes in England'. Boars like purple mountains, maidens with lotos feet and the gait of she elephants, giants with removable and renewable heads and bodies accommodating as the stomach of the sea-cucumber, are scattered broadcast throughout its pages. The high thoughts, the noble sentiments, the outcomes of human genius which we have been taught are to be found for the seeking, are few and very far between. It is necessary first to peruse an infinity of trivialities before we arrive at anything which may fairly be held to represent oriental *thought*. The rest is dream piled on dream and phantasm on phantasm — unprofitable, and to [the] Western mind, at least, foolish.

To orientalists, the two national epics have their own special value, as the *Rig Veda* has for students of early forms of religious belief; but the working world of to-day has no place for these ponderous records of nothingness. Young India, as we have said, avoids them altogether, knowing that life is short and Arts examinations long; the bare outlines of their stories are known and sung by the village folk of the country-side, taking the same place as folklore and love ditties; but as living forces, they are surely dead and their gigantic corpses, like whales stranded by an ebbing tide, are curiosities to be regarded from a distance by the curious, and left alone by those who look for any solid return from laborious reading.

# [Tommy Atkins in Burma]

*Civil and Military Gazette, 1 January 1887*

**Attribution: Sussex Scrapbooks 28/3, p. 65**

The episode described in this article reappeared some months later as the second of the Mulvaney stories, 'The Taking of Lungtungpen', *CMG*, 11 April 1887.

The British had been fighting in Burma since late in 1885.

Private Thomas Atkins of to-day may be five foot four in his ammunition-boots, less than thirty-three inches round the chest, and hard to keep in hand; but he has still a good deal of the spirit that sent his predecessors of the Light Division up the shot-torn vineyards of the Alma. Twenty soldiers in the Ninghyan district are ordered to cross a river and burn a village. The boat in which they are to cross is pointed out to them. Unfortunately the boat has its bottom knocked out of it by dacoits. Obviously it is the duty of the party to return and point out this distressing fact to the authorities. But the party continues to go on; and a detachment of five men and a bugler, a small boy, take off their garments and proceed to swim the river; losing one man as they cross. Then, clad as was Lady Godiva on a certain memorable occasion, they walk up the bank, advance upon the village, wherein, for anything they know, there may be a hundred dacoits, and set it alight. Luckily the village is deserted, and the dacoits are flying further into the jungle; so no one is hurt, and the little band returns naked, but not ashamed, having done what they were told to do. The idea of Thomas, whom a paternal Government has supplied with a rifle and a uniform, discarding these trifles, and running about the country with nothing on in pursuit of dacoits, is very ludicrous; but the little affair has its more solemn side, and it is impossible not to admire the reckless bravery of the four men and the bugler of the 2nd Queen's on the Sittang river.

# Of Criticisms

*Civil and Military Gazette, 22 January 1887*

**Attribution: Sussex Scrapbooks 28/3, p. 5**

A review — not by Kipling — of an amateur concert in Lahore,
published in the *CMG* on 20 January, expressed some polite
reservations about parts of the performance — 'The Orpheus
glees,' for example, 'did not show the amount of practice which
unaccompanied part-singing requires.' The next day a correspondent, X, defended the glee-singing on the grounds that the
tenor was indisposed and had to be hurriedly replaced. This
mild conflict gave Kipling his occasion for 'Of Criticisms'.

He was by this time a thorough veteran of reviewing, both in
Simla and in Lahore, and of both amateur and professional
performances. The same paper that contained this squib also
contained his review of some amateur theatricals by the artillery
officers at Mian Mir cantonments. 'The whole evening's entertainment was light, amusing, and not too long. What more could
one wish?' Kipling concludes his review, obviously following
the precepts laid down in 'Of Criticisms'.

**To the Editor**

Sir, — I object to music — sacred music especially — and I did
not go to the Montgomery Hall concert. These are my claims
for intruding on a discussion which doesn't in the least concern
me. Many years ago I used to write criticisms on things that
other people inflicted on their friends — concerts and theatricals,
and readings and recitations and operas — and in the course of
my ill-considered writings I made two or three notable discoveries, and contracted a deadly hatred, which I have still, of the
Indian Amateur. He or she is impossible to deal with except on
one line — that of unlimited adulation. When I read your correspondent's account of the concert I chuckled; because I saw
that he had erred, and I knew what awaited him. He tried critic-

ism — very, very mild it is true, and set about with praise that would have made a professional rejoice — but none the less it was criticism. He did not admit, as is my invariable custom, fully, frankly and without reservation, that never since Pagannini composed the *Dead March in Saul*, or Jenny Lind sang *Twickenham Ferry*, had there been such superbly phrased and magnificently *teneramente maestuoso prestissimo* arrangement of symphonies and plagal-cadences. The Indian Amateur understands that sort of criticism; and, since nothing is impersonal in this wretched country, respects the critic as a person of judgment and sound knowledge. 'Altogether,' says your correspondent, 'the concert was an admirable one and reflected credit on all concerned.' That is, not one half enough. It might go down with an ordinary hardworking singer at home, but the Indian Amateur demands more — and why on earth should he not have it? To-day my conscience is some degrees less tender than a brickbat; but I remember a misty and far off time, when I conceived it was the duty of one who had paid two, three, or four rupees to a public entertainment for two or three hours' stolid sitting on a bench in more or less comfort of mind, to treat the dispensers of that entertainment *au grand serieux*; to take some trouble in what he wrote; to compare their performances with others that he remembered; and as delicately as possible to point out here and there it might be, the possibilities of amendment or further perfection. I was wrong — bitterly wrong, but I did not discover my mistakes before I had lost two or three very pleasant friends, had been branded openly with the brand of half knowledge and outrageous conceit, and raised a healthy crop of piques and spites. The award of such praise as I bestowed was put down to purely personal and private motives, etc., etc., etc. Next [came?] my second discovery. Notice the Indian Amateur, he howls; do not notice him and he foams. He will of course deny all these accusations but that is a small matter. The safest plan is indiscriminate eulogy. The Indian Amateur demands ostentatiously, 'honest criticism, you know'; but if he gets even an expurgated — a triply Bowdlerized — edition of what his soul professes to yearn for, he — well, is unhappy. I have written — I glory in my shame — of the Indian Amateur till I feared that my pen would turn up at the point in disgust, or that the man himself or the woman herself would see the gross insult of unstinted praise. But I was wrong. The pen continued its toil and the praise was accepted, on my honour, as a right, as a bare instalment of a just due. It was absolutely petrifying! Did I say So and So was Faust, Irving, Terris, and Toole combined, So and So was hurt because Wilson Barrett had been omitted from the comparison. I have compared — may I be forgiven for it — a lady actress to Ellen Terry, and she pointed out that since Ellen Terry was old and she young, Mary Anderson must have been the star I had in my mind. I said it was so, and the floor did not open under my shameless feet. Later on I became absolutely callous, and am now open, for Rs. 2.8.0. in stamps, to prepare twenty lines of graduated, Corney-Grain-Santley-Sims-Reeves-Mario musical criticism (small type) *or* for ladies Rs. 3.4.0. ranging from Hortense Schneider, *via* Lola Montez to Adah Isaaks Menken, Patti, Albani, Norman Neruda, or two others. Dramatic ditto for men (old style English,) Kean, Kemble, Macready, Rs. 2.12.0. New style, Irving, Wilson Barret, and three other minor stars Rs. 3.2.0. Ladies: — Mrs Siddons, Connie Gilchrist (passing allusion only). Nellie Farren, Ellen Terry, 'whole gamut dramatic expression' 'thunder[ou]s applause' 'absolutely perfect rendering,' etc., etc., by private arrangement. Address

THE ANANIAS
Care of Manager of this paper

# Of Criticisms

*Civil and Military Gazette, 25 January 1887*

**Attribution: Sussex Scrapbooks 28/3, p. 81**

The reviewer wrote to defend the justice of his review against the response of X (see the preceding item), allowing Kipling to continue his remarks. The contempt of the craftsman for the dilettante comes out in Kipling's distinction here between 'gentlemen and ladies on the Government House List' and the 'professional living by his talents'.

(To the Editor)

Sir, — I have read 'Your Contributor's' letter of Monday with sorrow and sympathy. Ages since, I also used to write exactly the same sort of reply as he has done to exactly the same sort of letter as 'X' has written. I essayed to reason with the Indian Amateur — to convince him of the error of his ways — and to justify my remarks on his orchestral, operatic and theatrical performances. In short I treated him seriously. To what end? It only hurt his feelings, and I am specially averse to hurting the feelings of any man or woman. From the Nirvana which I have attained, I look down with more than rhinoceros-like calm on the strife. — Occasionally I smile dreamily, but that is the only emotion the well known scuffle creates within me. As Bayard Taylor, or someone very like him, says: —

I do not yearn for that I cherished most,
I give the winds the passionate gifts I sought,
And slumber fiercely on the torrid coast
Down there in Hadramaut.

I see the Indian Amateur give himself away, bound hand and foot, into the power of his critic; as he did into my power of old. I see the critic hit him tenderly over the head with a padded sofa-cushion letter as I did *not* do; for, in the years of my error I smote with the knobbiest bludgeon I could lay hands on. I feel sorry for both disputants because I know the futility of the struggle. If I cared to rouse myself from the deep peace which is now my portion, I would whisper: — 'Let us O my "Your Contributor" go forth together along the flowery path of "criticism", with a very soft C. Let us, if such a thing be possible, so cover and coat and tar and feather and beslaver the Indian Amateur with praise that he shall at last see, or his friends shall kindly tell him, that his leg is being pulled by a brutal and wanton press, clique or what you will. So shall it, in the course of the ages, be borne in upon his soul that the songs which he sings, and the plays which he plays, and the operas which he operates must be judged wholly by the standard of polite private and well-bred drawing-room criticism; that the outcome of his leisure moments and his attempts to please must be taken for what they are — the efforts of gentlemen and

ladies on the Government House List — *not* the labour of a
professional living by his talents and, as such, entitled to the
weighed and careful comments of a public journal'. Having
entangled myself hopelessly in this last ungrammatical sentence,
I will sleep again while the Indian Amateur points out the want
of knowledge, taste, manners and general unworthiness of

THE ANANIAS,
(Surnamed 'The Great')

# Anglo-Indian Society

*Civil and Military Gazette, 29 January 1887*

**Attribution: Sussex Scrapbooks 28/3, pp. 73/4**

Since this is written in imitation of what a tourist might be
imagined as writing about India, it cannot be taken as Kipling
speaking in his own voice. But as with other writers who have
used the traveller from afar as a way to secure a hearing for
their own ideas, Kipling has probably put a good many of his
own convictions and observations into this commentary on the
Indian scene. Which parts are testimony, and which parts are
dramatic imitation, the reader may determine for himself.

The birds of passage who annually flutter through India in the
cold season, look about them a good deal during their short
stay. Many of the wanderers will, perhaps, try to write books
about what they have seen. Meantine, as a specimen of the sort
of notes they are collecting, we are able to publish a few extracts
on India generally, and Anglo-India in particular, from the
home letters of one tourist who lately spent a few months in
India, but who is now beyond the reach of vengeance. The
matter may be interesting, as showing, in some measure, ourselves as others see us: —

You believe that Anglo-Indians are domineering and arrogant
in their habits. So do — or rather so did — I. What I had read in
the Anglo-vernacular newspapers — and you know I used to be
a careful student of them — certainly prejudiced me against the
men with whom I am staying. I fancied that, though the complaints were exaggerated, there must be a solid foundation of
brutality to account for them. You may imagine, of course, that
I looked out keenly for anything of the kind among my hosts,
especially in regard to their servants, about whom I have heard
so much. So far as I was able to judge, my first notions were
altogether wrong.

Every Anglo-Indian house is, as you know, full of servants,
but the amount of work exacted from each is very little indeed.
In one household of three people, something like £100 is paid
yearly for service only, out of an income of perhaps £900 a year.
But to return. The relations between master and servant are
peculiar, and closer, it seems to me, than with us in England.
A man who has been five years or so in India, has generally
gathered round him a little knot of dependents and their families, and never thinks of changing them, or they of leaving him.
They come to him as a matter of course for medicines when
they are ill, and in many cases he is the arbiter in their disputes
— as I have seen. He knows, more or less, about the state of
their families and the ailments of their children, and, I think,
interests himself in their welfare. In one instance the wife of
one of my host's table-servants was seriously ill, but the husband objected to taking her to the hospital, which I was told
was the only chance of saving her life. My host delivered himself
of a string of abuse in the vernacular, and then and there,
threatened his servant with a sound thrashing and instant dis-
missal, without payment, if the woman was not at once taken
over. The threat told, and the woman was eventually cured.
What seemed to irritate my host most, was his servant's pre-
tension to caste prejudice. 'The man' he told me 'is a low-caste
Mahommedan — I knew his father before him. The idea of his
swaggering about his caste!' According to my host, the man
would sooner have let his wife die, to gratify his vanity in keeping the women of his house — such a house, a mud hovel, with
a little screen of rags and bamboos in front! — than allow her

face to be seen. Curiously enough, my host admitted frankly, that had the man been a high caste man, he would not have done anything in the matter. This I own I cannot understand; for where a human life was involved, I should have felt justified in forcing my way into any zenana or whatever they call it, with a doctor. Their acceptance of caste scruples of one of the most striking things about Anglo-Indians. I confess that the refusal of a native – Hindus I think have this prejudice – to take away an empty plate, would make me very savage. But as the case above shows, Anglo-Indians of any experience resent at once any attempt to establish caste scruples where the position of the man does not entitle him to it.

There is no society in India as we understand the word. There are no books, no pictures, no conversations worth listening to for recreation's sake. Every man is in some service or other, has a hard day's work to do, and has very little inclination to talk or to do anything but sleep at the end of it. The officers of the many regiments are the only people who seem to have any leisure; and it is mainly to them that any little social festivity is due. They organise the races, dances, balls and picnics, and seem to manage most of the flirtation in the country. Nothing can exceed the hospitality and kindness either of a Mess or any officer of one. It is curious to think how little we in England see or know of our army. In India they are one of the most prominent features of the social landscape. I owe them many kindnesses.

Indeed, throughout my tour I have been everywhere received with frank and cordial hospitality. Armed with a few letters of introduction, I travelled from one end of the country to the other; men taking it as a matter of course that I should stay at their houses – never asking me at all, but simply directing that my baggage should be put down in such and such a room. All the same, though I was in their life, I felt that I was in no way of it. Every one seemed so busy. I got quite accustomed to the announcement the morning after my arrival: – 'Well, Mr – , I must hand you over to the care of my wife, I've got to go to office.' And to office at ten my host went; returning at five or half past, tired and jaded. It seemed almost an impertinence that an idler for the time being should intrude himself on so workful a life. The strain even in the cold weather must be severe. In the hot weather it must be heart breaking. Men age very rapidly in India, and I have seen young men of even five and six and twenty wrinkled, and grey on the temples. Looking down a dinner table, it is curious to notice the decisiveness and look of energy in the faces of the men — especially the younger ones. In England there is a certain flat uniformity of unformedness about our young men that covers them all. The older men *invariably* talk of their own work or pay or prospects when two or three gather together; and the young men, if in the army, talk of their horses. In a country where every Englishman owns at least one horse, this is natural but monotonous. No one talks lightly and amusingly as in England. Every one works and talks and thinks about his work. it must be a ghastly existence, when the brain and body both begin to tire with the approach of old age. Very few Englishmen in India seem at all contented, though they are enthusiastic enough about their work — always their work; though, to do them justice, they don't talk about it with a capital W.

You know the sailor's answer to the Gospel Reader's question as to whether he liked his profession? The man looked at the deck, looked at the masts, and then into the hold — lastly at his scarred hands and said: — 'Like it! D——n it, I *have* to like it'. This somehow seems to be the mental attitude of many Anglo-Indians. They have to like their work, and they do it well; but, according to their own account, it must be hopeless enough, with no prospect to brighten it beyond that which power and authority confers. And power and authority are not everything.

The curious clinging dependence of the native on the Anglo-Indians is very striking. Everything that has to be done must be supervised and pushed along by an Englishman; or the 'labour is naught'. For instance, directions which an English carpenter, tailor, smith or builder would grasp at once, have to be repeated again and again before natives can understand their purport; and throughout the whole progress of the job the puzzle-headed man comes a dozen times at least to his employer for help and explanation. You know my weakness for machinery in any form, as the highest concrete expression of man's intelligence. Natives — here I can speak authoritatively from what I have seen — have no conception of the proper care of the machinery.

This seems beyond their scope altogether. I have seen engines
running under charge of native drivers, which, according to
English notions, should never have left the cleaning-shed, and
which bore in every part of them, from the axle-boxes upwards,
marks of gross mismanagement and neglect. An English driver
or fireman, who dared to run his charge in such a condition —
but no driver would, so my indignation is wasted. The stories
I have heard of native management of good, first-class locomotives made my blood boil; but everything is accepted out
here as a matter of course, because the general policy seems to
be to give the natives as much work as possible, at any cost.
That is the keynote of everything, and allowances are made
accordingly. Perhaps it is wrong to generalise from one class
only; but if I were to judge India from the engine-drivers I have
seen, I would avoid it for ever. When I first came to India I
fancied, from the tone of the native papers I had read, that all
Indians were independent and self-helping. A good many things
have made me change my mind since. One never hears anything about the independence of natives from Anglo-Indians;
but a good deal about their helplessness. Every Englishman I
have met seems to say the same thing, and to put up with short-
comings that would drive an English employer of labour mad.
Here is an instance. A native clerk, the other day, was set to
copy some pages of printed matter for a gentleman in whose
house I was staying. Remember that the clerk had had, what
they call here, an English education, and could speak English
fluently. He missed out, through sheer carelessness, *three* lines
in one page, *one* in the next, and *two* in the third; thus making
the whole stuff nonsense; and he also did not put in a single
stop from beginning to end. I saw the paper, and if a boy of
sixteen, on fifteen shillings a week at home, had done it, I
should have dismissed him at once. And that same clerk was as
vain as a peacock, and talked to me about the 'political future
of India'. He may be an exception to his fellows. I hope he is.

All the work that I have seen turned out by native hands is
bad. Doors don't come up properly to the jambs; windows are
never straight; there is no finish in the roofs. Floors and plinths
are badly put down, and timber is wastefully misused without
any increase of strength. Native hinges and locks, and iron-
work generally, are all abominations to English eyes. There is no

correct rabbeting, mortising, mitreing, dovetailing or joinery of any sort in the land — as far as I have seen; and this disgusts me a good deal. The English newpapers, excepting two Bombay ones — where they use steam — are badly enough printed, even under European supervision; but the native papers are something atrocious. Some of them would be a disgrace to a tenth-rate bill-sticker. It is very funny to read all the flowing and civilized sentiments set up and printed in a manner which proves, literally on the face of it, that savages have been playing with English machinery and type. I enclose you one or two specimen cuttings — not the worst by any means. Aren't they shameful? Also I send you by post a hinge, a lock and a couple of links of chain turned out by natives and sold to Englishmen. These will tell you a good deal more than I can. Really these Anglo-Indians might make some attempt to teach the natives to turn out work properly. To me at least the natives are exasperatingly stupid, but something ought to be done. There are no large centres of supply anywhere, and if you want anything made, outside the towns of Bombay and Calcutta, you must advance the workman the money and he takes from one to three weeks over the most petty job. A cheerful and barbarous country for our purposes, isn't it? And these Anglo-Indians go on talking and writing about the 'political education and advancement' of the natives, and the educated natives do the same thing in those infamously printed papers! Just look at my cuttings! No English house would turn out an ABC for pauper children as vilely as this rhodomontade is printed. They may want political education — that is no business of mine, but I *do* know, before they are fit for anything, they must be taught to use their hands and English machinery a little less like Australian aborigines.

This slackness and want of straight lines goes all over India. The very keys on the railway lines seem as if they had been hammered in by a man who did not know which end of the hammer he ought to use. Everything here is raw, unfinished, misjointed, slack and wrongly built. The Anglo-Indians have a beautifully expressive word for all this — '*kutcha*'. Everything is '*kutcha*' — which means everything is just as an English workman would not turn it out. The natives talk — talk immensely. My hosts introduced me to a lot of English-speaking native gentlemen everywhere. They were all very much alike to look at, and they all spoke English beautifully. Also they all talked in much the same strain about the 'disabilities of natives', and my views on the Government of India. I heard an enormous amount about the reforms they wished for, as they seemed to think I was a man of influence at home or in Parliament; but all their reforms are purely political, and seem rather purposeless. They say India would be better for natives in the Legislative Council, and for the employment of natives in most of the posts where Anglo-Indians are now. Perhaps this is true, but they would have to be quite different natives from the printers and engine drivers and locksmiths I have met. I used to begin by asking these gentlemen about manufactures and so on — you know why I came out. (I hope the shareholders will take my advice, that's all.) But I found out, after a little, that none of these men knew anything about what I wanted, or the possibility of starting a factory in India with agencies at all the seaport towns. All the information I got, came from the Anglo-Indians, and they discouraged me a good deal. (My other letter contains my views on the purely business part of my tour — at length. You will see what I had to contend with. But to go back to my friends in turbans and velvet skull-caps.)

They did not know anything about their own country from a commercial point of view; but they prosed away about politics for hours. Now their kind of politics didn't interest me, though I tried to seem interested in order to get them to talk business later on. But they were a misty, cloudy lot altogether, and I had to go back to the Englishmen. Indeed, they told me that the Anglo-Indians knew more about that sort of thing than they did, and I found they were right. My hosts were exceedingly courteous to these gentlemen, but somehow there seemed to be nothing in common between them. I didn't wonder at it. The natives simply revel in words, and I don't think they understand half they say. They certainly are not at all connected in their conversation, and contradict themselves over and over again. A man must have a head for business before he can take up politics successfully. However, I'm out of my depth here.

You want to know what Anglo-Indian women are like? Well, they are very much like English ladies all the world over; but they aren't pretty. The climate kills good looks, and, taking one thing with another, they are as plain as they can be. Where they aren't plain, they are sickly and sallow. A little beauty goes a very long way in India. Nevertheless, they are exceedingly nice, and have much more individuality than English women. They know more of life, death, sickness and trouble than English women, I think; and this makes them broader in their views — though they talk about their servants as much as women do at home.

All the stuff that one hears and reads in England about their being 'fast' is utter rubbish. Of course there are some exceptions, but the bulk of them are a good deal steadier than women at home. Their life is very quiet, and everybody, everywhere, knows everything they do. Besides this, married couples live year after year alone by themselves in forsaken places, scores of miles away from anything like civilization; and I fancy that woman who has helped her husband through an abomination of desolation like this 'out-station' life, as they call it, gets to be exceedingly fond of him. This is rather curious, but I believe it to be the fact. If they were prettier, the English-women in India would be delightful. I admit that their 'belles' startle one rather. They would be out of consideration in a small county town in England. As a general rule, only the older women try to be 'fast', and their fastness is very modified; but it lasts for many years. Women of from forty to fifty and upwards — I'm not exaggerating, I assure you — are the Lillie Langtrys of India, and the youngest men are their worshippers in a lukewarm sort of way.

Nothing seems to impress the Anglo-Indians except their work. They call the Himalaya mountains — 'the hills'; when a man dies he 'pegs out'; when he is ill he is 'sick'. When a mother nearly breaks her heart over the loss of her first child, they say 'she frets about it a little'. They are more than American in their curious belittleing of everything, and they take everything as a matter of course, and when a man does anything great or heroic — and I have heard of some wonderfully grand things being done by officers and civil servants — they say 'not half bad'. That is their highest praise. I don't think you could startle an Anglo-Indian under any circumstances.

He is a very queer person, and I don't see what there is in his life worth living for. His amusements are very forlorn affairs, and there never seems to be any 'go' about him; though I have been told that this is not the case. All his jokes are old ones from England, and the local jokes can't be understood, unless you have been years in that particular place. He hasn't even any vices worth speaking of, and he smokes tobacco strong enough to blow your head off. Nearly all Anglo-Indians smoke heavily, and they all ride – down to the children. They have no notion of walking; but as a class they ride beautifully. I never wish to be better or more kindly entertained than I have been; but somehow their life repels me – it's so dreary. You would understand it better if you were out here. They don't seem to be paid as well as I expected, and the prices of any English-made things in India are absurdly high. All their money seems to go in insurance and remittances for their children; and you have no idea what they lose by exchange.

But this is the one country where they know and practise charity. The towns are full of subscription lists – an institution unknown at home. I honestly believe, if I were to take a piece of paper and write at the top 'Subscription required for a worthy object. Please pay bearer', I should get money from nine out of ten men. They subscribe to charities, and for orphans, and beggars, and widows and churches – for anything in short in a wonderful way, and they never stop to think about the creed they are helping. Roman Catholic, Baptist, Wesleyan, Episcopalian is all the same to them. I can't see why they subscribe, because it doesn't amuse them, and amusement is what they want most. Their play is as depressing as their work.

If I weren't afraid of seeming to despise the men and women who made my trip to India so pleasant for me, I should sum up all the Anglo-Indians as – 'poor devils'. Yet if I were brought to book, and made to answer for my words'. I couldn't say exactly why I thought of them in this light. But it is so. Men and women alike, one feels sorry for them, though I believe they would be the first to resent any pity. They have a very high opinion of themselves, and I think they have a right to, so far as work goes. But they don't seem to realize any of the beauties of life – perhaps they haven't time. It's a queer country. If you can dissuade any youngster you know from coming to live and work here – do so. I can't tell you why you should exactly, but I know you will do well.

P.S. This letter has been full of Anglo-Indians – not natives – and you wanted to hear about natives. I'll tell you frankly, I can't get on with them, and I am not going to support any people that turn out work as bad as the samples I have sent you. My private belief is, that nothing short of a new Deluge and a new Creation could improve them — at least the ones I've seen. They talk too much and do too little.

# The Jubilee in Lahore

*Civil and Military Gazette, 18 February 1887*

**Attribution: Sussex Scrapbooks 28/3, pp. 79–80**

The official jubilee of Queen Victoria was on 21 June 1887, but out of deference to the Indian hot weather the ceremonies in Lahore were considerably advanced. Sir Charles Aitchison, lieutenant-governor of the Punjab, presided.

Another side of Kipling's response to the jubilee is expressed in the conclusion of the verses called 'What the People Said', originally published in the *CMG*, 4 May 1887, as 'A Jubilee Ode. (Punjabi Peasant's Point of View)':

And the Ploughman settled the share
More deep in the sun-dried clod: —
'Mogul, Mahratta, and *Mlech* from the north,
'And White Queen over the Seas,
'God raiseth them up and driveth them forth
'As the dust from the ploughshare flies in the
    breeze.
'But the wheat and the cattle are all my care
'And the rest is the will of God.'

As for what the soldiers said on the occasion, Kipling gave a somewhat different account in a sketch he contributed to the regimental magazine of the Fifth (Northumberland) Fusiliers some fifteen years later. The regiment, he recalled, had been hit by fever:

When they trooped the Colours at the First Jubilee, outside

Fort Lahore on a February morning in '87, there were many blue-gowned invalids hanging over the rails and explaining with the proper nicknames the merits etc., of their company officers. Thus (for it doesn't matter after fifteen years): 'Collars and Cuffs is a good little man, but I *do* wish 'e didn't smell 'is sword so, at the salute. *There* 'e goes, as if it were a bloomin' posy.' Or judicially: 'The Major's running to belly something shockin'. 'E's 'ad that old tunic let out again,' or pathetically to a friend: 'That's Amelia! 'Im an' 'is pet Sergeant 'ave been persecutin' me for the past three months; an' look at 'im now — trailin' 'is company 'alf over the *maidan* like a kite with the string cut' ('Quo Fata Vocant', *St George's Gazette*, 5 November 1902).

### (From our own Correspondent)

#### Lahore, Wednesday, Feb. 16th

The Fort guns at dawn woke the City, and in their salute, sounded the key-note of the day. There are ways and ways of rejoicing. The Capital of the Punjab had chosen for its first day's merry-making the pleasure of a review; had decided, rightly and justly, that the Army of the Empress should be the first great feature of the hour.

Even the troops themselves — and by troops I would refer to that very faithful servant of Her Majesty, Private Thomas Atkins — though they grumbled with exceeding fervour at their share in the Jubilee, recognized the propriety and necessity of this.

They were to parade — the 5th Fusiliers, three batteries of Artillery, K–3, 0–4, L–1, the 5th Bengal Cavalry, the 24th Native Infantry, and the 32nd Punjab Native Infantry at mid-day on the *maidan* in front of Fort Lahore, between the tomb where the one-eyed Lion of the Punjab sleeps among his eleven wives, and the nobler structure where Jehangir lies under the red minars of Shahdera.

Meean Meer parade-grounds lack dignity, however convenient they may be; but the plain outside the Huzuri Bagh, between the Fort and the river, is rich in historical associations. It was good that our troops should come there; and evidently all Lahore thought so, for the city people turned out in thousands, and the station went [as] one man to see the show.

Skilled by past knowledge and experience, the Police and the Municipality alike had done everything to handle the crowds and the carriages comfortably and without confusion; for a flustered native, be he driving or walking, promptly loses his head, and is a helpless stumbling-block for ever afterwards. Stands had been built, enclosures roped off, and temporary roads run off the Fort road on the *maidan*, so that every one might come in peace to and depart with dignity from his allotted place. But dignitaries are not interesting. They lack originality, and their opinions on the Jubilee are monotonous. It was among the crowd of natives, melting and reforming at the wave of the constable's baton, that one heard the amusing things; and it was among the ranks of Her Majesty's very faithful servant — Private Thomas Atkins — on duty at the Fort, and on leave to watch his comrades in the Fifth march and countermarch — that one felt most thoroughly the spirit of the day. Native and Private are the foundations whereon the pillars of the Empire are put, and there is small fear of either proving unsound.

'This *tamasha*' explained an enlightened gentleman with a wave of his hand to the empty plain — for the troops had not come yet — 'is because the Queen of England is now fifty years old. That is the true talk.' 'No! It is because she has been Queen for so long' — a gentleman in a skull cap shot himself into the discussion. The argument became heated, and another byestander in a flowered dressing gown assured the disputants that the tamasha had been ordered by Sir Charles Aitchison to please the Queen, and all the lamps in the City would be lit that night for the same reason. The first speaker seized on the weak point triumphantly. 'Why should the Queen want to be pleased for nothing? I tell you this is because she is fifty years old. They are having tamashas everywhere; even at Delhi and Umballa!' Said the skull-cap angrily: — 'Ask the Englishman. It is because she has been queen so long.' And the Englishman gave it as his verdict that the skull-cap was right. But, you see, everyone in that group knew that the day was in some way connected with our Queen. The ticca-gharri drivers knew, the bhisties watering the parade-ground knew, a municipal *meh* — Sub-Assistant Director of Conservancy — captured as he flew by on some mysterious errand — knew; the students of the schools knew (they are, by the way, running the sentence 'Most Gracious Majesty' into one long hydraulic word that will become naturalized in the Vernacular if the Director of Public Instruction does not look to it), the clerks of the Public Offices knew — everyone knew except the outstation visitors, the 'huge thighed Jats', in blue turbans, speaking strange tongues. They said, referring to the highest power they knew on earth, that perhaps the Deputy Commissioner had ordered the entertainment, and were with difficulty restrained from flocking like sheep on to the parade-ground.

Then in the middle of the babble the guns swept on to the ground with a jingle and clatter, white with the dust between Mian Mir and Lahore, and took up their position on the extreme left. Thomas of the Fifth at the ropes said, *apropos* of nothing in particular and the army in general, 'wait till you see us'. Then he looked to the far right, where two hundred of the 3rd (Railway) Punjab Volunteer Rifles were drawn up under the shade of the trees, and hinted condescendingly to a friend that they would 'pass muster — leastways as they stood'.

Then the 5th Bengal Cavalry, very dusty, came along the Fort road and filed in two by two, and behind them marched a hundred and twenty of the 1st Punjab volunteer Rifles, also dusty. 'We' explained Thomas, with an air of one who had been reared in a C-Spring barouche, 'comes in by train', and he pronounced 'train' with a long drawn, Northern burr that endeared him at once to a north countryman. Sure enough 'we' did come in by train — a long train at the Badara Bagh Station, which was only at the other side of the ground. With 'we' came the native regiments, the 24th and 32nd — or at least the three turned up together on the far side of the ground mysteriously — and moved from the little station platform into the open; the Fifth taking up ground on the left of the guns.

Now the Fifth are a thousand and some odd strong, and allowing for the men in the Fort and contingencies, came in something over eight hundred strong — a long, red-backed, black-legged caterpillar moving its myriad legs with dizzying regularity. Familiarity, which is supposed to breed contempt, can never lessen the admiration one feels at the appearance of a regiment of British Infantry — that unfortunate arm which, having been logically proved to be badly recruited, weak,

infamously-armed, expensive and the daily newspapers only
know what all besides — illogically persists in winning victories
that by all the lore of the schools it could not have won, and
doing things which it is theoretically impossible for it to do.

At this point the spirit of the day asserted itself. Thomas
felt it for he spat vigorously, knocked out his pipe and leant
against the ropes while the flag at the saluting-base was being
fixed — not run up for it was larger than the staff — and the
Lieutenant-Governor came in as the brigade wheeled into line
across the ground, and the batteries on the far left opened
with the royal salute and the horses got ready, after their
amiable wont, for the *feu de joie*. The Native Infantry Regiments formed up on the left of the Volunteers behind whom
were the 5th Bengal Cavalry and the 5th Fusiliers were on the
right of the Volunteers; making a broad band of colour — red,
khaki, red and white, red.

Then came the salute and the triple *feu de joie*; a high chill
wind driving off the smoke: and next the trooping of the
Colours — a thing, here Thomas at the ropes explained, 'you
don't see done every day'. Decidedly it was with the British
Infantry that the lion's share of the work and the interest
rested, for it was their Colours that were trooped and on them
everyone's eyes were turned.

And here an apology. If through the poor account that
follows, it should seem that the writer has slurred over and set
aside mention of the other troops and has confined himself
more specially to the British Foot Regiment, let him be forgiven; because surely the thoughts of such a day as to-day turn
to the oldest arm of the state — the power through which the
Empire was made in the beginning when 'the guns that can go
anywhere, the Cavalry can and' — how does the Gunner's un-
official motto run? — were 'fireworkers' beginning to write
their name in history. And further, because the ceremony he
saw that day was strange and vivid, and touching beyond words
— a presentment of all the dignity and honour, and devotion
of all our little army. May be, the military eye — though it is
hard to think so — sees otherwise. This must be an excuse for
dwelling at undue length on one part of the Review.

The Fifth came forward, the Volunteers and Native Infantry
forming at right angles on the left and right of the regiment
making three sides of a square open at the corners — the Colours

on the left on the regiment under sentries, the drums in front of the colours, the regimental band on the right of the regiment; and the officers for duty standing near the saluting base. Then, to avoid being unnecessarily technical, eight non-commissioned officers marched out to near the saluting base; turned inward to the line, and the drums marched from left to right beating the 'assembly' while the officers fell in with the sergeants, and, divers orders being given, marched slowly to their men; the band playing meantime. Here the band and drums moved across the face of the regiment from right to left playing a slow march, till they reached the colours; came back a second time to the right and their original station, while the drums beat for the escort — one company — for the Colours. That company moved out clear of the line and, preceded by the band, wheeled left and marched to the Colours which they took over in the prescribed form; for the colours are a great and sacred charge with which there can be no light tampering. The ritual of the ceremony, the dead immobility of the troops in front, the plaintive wail of the fifes as they marched and re-marched, the slow throb of the band, even the stately step of the Drum-Major at the head of the band, all combined to impress and even to startle an on-looker. It seemed as though one saw the great heart of the Army beating, and through that wall-like line of red and black, were privileged to catch the whole essence of the institution — pride of country, pride of service, pride of tradition, past honour, and glory to be won hereafter. Beyond that, too, looking at the strange country, with the Shadera minars behind, came an overwhelming sense of the pathos of the whole, and thoughts of the thousands of men who in two hundred years, had died in the regiment — that immortal 'we' Thomas by the railing referred to, who never dies.

And the escort halted and the Colours were saluted, and guard and Colours moved up from the left to the left of the line and carried the Colours along the length of the regiment, between the first and second ranks, that all men might see them. Every military man knows the order, and the unmilitary man would not understand an explanation made profoundly mysterious by that singularly lucid publication with the red back and the brass clasp.

Perhaps this was the most impressive part. But it is hard to say. All was strange and sobering in this rite born of many years.

The day of all others was best fitted for it and it was good for a time to wax wildly enthusiastic over the sight. Thomas is Thomas, whether he is hanging his legs out of an ekka on a shooting expedition, or spotless, white gloved and pipeclayed, taking his part in the dust and heat of a review; but for that little space while the band wailed, and the slow stately marches and salutes were being 'got through' — profane and irreverent expression! — it seemed that Thomas was another and a glorified Thomas and he was, in the presence of the alien, praying to his God and his Queen.

But it is *not* good to gush nor would it be wise to troop the colours too often — as the finest Mass loses its effect through mere repetition. Still that particular ceremony was grand and did most effectually dwarf what followed. Even the march past, the trot, and the thunder of the guns — three batteries make a very respectable little earthquake — seemed stale in comparison; and the blown dust was an intrusion on a sumptuously loyal strain of thought bred by the spectacle. Thomas by the railings said again as the Volunteers went by that they would 'pass muster' and made unflattering and personal remarks about his particular company of the Fifth — most likely because he was in the stalls, so to speak. Indeed another Thomas wondered sarcastically how the 'General' got on without him; and offered introductions to the Lieutenant-Governor.

Then came more dust and more marching, in mass of quarter columns, I think; but the dust hid everything until the Lieutenant-Governor rode out and spoke to General Murray and the officers of the Staff, and the Brigade dispersed, and Thomas-by-the-ropes went away apparently not in the least impressed. He said he wanted something to eat — the Philistine!

This was about half past two o'clock, and the Durbar near the site of the new Town Hall would take place at four. That was the civil element of the day, the popular coming at night, and was not imposing. Native States know how to manage durbars, and to splash colour and gold and brocade with proper lavishness; but the Englishman, in his heart of hearts, takes no delight in these functions. Therefore his carpets are devoid of gold, and his shamianas like unto mess-tents; nor is he particular about the beauty of his chairs. Five hundred native gentlemen attended the Durbar which was enlivened by the Jubilee honours being proclaimed, and a flow of congratulations for those whom the Government had honoured. Further, very many native gentlemen were presented with gold-printed certificates and lengths of *khinkhab* for services rendered to the State, as notified elsewhere. They bowed and retired as the Lieutenant-Governor of the Punjab smiled upon them, and the Secretary read their names and stated what they had done to render themselves amenable to — deserve the favour of the Government.

At the conclusion of the Durbar, His Honour passed out and laid swiftly a slab of red marble, coins and a copy of the *Civil and Military Gazette* buried below, which is the foundation stone of the Town Hall to be built late on. Then he departed, and the Artillery saluted — time, 55 minutes for Durbar and foundation-stone under a hot sun.

A Lieutenant-Governor in a Jubilee is much to be pitied. His Honour had just time to breathe before turning round again and coming down the Mall at seven o'clock to drive round the city and inspect the illuminations prepared in honour of the day. The Police — well, the Police had no time to do anything at all except marshall people from noon till eight.

Everybody who could come, came to see the illuminations; and at one time at least six hundred carriages must have been stacked on the Mall, pointing Anarkullee-bazaar-wards. The programme, which was adhered to, was a drive from the Telegraph Office, *via* the Museum, the Secretariat, through the Anarkullee Gardens, past the University, the Deputy Commissioner's Kutcherry, down the Cemetry road, round the Fort, and so round the city to the Railway station, and then home as you pleased. Thanks to the Municipality, any man might get earthen *chirags* — gratis, as many as he pleased, provided he filled them with oil and set them on his house. Of this privilege, Lahore had availed itself largely: there were no fireworks, few set pieces, nothing but lakhs of *chirags*.

And the effect was superb. Of all ugly buildings, the Accountant General's Office is one of the ugliest, but the myriad twinkling *chirags* transformed it utterly into a fairy palace, a wonder of art and perspective. So with all the other buildings — mean and sordid as they looked in the day time. The Museum was adorned with transparencies in addition to *chirags* — a really beautiful picture of the Queen's head, flanked by English and vernacular mottoes in floral borders, which attracted a great crowd by day as well as by night. Artistically, this was undoubtedly the best decoration, being popular with the people; but the whole city was changed beyond knowledge by the lines of flame. It rose out of the darkness a thing of wonder and mystery. Little bits of walls, or house-tops, too insignificant to be noticed by day-light, showed, in lines of fire as parts of one great whole; came forward as the last touches in some marvellous perspective drawn in golden lines against the night. The face of the Huzari Bagh, the Fort, and Runjeet Singh's tomb were, but for a most prosaic smell of oil, sublime, and above the walls, towered domes, indicated more than outlined, suggesting a huge city of illimitable distances. If Lahore is to be shown to a King, he should see it, beautiful as it stood last night, between the dusk and the dawn. The harshness of the new buildings, the squalor of the old, and the narrowness of the ways were gone; and in their place was neither a town in Fairy Land, for that is trivial, nor a roaring city in the Land of Darkness, for that is terrible: but something between the two, a place to dream of, royal, unapproachable. But it was Lahore, with so many miles of drains and paved roads, and the North-Western Railway had used thirty thousand *chirags* and two tons of oil for their decorations, and some-one else had used ten thousand, and some one else seven; and the dust of the long gharri procession was choking, and it was better to go home than to stay out in the stench and the glare.

But afterwards, when most people had gone to help His Honour through with the loyal and lengthy addresses that were his portion that night, what a city our city was! The dust had settled, the streets were full, and the lamps were shining faithfully; while from the dark heart within the walls came the roar of powder-gurrahs exploded in honour of the Empress. Surely no one of this generation will forget the sight. From the Delhi to the Taksali Gate, from the Taksali to the Delhi Gate, and far away in the Civil Station, the fire-lines ran in and out of the trees, and the domes of the mosques blazed in the still night-air. Over the city itself played a pale golden light turning the darkness into deep violet; such a light as one sees at night playing over Brighton from far away on Lewes Downs. There were lights twinkling on the Shadera side of the Ravee, and along the Mian Mir road, and from one distant village shot up a single rocket.

As the fire broke and decayed, and the great city dropped

back into itself again, with the falling lights, a muezzin from a mosque began the call to prayer.

Here follows the sermon, if any reader have patience to work it out for himself.

# In Reply to the Amateur

*Civil and Military Gazette, 24 February 1887*

**Attribution: Sussex Scrapbooks, 28/3, p. 82**

This is the last of Kipling's mock-diatribes against the Indian amateur (see 22 and 25 January 1887), written in response to a belated letter signed 'Amateur' in the *CMG*, 23 February. 'Amateur' complains of the 'amateur critic' — the 'Lieutenant Quilldriver or Captain Steelslasher' — as just as much a plague as the amateur singer. He then concedes that no amateur should ever sing 'except for a charity', giving Kipling his opportunity, and ends with a plea for simplicity and honesty — the part that Ananias says 'I have forgotten'.

'I have seen four-and-twenty leaders of revolts in Faenza' is from Browning's 'Soul's Tragedy', a line that Kipling evidently liked, for he quotes it (or misquotes, as here) more than once.

A[mateur] C[ritic] — Does it matter? Is it worth it? On second thoughts, yes. He has spoken lightly of Me — the Great Ananias, neither Quill-driver nor Steel-slasher, nor another, but Myself. Therefore I will pulverize him. No! As I am strong, I am merciful.

Listen, O man, you should have asked me to draft your letter. Between the seventieth and ninetieth line thereof you have set down, in black and white, that you and your kind are only worth hearing for charity's sake: being deservedly valueless on your own merits. Why this abasement, when I could have saved you? There are three men and five women in India whom I, worn with many years' bad music, would go far to hear — would go even through the preliminary shoutings of the Lesser Stars. Believe Me, my enemy — for I count, with the eight exceptions aforesaid, all makers of music as my foes — that in rare instances the Indian Amateur is worth listening to, even when he amatortures, that orphan boys may have magenta comforters or the inebriated loafer a more easy *charpoy*. Why did you not say this? Why did you not come to Me?

The rest of your letter I have read before . . . ages ago. Perhaps your father or his father wrote it. I have forgotten. 'I have seen four-and-twenty leaders of revolts in Faenza', and the complaint of the Amateur rises with the rising generations.

But the Amateur is none the less evil.

Yours, magnanimously,

ANANIAS (surnamed THE GREAT)

# [The First Empress of the East]

*Civil and Military Gazette, 28 February 1887*

**Attribution: Sussex Scrapbooks 28/3, p. 84**

Brigade Surgeon Macdowall's volume of verse drama, *The First Empress of the East*, London, 1886, had been preceded by his *Lady Margaret's Sorrows: or, Via Dolorosa, and Other Poems*, London, 1883.

Kipling must have seen much of the vain and amateurish literature generated by the lonely poets in the service of the empire. Only a few days before his review of Dr Macdowall's poem he published this brief notice of another, comparable, work:

A soldier of the 1st Worcestershire Regiment at Karachi has committed poetry — a first canto of an epic called *'Henry Gould'*. In all honesty, it can be said that there never was a poem like *Henry Gould*: who was a subaltern who

smote his Adjutant on the nose at Mess because the subalterns 'chaffed' him in their usual gentle manner. This, with
some few digressions, makes up the first canto. In spite of its
wild extravagance, wilder rhyming and excruciating bathos,
there is a queer crooked sort of power in some of the touches;
notably in the account of the descent into Hell of Tom Pepper,
one of the digressions aforesaid. In the fervent hope that this
much commendation may not [*sic*] induce the writer to
finish the epic, we would recommend people to get *Henry
Gould* — printing office not stated — and read it. It is curious
(*CMG*, 22 February 1887).

Thomas Holley Chivers, mentioned at the end of the review
of Macdowall, was a favorite extravagant poet of Kipling's and
is quoted in two lines of 'The Files':

'When the Conchimarian horns
Of the reboantic Norns. . . . '

We have received a 'story in dramatic form', from the hand of
Brigade Surgeon Cameron Macdowall, entitled '*The first Empress
of the East*'. Dr Macdowall has appeared in print before. Last
time, if we recollect aright, he was — in print, *bien entendu* —
engaged in kissing the hands or feet of a female relative; his
cousin was it, or aunt? This time he is murdering a young girl,
in a few hundred lines of blank verse. He explains in his preface
that he cannot help writing verses, and he prints his imaginings,
because 'manuscript poetry gives a most restricted pleasure'.
Further, he hints incidentally that he has a good conscience.
How he can reconcile this with the verse he makes, is a question
which concerns himself alone. Here is some of his verse. A person,
called Longinus, is showing his stable to one Glaucus — also
horsey. Longinus says: — 'A noble race these horses of Arabia,
Glaucus; they're the sublime of all equinity'. This makes Glaucus
jealous. He shows that he also can 'sublime equinity' in more or
less rhyming, more or less ten-syllable verse. Glaucus prefers
the Arab, or 'the freeborn desert child': —

His quarters almost horizontal lie
This gives vast power — it boots not how or why.

His muscular haunches sheer beneath him point.
A plummet line would almost touch each joint
His legs are flat and broad from front to back
Even at the knee, and clear marked by the track
Of three divisions.

This must be Macdowallese for being fired; but there is no footnote. After 'stables', Longinus and Glaucus begin to explain things. Longinus is a cavalry officer in Zenobia's service, and his 'sublime equinity' is a good deal cut up in a charge against the Romans. As Longinus explains: — 'It was a wondrous charge but t'was not war'. Longinus was a little bruised; but what really hurt him was — 'to see such gross, such palpable mis-management'. This fragment seems to have been borrowed from a sanitation-report; but there is no footnote, and the author, as a rule, is lavish in this respect. Longinus has been recommending alterations in arrows and spears to an Equipment Committe who had disregarded his suggestions. In the scuffle aforesaid: —

There actually were no reserves of archers
Nor even of arrows; or if such there were
They were so far removed in rear — alas!
As to be practically useless. Then the men
Their quivers empty quite could not resist
With a short dagger the Roman legion's spear
    Yet I've often urged
Better equipment for them; and reserves.

Longinus is very nice, and the stage directions are very funny. People stab themselves and fight very freely. When Dr Macdowall runs dry, bits of Gibbon are brought in. This adds immensely to the effect. Footnotes career about the pages to clear up historical allusions, or to point out where the author has got an original notion and wants to work it. He compares the Dawn to a spirit rising from the grave, and believes the comparison to be original. It is original — aboriginal in fact — being at least as new as the Solar Myth. There are many startlingly original things in the poem — notably the verse. At the end of the book are notes; and the notes alone are, in their petrifying audacity, worth the price of the volume. The author is afraid people will reproach him for his 'freedom of metre and accentuation'.

On the contrary, they like it. Lines like these are not met every day: —

> 'Lo! to save the temple from destruction.'
> 'Monotony of too much sameness.'
> 'Methinks 'tis no such wondrous place. Hast
> seen Palmyra?'
>    'Have yielded at Antioch.'

and so on. There is no monotony about such verses, nor any 'cloying surfeit of reiterated cadence'. *The First Empress of the East* is a fine, rugged, veterinary, military, amatory, blood-thirsty, Gibboned, Saga. There was an American doctor called Holley Chivers, once, who wrote poems — *'Facets of Diamonds'*, *'Eonchs of Ruby'*, and the *'Lost Pleiad'*. The only perfect copies of his works are in the British Museum. There is a likeness between his style and Dr Macdowall's. But we prefer the Indian Doctor.

# The Sutlej Bridge

*Civil and Military Gazette, 2 March 1887*

**Attribution: Sussex Scrapbooks 28/3, pp. 85—6**

The name 'Punjab' means 'five rivers': the Jelum, Chenab, Ravi, Bias, and Sutlej. They unite to form the Indus. Of these rivers, the Sutlej, the southernmost, drains the largest area. Ferozepore is about fifty miles to the south and slightly east of Lahore. Raewind (Raiwind), which Kipling also mentions, is roughly midway between Lahore and Ferozepore.

The bridge that Kipling so vividly describes in this article, crossing between Ferozepore and Kazur, was called the Kaisarin-i-Hind (Empress of India) and is clearly the main prototype of the bridge in 'The Bridge Builders'. Like the bridge over the Ganges in that story, the actual bridge over the Sutlej was built on twenty-seven brick piers, carried a railway line fifteen feet broad and a cart road of eighteen feet, flanked by footpaths. After that much matter of fact, Kipling develops his story on its own lines.

### (From our own Correspondent)

Like its four brethren, the Sutlej is a profligate stream; never keeping to the same bed for two years in succession. Like its brethren, too, the Sutlej has to be bridged by order of the Indian Government, which does not approve of interference with its frontier communications. And this is the story of a visit paid to the Sutlej Bridge at Ferozepore, in the month of February 1887, by one who knows nothing whatever about engineering.

Three years ago, the same visitor went down to an abomination of desolation called Gunda Singh, a few miles on the Raewind side of the Lahore-Ferozepore line; and there rose a dust-storm which covered the temporary line with fine sand, and the trolly ran merrily off the rails in consequence; sitting down on a hillock like a hen. This proved the nature of the country to be worked upon, and severely bruised the visitor who went his way foreseeing the downfall of the bridge and the Government and everything connected therewith.

Three years later, there was a fair embankment where the trolly had spilt him; and from Gunda Singh, the road that runs by the side of the line to the Sutlej banks, was filled with bullock-carts and ekkas and foot passengers all streaming riverwards to where a cloud of dust rose like the smoke of an engagement. That 'pillar of cloud by day' never fails; and marks where the traffic is running through the bridge-of-boats and over the two-foot tramway that the Bridge will, a few months hence, supersede. Those in search of a new sensation would do well to go over the tramway that runs over the bridge-of-boats.

Arrived at the transhipping station for the tramway, the train pulled up in the middle of what, to an unprofessional eye, looked like a most royal mess. Lines of every gauge — two-foot, metre and broad — rioted over the face of the pure, white sand, between huge dredger-buckets, stored baulks of timber, *chupper*-built villages, piled heaps of warm red concrete-blocks, portable engines and circular saws. High above everything, the great main

embankment heaved itself, which is to take the cart road on to
the Bridge-head. At the lower end of this embankment, a
snorting train was getting rid of girder-booms on to a sloped
platform, whence they would in time be taken down to the river-
bed by the temporary lines. The face of the country swarmed
with toiling men.

The Sutlej Bridge, which, as every one on the works is at
great pains to assure you, is 'of a very ordinary type', is something over four thousand four hundred feet long, and is made
of seven and twenty brick piers which will carry first, a railway line fifteen feet broad; and, above this line, a cart-road
eighteen feet broad with a foot-path, four feet six broad, on
each side. That is to say, that the railway-line is covered in atop,
and the whole of the girder-work resembles a huge oblong box
latticed at the sides. This is not a technical definition at all; but
the technical name of the system on which the Bridge is built is
quite unfit for publication outside of *Indian Engineering*.

But the building of the Bridge comes hereafter. All the piers
are up and also 'down' — which is intelligible only to engineers
— and the girder-work alone remains to be done. Now, each
girder weighs some two hundred and twenty odd tons, and is
made up of fifteen hundred loose pieces, exclusive of fifty iron-
bound boxes of bolts and rivets. For this reason it is at first
difficult to understand the exultation of engineers, who speak
so lightly of a few spans of girder-work.

The difficulty grows as one travels along and under and by
the side of the Bridge — on the great iron plates of the flooring,
in the shadow of the piers, or ankle-deep in the silver sand.
Several spans on the Raewind side are already begirdered, more
or less, and a few hundred workmen are hard at work rivetting.
The clamour is startling, even a hundred yards away from the
Bridge; but standing at the mouth of the huge iron-plated
tunnel, it is absolutely deafening. The flooring quivers beneath
the hammer-strokes; the roof of corrugated iron nearly half an
inch thick which will form the floor of the cart-road, casts back
the tumult redoubled; and it bounds and rebounds against the
lattice-work at the side. Rivetters are paid by the job, not by
time. Consequently they work like devils; and the very look of
their toil, even in the bright sunshine, is devilish. Pale flames
from the fires for the red hot rivets, spurt out from all parts of
the black iron-work where men hang and cluster like bees;

while in the darker corners the fires throw up luridly the half nude figures of the rivetters, each man a study for a painter as he bends above the fire-pot, or, crouching on the slung-supports, sends the rivet home with a jet of red sparks from under the hammer-head.

At first sight, the stern build of the Bridge seems ludicrously disproportioned to the shrunken placid river it spans. It is as if the Government, true to its education policy, had thrust the garments of a full-grown man on the limbs of a child. So peaceable is the Sutlej, in the cold season, that the Engineers have won from it two great tongues of land which nearly meet in the middle — have all but dammed it in fact, to get space to bring up materials for their girders. It is true that the tongues aforesaid are faced with concrete blocks, but even that precaution seems out of place. Men brought sand and silt by the hundred thousand donkey-loads and cast it into the stream, and the river gave place. Lines were made on the land, and now the whole Bridge seems as if it were spanning a small Sahara for no other purpose than its own glorification.

But the Engineers, and any man who has had dealings with an Indian stream in flood, know better. A quarter-mile journey in the shadow of the Bridge where the temporary line runs, brings you to the end of the first spit. The red concrete blocks go down sheer into the stream, and there is a break of four spans, or two hundred yards, before the beginning of the next tongue. Here the stream of the Sutlej tells its own tale of pent strength and murderous possibilities as it drives through the opening under the pile-supported 'material' line which spans the contracted river. There is a swirl and thrust about the green water unpleasant to look at.

The four spans must be girdered somehow across the break, and the made ground on either side cut through, before the snows melt and the Sutlej comes down in earnest. At present, the Engineers explain that 'a child might play with the river'. As safer measure, a gang of coolies and a pile-driver are at play on the end of the Raewind tongue. Their business is to punch certain huge logs, profanely called 'fifty-foot sticks', into the two hundred yards of twenty-seven foot water, and so form a foundation for the overhead crane to travel along with the girders.

On the made-ground portion of the Bridge, the girder spans

are supported by huge piles of sleepers filled inside with sand in case of fire falling from the rivet furnaces. Four such supports stand between pier and pier. The girders rest on these and are pieced together, all their fifteen hundred parts, before the support is withdrawn or the girder-ends let down on the great blocks of red Agra stone prepared for their reception in the head of each pier. With sand in their bellies, sleeper-stacks do not burn readily.

Round the great piers — they look like gigantic chess-castles — in the remnant of the stream, lie concrete blocks mixed with silt, much worn and rubbed by the water-rush. These are the remains of islands which had to be made before the piers could be sunk.

And here is a fit place to introduce the story of the Bridge. In the beginning, the Government devised its plan, which grew foot by foot on paper while it was hatching itself among the offices; here swelling out two or three feet in the dimensions of the piers; there spreading a foot or two in the width of the roadway; and so on, as is the custom of most schemes. Later, the Frontier scare arose, and then the order was to push on with all speed, and be sure to finish within three years. In October 1885, work was begun with the avowed intention of putting up and 'down' only one-half of the piers during that cold season, and so proceeded till January 1886, when the strong hands which control the North-Western Railway grasped the Engineers' matured opinion, that by a supreme effort all the piers could be undertaken, and at least a whole year saved.

Now a Sutlej Bridge pier is made something after this fashion. A huge iron ring or shoe, called technically a well-curb, twenty-three feet in diameter, is put into a grave on the river-sand, exactly as the wooden well-curb of a Punjabi well is laid down. On this shoe is built a circle of brickwork, with walls four and a half feet thick; leaving, therefore, an internal circle of fourteen feet. You have, then, an iron-shod, hollow-cored, brick pillar twenty-three feet across, to let down through the unstable sand, to firm foothold below the lowest depth that the Sutlej can gouge out for itself in its bed. Here the fun begins; for the tube has to be treated exactly like a well on a gigantic scale, and must go seventy-six feet down, foot by foot, as the sand and silt is dredged out at the bottom of, and brought up through the heart of, the fourteen foot shaft aforesaid. Moreover, the pillar must be mathematically straight; and endless are the ways and means devised for dredging out and pressing down when a pillar shows a tendency to list. As the brickwork sinks, more is built atop, until the whole shaft reaches its full seventy-six feet — bedded like a tooth in the jaw. At this point the circular shape of the pier is altered to ovoid, for four and twenty feet — that portion which is above the river at ordinary times — the better to resist the rush of the water; and the conclusion of the whole matter is the filling up of the fourteen foot shaft with rammed concrete. This is, more or less intelligibly, how a pier is built on more or less dry land. But twelve out of the twenty-seven on the Sutlej bridge had to commence where as much as fifteen feet of water ran over the shifting sand, and those twelve were the last to be begun. Therefore, men let down into the stream concrete blocks till they made a circle of forty feet diameter above water. Next they got rid of the water, replaced it with approximately dry land, by filling in the circle with silt, and through this artificial island drove their pier.

To begin such piers in the end of April was an insult, flat and flagrant, to the experience of the Bridge building elders, and to the majesty of the Sutlej alike. But the river was the more important of the two. There was the dead certainty that it would come down not later than the end of June, and the lively possibility that it might do so earlier. Not only was it necessary to get the piers in, but to get them sunk well beyond the reach of the scour of the flood. In short, the reputation of the Department, a few hundred thousand cubic feet of masonry and concrete, and some lakhs of the public money, were at the mercy of a reprobate stream. Men worked in those days by thousands, in the blinding sun glare, and in the choking hot night under the light of flare-lamps, building the masonry, dredging and sinking, and sinking and dredging-out. By the first week in June all the piers were down to the reasonably safe distance of fifty feet; and a half were sunk to the full depth of seventy-six feet. The Engineers took breath and waited.

Then the floods came, and many lively things happened, including a small cyclone which smashed up a bridge-of-boats; but the piers stood firm, being protected from the scour of vast quantities of concrete blocks which had been piled round them. In August the depth of the river, within fifty yards of some of the piers, was over forty feet, or nearly as deep as the foundations of some of the shallower sunk piers. Then the Engineers watched and prayed day and night, and slept uneasily in their beds. After the floods and the rains, came fever of a malignant type, and many coolies died. It was the price the Sutlej took for allowing the piers to stand. After September there was no serious difficulty to be encountered, and on Christmas Eve, 1886, the last pier was home to its full depth, and there was rejoicing in the little colony above the river bed. For the Sutlej had given them their Christmas-box.

Indeed, hearing the Story of the Bridge, bit by bit, from one man and another, it is impossible not to catch the enthusiasm of these hard-headed men of girders and masonry — to see the labouring stripped gangs yelling and screaming under the still lamps through the hot May nights, while the whisper of the river between the piers bade them make haste, and the clank and rattle and grind of the dredgers, answered the voice of the stream. When these men pat caressingly the huge flank of some pier, well nigh throat-deep in sand, and say: — 'She gave us a lot of trouble last year' — the inclination to smile does not come over the unprofessional mind till it is out of the range of the influences of the Bridge — out of the bitter chill shade, the keen dry wind that twangs like a strained wire as it hurries over the sand — out of the raw untempered white sunshine, where each rift and borrow-pit throws a deep indigo-blue shadow — out of the hearing of the clang of the rivetters, the straining and clanking of the cranes, and the grumble of the concrete-blocks shot over the barge sides into the river — till it is disconnected, in fact, from the terribly eager, restless, driving life that fills the river-bed, and falls back once more on everyday existence.

But to escape the tumult, one must go far, for the works extend in some shape or other over seven or eight miles. At either end of the Bridge they are building two great embankments of different levels — the lower to carry the train, and the higher the cart-road that runs above the train. Here the whole face of the country is scarred and scraped and scooped for the earth of the roadways. There is a faint feverish smell from the damp silt soil, and everywhere the eye falls on interminable processions of donkeys and donkey-drivers — laden beasts climbing up, and unladen ones going down. The sound of the thousands of little hoofs on the soft earth, and the

never-ending 'thud' of the loads as they are tipped off, makes
a bass drone, to which the rattle and thump of the donkey
boys' sticks supplies a staccato treble accompaniment. The boys
do not seem to talk, or the donkeys to fight. There is nothing
but the hot sun overhead, the sickly reek from the ground, and the
subdued sound of toil. From the cart-road that is to be, or higher
embankment, one looks out over the Bridge works generally,
and understands in some small measure how vast they are. Far
as the eye can reach, through the sand-haze up stream, stretch
the protective works — two massive bunds, twenty feet across
at the top, flaring away like a huge V from each end of the
Bridge, till they enclose, three miles off, a space of five miles
in which the river can riot as it please — certain of being guided
straight at the Bridge. These bunds are faced with concrete
slabs, and planted with *shisham* seedlings. On the top of each
runs a railway, which can carry at once material to any portion
of the face that may need strengthening, or supply stone to
the ten spurs with which each bund is studded. These spurs
run parallel with the line of the bridge, and take their share in
curbing the river. The quarries of Rohri, Tarakhi and Tusham
were laid under contribution for the material here, and one
sees, on the Raiwind side, snowy white, and on the Ferozepore,
dull brown spurs standing out against the dusty background of
the bund — miles away across the levels of the Sutlej.

There are something like one hundred and fifty lakhs of
cubic feet of earthwork in the protection bunds. There are
sixteen lakhs of cubic feet of quarried stone in the twenty
spurs and the noses thereof. There are fifteen lakhs of
cubic feet of concrete blocks, made on the banks of the river,
in the facing of the bunds. The appetite for figures is an acquired
and American one. Turning from the bunds to the Bridge itself,
waiting to be joined on to the embankment, one asks for more
figures and gets them. There are fifteen lakhs of cubic feet of
masonry and concrete in the twenty-seven piers of the Bridge,
and on top of these lie six thousand tons of iron-work — all of
which, here comes the inevitable reminder — 'is ordinary you
know — quite ordinary. You should see the Hugli bridge, or the
Sikkur, if you want heroic engineering'. The same insular pride
prompts Englishmen of all professions to say of any work done,
'It is nothing to what we can do or have done somewhere else.'
Public Works Departmentally speaking, the Sutlej Bridge is

nothing out of the way; the only point about it being the short space in which it will be finished; for it will be opened, they hope, in April or thereabouts. But it is fitting enough at the price in all conscience — this stern line of brick and iron, guarded by bund and spur, throbbing from end to end with human life, and set in the centre of a town of ten thousand folk of all kinds, from *changar* earth-workers, to Suratee men learned in ropes, tackles, blocks, and falls, and West Indian creoles controlling the pile-driver. At one time the Bridge took fifteen thousand men to attend to its needs. Bricks and concrete blocks are made five miles from the Rewari end, and are brought in by rail; girders and material lie along the line three miles from the Ferozepore end; and between the two points a large floating and permanent population is scattered.

In a couple of months or so everything will be done with, used up, dispersed or turned to fresh ends; for this lazy Government of ours is never at rest. (It ordered the Bridge to be built, because it wished to connect Ferozepore Arsenal and the Rajputana Railway system with the Frontier.) The *changars* will disperse to where fresh embankments call for their baskets and strong arms; the services of the straddling cranes, vicious pile-drivers, and sun-baked Engineers will be 'replaced at the disposal of their respective departments'; the gear-strewn river-bed and earthworks will be cleaned up and smoothed down, and the stories and associations connected with the building of the Bridge will die out with the marks of the temporary lines. Perhaps a Viceroy or a Lieutenant-Governor will come and open that Bridge.

Lastly, over the place where men toiled and sickened and died, and fought with the turbulent Sutlej, the train will pass with a rattle and a roar; as the first-class passenger, too indifferent to look out, yawns: 'Hullo! There is a bridge!'

# The Chak-Nizam Bridge

*Civil and Military Gazette, 18 May 1887*

**Attribution: Sussex Scrapbooks 28/3, pp. 115–16**

The bridge over the Sutlej (see the preceding article) had been
opened at the end of April inauspiciously; the ceremonies were
delayed and protracted by various failures, the heat was troublesome, a sandstorm blew up, and the Lahore contingent, exhaust-
ed, did not get home until three in the morning. Accordingly,
official Lahore was not eager to attend the opening of the bridge
at Chak Nizam, the Victoria Bridge, especially since the region
is one of the hottest in India. Such is the background of Kipling's
account, which neglects technical details and concentrates on
a narrative of the preliminaries to and the aftermath of the
opening ceremonies as much more to the point for his Lahore
audience.

The bridge at Chak Nizam lay about a hundred miles north
and west of Lahore. The lieutenant-governor presiding was
Sir Alfred Lyall.

### (From our own Correspondent)

May 6th

Incidents which one may now regard as closed, have somewhat
discouraged the residents of Lahore from journeying abroad to
open bridges in the summertime. They have said that Abana and
Pharphar, dust-storms of their own country, are sufficiently
amusing; and that in future, the arteries of traffic may open
themselves 'whenever they feel inclined', uncheered by the
presence and applause of Lahore. But the capital of the Punjab
generalizes hastily, and does not always mean what it says.

There was a bridge — an unbaptised bridge — at Chak-Nizam
which is on a stretch of the Jhelum, which is near the Salt
Range of the Shahpur District, which is at the 'back of beyond'
— completed a few weeks ago under the direction of these four

gentlemen mainly — Mr James Ramsay, Engineer-in-Chief Sind Sagar State Railyway; Mr F. R. Upcott, Engineer-in-charge of the Bridge; Mr Boydell, Executive Engineer; and Mr J. Spence, Sub-Engineer.

Now this bridge, though neither excessively long nor immoderately expensive, was an important, a strategical arrangement, inasmuch as it completed one line in a great circle whereby Lahore, Multan, and Dhera Ismail, will eventually be linked together, and troops will be thrown, that is the technical term, from Pindi to Dhera Ghazi Khan on the North Bank of the Indus, without having first to run down to Lahore, and thence *via* the old I.V. State to Multan. The last coupling-link — a bridge across the Indus at Sher Shah yet remains to be forged — possibly by Mr Mallet. This was one among the many things which the Chak-Nizam bridge accomplished; and it was necessary, therefore, that His honour the Lieutenant-Governor of the Punjab should open it, as he had opened another strategical commercial bridge at Ferozepore a few weeks before. Bridge-opening in May is, to put it mildly, a risky performance, and is fairly certain to be warm.

Wherefore the engineers of the Chak-Nizam Bridge, having the fear of consequences before their eyes said: — 'We will invite men only and peradventure they may enjoy themselves'. To this end, the engineers took measures — measures of ice, and soda-water by the hundred, and all the materials of a feast, beside the dining-saloon of the 'Homeward Special' which goes down the Indus Valley to catch the Hall Line steamers. Then they issued their invitations to Pindi and to Lahore; keeping the list down because they were afraid that their guests might be seduced into an oven and there die, *budndming* [sic] the Sind Sagar Railway and everything connected with it. Their fears were groundless; but they wished to be on the safe side. His Honour the Lieutenant-Governor of the Punjab promised to attend, and kept his promise, though he was forced to jam the trip into the forepart of his journey to Simla. With him came Captain Davies, Private Secretary, Captain Johnstone, A.D.C., and Mr Mackworth Young. Also, from Lahore, Colonel Conway Gordon, Director General of Railways, Messrs. Mallet, Sandiford, Williams, List, Jacob, Colonel Menzies, Mr Arundel, Mr Mercer and others. From Pindi, Colonel Nisbet, Mr Harrington, Lieutenant Thackwell, Mr Browne, Colonel Lovett, Mr R.W.

Roberts, Mr L.N. Broome, Mr Bicquet, Dr Dennys, Mr Dennys, and many others. From all about generally Mr H. O'Connor, D.S.P. Shahput, Mr Wilson, D.C., of Shahpur, Mr O'Dwyer, Assistant Commissioner of the same cheerful district, Major Bartholomew, M.J. Anderson, and other Civilians, engineers, and sight seers. But the point — and on the night of the 15th May this was a very great point — of the list was that there was no crowding; each guest sprawling on his own bunk as was right and proper.

So we left, actually to the minute, at 9—26 p.m. from Lahore, in the middle of a riotous dust-storm, which blew half a gale throughout Sunday night, and secured the Lahore section at least a comfortable night. We possessed the 'Homeward Special' dining saloon — a huge car which reminded one of a P. & O. saloon — and in that car might, at all hours of the night, be found pleasant drinks to wash down the flying dust. It was here that the Lahore section first realized that the Chak-Nizam Bridge opening was going to be a success. At Lala Musa Junction, the Pindi detachment must have 'hooked on' to the train in the night; and at most of the stations the natives must have believed that His Honour would descend and talk, for they saluted the train reverently and vigorously all the time it stopped.

Very early in the dawn a ghost-like white colt mistook the train for its mamma, and in that belief ran, screamed shrilly, ran swiftly for two miles on the ballast, where it nearly committed suicide over sleeper-tails. At five forty-five on Monday morning — again to the minute — the special pulled up in a grey, wind-blown, sandy, desolate waste, whence all the crops and apparently most of the cattle had been removed. There was no sunrise, nothing beyond a weak watery light behind a veil of cloud and dust, and the early morning air was almost chilly. On either side of the embankment up which the engine had toiled, lay the swept-up *debris* of construction works and service-lines, wheelless trollies, stationary engines, baulks of timber and piled sleepers. In front, grey mist against grey mist was the line of the Jhelum, full from bank to bank; but a most mournful and melancholy river that had somehow entangled itself among plashly green fields, and did not quite know how to get out again. The banks were low and mean, the water was nearly flush with their crests, and the river in its muddied monotony of grey, sage-green, and silver-white did not look dignified. No more did the new bridge. The water was within fourteen feet of the girders and there were no imposing guard-houses at either end. It was a straight black, sullen, business-like line ruled across a turbulent river for the convenience of man, and not for the pleasure of his eyes; and it said as much in every span. Only the professional men in the train could know what amount of labour it represented, and they seemed to take it, after the custom of their breed, as a matter of course.

Your paper has already given details of the build of this Gradgrind of a bridge; and your readers know consequently that it is made up of seventeen spans of 160 feet from centre to centre of the 107-foot brick piers which bite into the bed of the stream.

The startling peculiarity of the structure is that it will be made for less than the estimates. Another feature is that the last two girder spans had to be fitted on their piers from boats by reason of the rush of water. This gave the Engineers many lively hours, as the river was not constant, and the booms rose and fell with the water, and needed attention. All this, however, seemed to be not worth talking about; and was only discovered after long and persistent questionings based on the assumption that every bridge, even an 'ordinary thing don't you know', has something noteworthy about it, and that the Engineer is the last man to know what he has done. For instance, *the* great point about the Chak-Nizam bridge in the eyes of its builders is that you can bathe and boat near it! The rest of the 'thing' came in the day's work.

The ceremony of opening the bridge was spun out of malice aforethought, for the Engineers had provided all the guests with a sumptuous *chota hazri*, and one cannot eat a still more sumptuous breakfast an hour after such a meal. One of the bungalows of the English colony was turned into a banqueting hall. There were no decorations worth speaking of on the Bridge — all were reserved for the table and took the form of — but this is gross and carnal. It was a delightful *chota hazri* and the mangoes were iced to the minute.

Next, His Honour began, I think, to see native gentlemen, but on this point I am not certain. There were may native gentlemen all anxious to be introduced, and as there was no formal durbar the introductions came off 'promiscuous' in the verandah of the bungalow. These, however, are the names of the leading men of the Shahpur District and Pind Dadun Khan Subdivisions of Jhelum and Shahpur; To wit: —

Malik Davi Dass, Vice-President of the Bhora Municipality; Mian Mohammed, member of the same important institution (Bhora has a population of 15,000, and makes break-knife handles of a pretty but brittle stone); Pundit Dewan Chand, Sultan Mahommed, of Shahpur, the Metropolis; Bakshi Ram Soobhya of Bhera, Hari Ram, and Radha Kishen, contractors of Bhera, and Hyat Khan of Kote Ahmed Khan.

Of Pind Dadun Khan, presented by Raja Jehan Dad Khan, Khan Bahadur, Chief of the Ghakkars, in charge of the Pind Dadan Khan sub-division, and down in the Civil list as an Extra Assistant Commissioner: — Sodhi Sher Singh, Sodhi Sheeran Singh, Sodhi Hari Singh, Sodhi Kartar Singh, Sadar Hare Singh, Raja Surif Ali Khan, Khokhar, Sultan Lal Khan, Sultan Ali Bahadur Khan, Raja Abdulla Khan, Raja Mahommed Baksh, Chandhari Gauhar Khan of Garibwal, Chandhari Shaba Khan, Mahommed Buish, Mirza Shakir Khan, Lala Duni Chund, Tehsildar, Pind Dadun Khan, and Diwan Lakhmi Dass, Munsiff of the same place.

These things having been happily accomplished while the Englishman smoked, His Honour took a trolly, which was filled according to all the laws of precedence, and being followed by the rest of the guests and a great concourse of native gentlemen, trollied from the Shahpur to the Jhelum abutment. All this time mercifully the sun was banked, and the air was cool and misty. There was nothing to be seen of the Salt Range, or of the stretch of the river; for the haze veiled everything at a few hundred yards' distance.

Arrived at the Jhelum side, His honour halted till a rivet in a fire-pot had been properly cooked, while the rest of the audience looked on; the more ignorant wondering what in the world His Honour would do with the red-hot iron. Then stepped out Mr James Spence, Sub-Engineer, and Andrew his son, chosen for this proud office by right of past zeal, and artistically sent that rivet home in a side-girder, put a head on with a 'snap' — this is the technical expression, a snap is like a corkscrew and a soda-water bottle-opener — and stood back.

Mr Upcott, Engineer in charge of the Bridge Works, handing a small testing hammer in wooden case to Mr Lyall: — 'Will Your Honour see that the rivet is firm and fast?'

Mr Lyall, tapping [the] rivet dubiously, as if he were afraid of destroying the handiwork of J. Spence and Son: — 'Yes; it seems all right. That's all the ceremony then? Well, gentlemen, I remember six and twenty years ago, travelling from Jhelum to Multan in a country-boat along this river. I found it then in its natural condition — nothing but waste land along the banks — and I only saw a few buffaloes and their herdsmen, and an occasional boat sailing up or drifting down. I fancy the river must have looked like that when Baber crossed it four hundred years ago, on the invasion which led to the foundation of the Mogul Empire — indeed it could not have greatly differed from the time when Alexander led his army here two thousand years ago. To-day the British Government, in the fullness of time, have set their mark upon the river, and have ornamented it with two beautiful bridges, one of which we are assembled here to-day to inaugurate. In the name of the Queen-Empress, I declare this bridge, the *Victoria* Bridge, open henceforth for public traffic. God keep it and protect it, and may it stand for ages for the use and profit of the people of the land, and a monument of the British Empire in India.'

Whereat, under the leadership of Mr J. Ramsay, we all cheered heartily, and added an extra cheer for Mr Lyall's sake. He needed encouragement, for at that moment a photographer appeared, and held the front ranks of the assembly in uneasy *cameraderie* for a few minutes. Next, a train bore us all back to Shahpur and, after an interval, breakfast of a sumptuous kind.

This was a breakfast to be remembered through the hot weather — a well arranged, perfectly iced, deftly served entertainment, to sixty or more people. The menu ought to be reprinted for 'information and reference'; but the one copy in this writer's possession was stolen. At the conclusion of the banquet — meal is a vulgar word — came Havanas and the health of the Queen drunk in the Royal wine. It is on such occasions that, soothed by champagne, and made patriotic by *pâté de fois gras*, both iced, that the humblest soul feels, he too, is assisting in the development of India, and the Progress of the Ages.

Then Mr J. Ramsay, Engineer in Chief rose and spoke: —

'Your Honour and gentlemen, I am very pleased to see you all here, and we are much honoured in having you, Sir, to perform the ceremony of opening this Bridge; and I sincerely trust that none will have any serious cause to regret having accepted our invitation to be present. On a printed card, of which I hope every one received a copy, I have given a brief description of the main features of the Bridge but there was not space to mention the difficulties and delays encountered in the well-sinking from the clay bands met with at sixty feet and more below low-water-level, requiring peculiar treatment to get the wells through them; nor of the delays afterwards, in having to wait for the girder-work not arrived from England; nor of the anxiety during the erection of the sixteenth and seventeenth spans which had to be erected on staging fitted up in country-boats moored in deep water, and in a strong current running at the rate of some eight or ten miles an hour. Looking at the completed structure, as seen this morning, with the full river flowing steadily through every span between the two abutments, the difficulties encountered and overcome during its construction, do not show up; many of them will remain only in the memories of the officers and others, who were actually engaged on the works.

On the afternoon of the 17th December we had an unique, or almost unique accident, at the second span. The erection-staging caught fire after both the main girders had been almost rivetted up, and, owing to the high wind blowing at the time, all efforts to subdue the flames were overpowered, and in about twenty minutes after the fire was first seen, both girders buckled under the intense heat and fell into the water upstream. The wreckage of one was cleared away, but the other remains where it fell — in the bottom of the river.

'New girders were at once ordered out from England, and these were erected on the 29th of last month, and the last rivet was driven in your presence this morning.

'I think, Sir, that very great credit is due to Mr Upcott and his staff of Engineers and petty officers, for the workmanlike manner and speed with which they have completed the Bridge.

'Their untiring energy and zeal about these works and exposure in all seasons at all hours are worthy of far higher praise than I can give and I sincerely hope will secure fitting rewards.

'To Mr Hiley, Port Store Keeper Karachi, our thanks are due for the orderly and prompt manner in which the girder work was all forwarded to us here. The officers who have been on the construction of the bridge are Mr Upcott who commenced and has finished it; Messrs. Brydell and Cole, Executive Engineers, and Mr J. Spence, Sub-Engineer. Messrs. Wynne and Messrs. Tait were also for short periods, in charge of the works.'

Mr Lyall in reply said briefly: —

'Before I came here Mr Ramsay assured me that there was to be no speech making, so I did not come prepared to make a speech. I did hope to receive a telegram from the Government of India congratulating us and the Engineers, on the completion of the Bridge, and giving credit to all the officers who took part in the work. It seems, however, as if some accident must have happened, and that the telegram must have gone astray. It may, however, come in due time to be put in the newspaper but I regret that I shall not have the pleasure of reading it to you here.

'Mr Ramsay in his speech has mentioned all the officers connected with the bridge, but he did not mention his own exertions. Nevertheless I hope that the Government of India will give due credit to Mr Ramsay.

'A remarkable feature of the present time is the wonderful speed and certainty with which works like this are now made. The Victoria bridge half a mile long and costing 25 lakhs has been built as you know, in less than two years and for less than the estimates (*Loud cheers*).

'A good many of the Lahore people showed the white feather when they were invited to come down here, but I am sure those who are present will carry away pleasant remembrances of their visit, and will feel grateful to the officers who have entertained them so pleasantly to-day. Gentlemen my toast is: — 'The Bridge and the Officers who made it'.

Mr Upcott replied to this toast: —

'Your Honour and Gentlemen. In thanking you for your attendance here to-day I can only say that it is easier to fix a girder than to make a speech; and I don't wish to detain you with one. I must, however, take this opportunity of thanking publicly every one of my subordinates, down to the lowest coolie, for the way in which they have worked — for you'll understand that without help from everyone this sort of thing can't be made. I trust you have all enjoyed yourselves (*cheers*) and I hope you will have as comfortable a journey back as you had down.'

Then the proceedings terminated — with a fresh rush of

native gentlemen I think, but am not certain, for, in an office round the corner, an excellent Telegraph Babu almost hysterical with wrath against an incompetent signaller up the line, was using language not to be found in any code, and to him my attentions were addressed. The Government of India Telegram arrived as Mr Lyall foretold, only in time to be put in the papers. This is what the Viceroy said, on the 16th instant, to the Lieutenant-Governor of the Punjab: —

'It is with the utmost satisfaction that I find myself called upon for the second time within one month to congratulate you on the accomplishment of railway transit over one of the great rivers of the Punjab. The Jhelum Bridge at Chak Nizam establishes continuous communication by the aid of the Sind Sagar State Railway between the northern posts of the province, the trans Indus Military Stations, Dhera Ismail and Dhera Ghazi Khan and Multan. The Bridge has been ably located and most rapidly constructed, and I desire that you will convey my satisfaction at the successful completion of their labours to the staff of all grades who have been directly engaged upon so important a work  and specially to Messrs. O'Callaghan, Upcott and Ramsay who have successively held the post of Engineer in Chief of the Line and Director of operations.'

At ten punctually we left — a long train — with many maunds of ice and one of our genial hosts accompanied us to Lahore. Then the heat settled on us like a mantle. There was no sun, but the grey sky held us like a hot dish-cover, and flying dust storms hunted the train and begrimed us from head to foot. Like Mr Ramsay's girders, we buckled with the intense heat for seven weary hours, but our host (may he attain Simla for his kindness!) was with us, and the journey was lightened by a perfect tiffin — all cold and iced — in the dining-saloon carriage. There was an unsuccessful cabal among the Pindi section to steal that car, but the conspirators were cut off at Lala Musa with four maunds of ice, and an Imperial cellar to get home at nine at night. We were only fried till five forty five; but we felt a Calcuttacute envy at seeing His honour go on to Simla from Lahore.

It was a great success in every way; for no man expects even the Engineers who built the Victoria Bridge, to muffle a May sun.

# Concerning One Gymkhana

*Civil and Military Gazette, 11 June 1887*

**Attribution: Sussex Scrapbooks 28/3, pp. 124—5**

The word *gymkhana* is an Anglo-Indian invention, meaning any gathering for sports, or the place where such sports are held. In Lahore, practically speaking, the word always meant horse racing; some foot racing might be part of it, too, as in the case of the gymkhana Kipling describes here.

Kipling had reported many a gymkhana before this one. Here, he manages to combine, in *faux-naif* style, a sharp observation of detail with the sense that such things, seen so many times before, make little sense in the hot weather.

## (By an Unsporting Correspondent)

This happened on Thursday at half-past five; and the thermometer in the verandah could not have been much more than 100°. Out on the Lahore race-course, where the hot wind romps in from Mian Mir, it was under 150. But not much. Such a Gymkhana is not made every day of the hot weather.

There were present one Band; thirty-five gunners and soldiers from various parts of the universe; forty natives with no ostensible means of amusement; seventeen people who had the privilege of sitting on the Grand Stand, which was red hot; and forty-one people who had not that privilege, and so sat in carriages which were only warmed through. There were also ponies on the ground, and the ponies hung out their tongues and begged for drink from soda-water bottles with leather round the tops. Main Mir ponies do this habitually on account of the weather. Some body has altered the Grand Stand a great deal. There is more brickwork about it now, and it looks very fine. If you accidentally spill a peg on it, it hisses. This is because it grandstands out in the sun. Near the Grand Stand is a circular, straw hut, with a gallows inside it, and a chopping-block and a meat-scales. It is called the weighing room, but it is just as hot as the

Grand Stand. If you wait more than a minute in the scale-things you begin to go up to the roof, on account of waste caused by insensible perspiration. Several people told me this; and they also said that it was necessary to dip the stirrups in iced water before mounting. They said that this was the origin of stirrup cups. All the Stewards were very affable. They told me everything I wanted to know, and they said that the ice was in the Honorary Secretary's office round the corner.

The Gymkhana was a very fine Gymkhana. The course was soft and powdery, and most of the ponies turned black when they came in. None of the ponies were allowed to run more than half a mile at a time. I think there should have been no compulsion on this head. The ponies did not say anything about it, but they thought a great deal. One pony tried to run all round the course. He ran very fast, but it was the wrong way round, and then his rider was rude to him, and he got rid of him and they separated, and he went away for a walk, and we watched him coming back again in top-boots; but we could not hear what he said. This does not sound correct somehow, but it is no use trying to explain the matter till that pony comes back? I think he went to the Club.

The first race was called a three-furlong race for 13—2 ponies, and some one gave you thirty-two rupees if you won it. The heat alone was worth all the money. It ended this way: —

Mr Temple's *Belladonna*, 10—6, Mr Stopford . . . . . . . . 1
Mr F's *Eugena*, 10—10 . . . . . . . . . . . . . . . . . . . . . . . . 6
Sergt. Brown's *Judy*, 10—6 . . . . . . . . . . . . . . . . . . . . . 3
Mr Roe's *Norah*, 10—6 . . . . . . . . . . . . . . . . . . . . . . . . 4

*Eugena* was four feet five and a half inches high, and I can't understand why she carried one hundred and fifty pounds when the others only carried one hundred and forty-six. They all sweated just the same, and I don't think it was fair. The first pony won by two lengths.

The second race was for Galloways — that is to say, any horse between five and six feet high. They ran for half a mile, but there was a horse who ran for several miles. He did most of it in the air, while going down to the place they start from. The rest he put in by running side-ways across the course, and trying to lace his hind legs together. He was ridden by a Driver of Artil-

lery, one of those men who are paid to sit still when a gun wheel
runs over them. I don't think any one else could have ridden
that horse. I could not catch his name exactly, but from what I
heard the driver say I think it was 'Dammimm'. There may have
been something more; but that was the bulk of the name. That
raced ended this way: —

Mr Temple's *Shahzada*, 10–2 Mr Stopford . . . . . . . . . . 1
Bombr. James' *Marquis*, 10–0 . . . . . . . . . . . . . . . . . . . 2
Mr Knapp's *Dammim* (I think; . . . . . . . . . . . . . . . . . . . 3
but you'll recognize him by his action anywhere)

They said this race was won anyhow. It seems all right to me.
*Shahzada* ran perfectly correctly, and took a nip out of a soda-
water bottle just like a real lady. It must have been the quadrille-
horse that ran anyhow. He goes best on two legs.

The next race was a polo-scurry, catch weights over ten stone,
to be run in three-quarter-mile heats; but one pony was not
going to waste his time and substance scurrying in June so he
went home. I think he was the only sensible pony in the lot, but
his rider was quite angry about it, and walked back from the
far end of the course. So the polo-scurry was a family affair
between the Punjab Police. They ran twice and the senior policeman won, which is right and proper thus: —

Mr Bishop's *Bob*, Owner . . . . . . . . . . . . . . . . . . . . . . . . 1
Mr Roe's *Tom*, Owner  . . . . . . . . . . . . . . . . . . . . . . . . 2

About that time there was a hundred-yards race between two
soldiers in fancy uniform, skin-tights and black belt things, and
another soldier in white uniform. I think he got in by mistake.
The winner of this race was Bandsman Coveney of the 5th
Fusiliers. I am not going to say who the loser was, or what the
time was, because the 5th at Ferozepore might see, and Coveney
is racing one of their men next month. A gentleman with two
red V-shaped things on his cap told me in confidence that
'Mian Meer was the tip'. I said I knew it from the first, but on
mature consideration I find that the information is of no use
to me, so I tell it to you. I haven't the ghost of a notion what it

means, but it's evidently worth having. Remember 'Mian Mir is the tip, an' our man'll give 'im socks'.

Then there was another race. All the races, by the way, except the ones where the men did all the running, were for thirty-two rupees. The foot races were ten rupees. This next race was a hurdle scurry. They can't do anything without scurrying or heating or something. There was a post down the course, a quarter of a mile away and some coolies put up two flights of hurdles. The horses started from the winning-post, and went over those hurdles, turned round the post, and came back again. This was not half so difficult as it sounds, because if a horse snorted at the hurdle, it came down, and the horse walked through. This was a most exciting race. All three horses began a figure of the Lancers in front of the first hurdles until some one breathed too hard, and a hurdle fell. Then they all made an example of that line of hurdles and the next, and after they had twisted round the post, a dear little, brown little animal four feet two inches high, scuttled home first, when no one was looking, and won by a head on the post from a mare called *Nana* who is not nice. She makes a fuss about small things, exactly as I am doing now, and she has nothing to show for it, except her heels. The official report of the race said: —

Mr F.'s *Bonne Bouche*, 8–11, Native . . . . . . . . . . . . . . 1

Mr Temples' *Nane*, 11–0. . . . . . . . . . . . . . . . . . . . . . . 2

Mr Roe's *Norah*, 9–12 . . . . . . . . . . . . . . . . . . . . . . . . 3

But Mr Temples's remarks about *Nana* were much more interesting.

Hereabouts, they had a hurdle race open to soldiers. Natives know what happens to them if they cause injury to a horse, but they know they can damage the *gorah log* as much as they please. Consequently, the coolies hammered in five lines of hurdles with a beetle, and they hammered them good — especially the last hurdle where a man might be expected to trip. But there was no accident, and a man called Wells, clad in beautiful blue drawers, won from Coveney. There was a little trouble here. You see, one man said the winning post was here and another there, and Wells was ahead when they were here, but Coveney beat him when they were there. Judgment against Coveney. I think this serves Coveney quite right for spoiling his 'flat' form by training for short-stride hurdle-races when he knows that he has [to] meet Bayliss in July, and it's all one can do to get one's money on at. . . . But this is a private matter.

The last race was for Non-Commissioned Officers' ponies, and that was the race of the evening. The men took an interest in it and shouted. It was a half mile race, and the men began issuing riding orders to no one in particular the moment the flag fell. 'Dan' was the jockey most in demand. They implored him by all sorts of regimental gods to 'whip her' and Dan whup all he know with a flail sort of thing used for stunning battery horses when they refuse to be shod. But she wouldn't or couldn't come. I don't know who she was, but I felt sorry for her. Dan knew how to whip. The result of this race was: —

Corpl. Ashworth's *Dulcibella* . . . . . . . . . . . . . . . . . . . . . 1
Sergt. Major Simmon's *Happy* . . . . . . . . . . . . . . . . . . . 2
(I think that was Dan's horse)
Sergt. Brown's *Judy* . . . . . . . . . . . . . . . . . . . . . . . . . . . . 3
Sergt. Galway's *Rupert* . . . . . . . . . . . . . . . . . . . . . . . . . 4

The winner was a queer, little, yellow beast with a white mane and tail, and, in the pride of his heart, the owner insisted on giving her nourishment from a feeding-bottle. I don't think *Dulcibella* was accustomed to that sort of attention; for never was an honest little country-bred so horrified.

Then the scene closed with another rider claiming foul, disallowed; a rush of *gharris* to the Hall, and *Dulcibella* trying to spit out the medicine she was sure she had taken in the soda water bottle.

# In the Clouds

*Civil and Military Gazette, 13 June 1887*

**Attribution: Sussex Scrapbooks 28/3, p. 125**

On 9 August 1884 the dirigible balloon 'La France' flew for twenty three minutes and managed to return to the point from which it had started: this was the first of several flights. The craft, designed by the French army engineers Charles Renard and Arthur Krebs, was 165 feet long and 27 feet in diameter, with a bamboo gondola 108 feet long. It was propelled by means of an electric motor, powered by batteries whose weight required almost the entire lifting power of the hydrogen with which the balloon was filled. Its best speed was 14½ miles per hour. The craft was technically an excellent design, but the battery-electric system was soon displaced by the internal combustion engine.

This article is the first sign of Kipling's interest in the possibilities of aeronautics, the best-known expressions of which are 'With the Night Mail' and 'As Easy as ABC'.

Dynamite dates from 1867; rack-a-rock and roburite are both later forms of blasting explosive.

Nearly two years ago, the military and scientific worlds were assured that the problem of aerial navigation had been definitely settled by the Krebs-Reynard self-propelling balloon, an engine that had actually flown, or sailed — whichever may be the correct expression — at a rate of nine miles an hour against the wind, and nineteen miles with it. Since that date, the balloon seems to have dropped quietly out of existence; for no mention of it has appeared later than the enthusiastic report of M. Hervé Magnon, who watched the experiments on behalf of the Academy of Sciences. If his testimony, and that of thousands of eye-witnesses can be believed, it is certain that an aerial ship has been made capable of manoeuvring in the face of a moderately strong wind. Where is that balloon, cigar-shaped, one hundred feet long, with a light dynamo-engine? Have the inventors dropped their work, or is the matter in the hands of the French Government? The questions are not so absurd as they seem at first sight. It is possible to make many improvements in a new machine, in twenty months; and men who have devoted their years to an idea are not willing to throw away their work as children throw away toys. In 1885, the Krebs-Reynard balloon could only carry the weight of three men; but, assuming its specification to be still on paper, it may have trebled its bulk since then. A balloon three hundred and sixty feet long and thirty in diameter can, theoretically at least, support a driving-apparatus of more than fifty-horse power, and a crew of from nine to ten men. A Screw propeller, twenty feet in diameter, revolving at the rate of eight hundred revolutions a minute, should give such a balloon, and on paper always does give it, a velocity of some twenty miles an hour. But, at present, the public mind is not educated up to balloons; believing them to be untrustworthy conveyances at the best; collapsing unreasonably or perversely drifting away. The fact, however, remains that one balloon has been made obedient to the rudder under not too trying circumstances; and in the hour of its triumph was considered to be the stepping-stone 'to discoveries which will render this means of locomotion of common and practical service'. If it ever reappears, we may be certain that its first employ will not be in the peaceful paths of civilization.

Setting aside for a moment the insular prejudice against 'this means of locomotion' — the volatile Gaul is your only aeronaut by instinct — it is startling to contemplate the possibilities of the steerable balloon. The leashed and fettered arrangement, hauled like a huge kite at the tail of a cart, may be valuable for reconnaissance, but it is, even with the most skilful handling, an unwieldy thing and liable to come to extreme grief, as to its guide-rope, among trees or telegraph wires. Moreover, a reconnoitring party suddenly driven back by the enemy would be in an unpleasant and ludicrous predicament. They could not run, for a tethered balloon is as deliberate in its movements as a tethered elephant; and they could not well cut the rope and abandon their comrades in the car, on the off chance of a favourable breeze blowing them into friendly camps, for a balloon of observation carries no provisions. To remain with the balloon would profit nothing, and the balloon would be a most valuable prize to the enemy. Air-reconnaissances in the field, therefore, must be bounded by strict limitations.

With the navigable balloon — with even such an imperfect article as the Krebs-Reynard — the scope of action is infinitely wider. At two thousand feet a balloon is said to be practically safe from rifle-fire, and it is not easy to send shells up to a quick-flying engine of destruction — for this undoubtedly the perfected balloon would be. The hundred varieties of dynamite, rack-a-rock and roburite are light and portable. A half-inch cartridge of the former exploded on a steel rail very effectually puts a stop to traffic for some time; and there is no reason to believe that its effect in a camp or among massed bodies of men would be less striking. Indeed, we may assume that the presence, over head, of an unassailable enemy, dropping explosives on to the heads of a force, already engaged with an enemy on foot, would be singularly disturbing. Even a light article, with a carrying capacity of not more than three hundred pounds, would produce an unprecedented moral effect. It could keep pace with a flying army as a hawk follows a terror-stricken covey of partridges. But there would be no swooping — nothing beyond a steady and continous steaming, and, from time to time, a message in the shape of some explosive compound.

The discipline that could stand against this form of attack has yet to be elaborated. The best troops in the world would break and scatter in the face of a death that literally fell on them from the blue. They would be scattered before they were attacked, exactly — to maintain the ornithological metaphor — as fowls run in all directions from the shadow of the hawk. Once the effect of a sky-dropped shell had been noted, no one would willingly wait anywhere directly under the balloon. Regiments and batteries might retire gracefully and in order, but, while so retiring, they would be useless for offence against the enemy on the ground in front of them. By natural consequence, then, we should in time arrive at the extraordinary spectacle of a battle, where tens of thousands were arrayed on either side, won, almost without bloodshed, by the power which possessed the balloons. It would be the most impressive example of moral effect that the world could offer — an armed host unable to strike, unable to move, because it knew that attack or manoeuvre was the signal for its disruption. Such a vision may be held to be too fantastic. Let us imagine then a flying war-balloon which, sublimely ignorant of frontiers or opposing chains of fortresses, waits, head to the wind, above a populous town or the main arsenal of an army corps, until the ultimatum which is dropped from the car to the earth has been accepted, and the town is abandoned and blown up. The idea is even more impressive than that of balloon attack against an army. The town cannot move. It can only wait while its inhabitants hide, as did the rebels who denied the suzerainty of Laputa, in their cellars. Once, and once only, it would be necessary that the balloon should make a memorable example in order to instruct the enemy in the nature of the weapons at its command. When the chosen town had been reduced to blackened walls, the rest would be easy; for the most patriotic burgh would prefer capitulation to unromantic destruction.

# Further Developments

*Civil and Military Gazette, 13 June 1887*

**Attribution: Sussex Scrapbooks 28/3, p. 126**

This spoof of the behaviour of the civil administration was prompted by a case in Bombay. The regular promotion of civil servants was slowed down by a lack of available positions, and the government had accordingly directed that the situation should be 'remedied' by appointing civil servants 'to offices other then those reserved for them by law' (*CMG*, 13 June 1887). In this way a civil servant had recently been appointed to a judgeship in Bombay. A group of Bombay lawyers objected to the appointment, and the governor, in denying the protest, had pointed out that the civilian in question, besides having some legal experience, was 'a Master of Arts of Oxford' and had 'qualified himself in Marathi, Gujarathi and Hindustani'.

**(Vide next column)**

'High in the ranks of the sixth form of one of the leading public schools in England and distinguished at Oxford, he has filled posts in the Revenue and Political Departments and has exercised the powers of. . . . a District Magistrate.'

*Pioneer* June 10th

'An M.A. of Oxford and a distinguished linguist.'

*Pioneer's Correspondent*, June 10th

*(Circa* 1935 A.D.*) Memorial from Unimportant Hamlet, with three quarters of a million of inhabitants, to Very Superior*

*Administration*: — 'Hi! Look here! There's one of your men administering our Port Trust. He says you told him to. He's
changed the Pilots' badges, and put 'em into white kerseymere
breeches with sword, and warehoused the steam-crane in the
dock-transit sheds and berthed all the Zanzibar *buggalows* at
the Apollo Bunder, and the Gulf horses are loose in the 'haz-
ardous goods' sheds, where the percussion-caps and kerosine are
kept. . . . and. . . and.'

*V.S.A.*: — 'Mind your own business. That gentleman is
Senior Wrangler and can repeat the Zend Avesta backwards.
You are a set of spiteful shop-keepers. Put your head in a
gunny-bag. Yah!'

*Directors of Obscure Railway Company, with capital of a
few millions, to V.S.A. aforesaid*: — 'Would you please transfer
the Assistant Collector who is driving, on the pay of his grade,
Loco. B.41 all over our line. He drives remarkably well, seeing
that he does not know the difference between a big-end and a
link-hanger, and blows the piston-rings through the blast-pipe;
but the traffic in our jurisdiction has been seriously impeded
of late, owing to his going through all the junctions without
lights or whistling, and with the brake-lever broken at the
shank.'

*V.S.A*: — 'We don't understand your workshop technicalities.
The official you allude to was, till lately, a distinguished light of
our Secretariat where he gave every satisfaction to those best
qualified to judge. You will, we presume, admit that the Government has some slight knowledge of the capacities of its servants;
though you will hardly be disposed to allow that vituperation
indiscriminate as yours is the characteristic feature of a debased
and narrow intellect.'

*Ignorant Engineer of twenty years' standing (By Telegraph)*:—
'Honour report earthworks section my charge being faced Agra
stone by lunatic asserts he once Sudder Judge. Line over howling
desert. Cost stone carriage only, four lakhs. Please arrange transfer person above mentioned.'

*V.S.A. (Also by telegraph)*: — 'Remove yourself Rann Kutch,
futher notice. Gentleman distinguished numismatist, poet, natural
historian and Sessions, not Sudder Judge. Protest evidently
outcome ignorance, jealousy. Letter follows.'

*Incompetent General, V.C. Mutiny, China, Abyssinian,
Ashantee, Zulu, Boer, and Egyptian medals in Command Brigade*

(*Confidential to V.S.A.*): — 'Awful mistake somewhere: whole cantonment laughing. Man in Political cap, alpaca coat and tennis-flannels, come in by this morning's train. Ordered me to hand over command of the Division and became dangerously excited when I handed him over to guard. He appears respectable and has been vouched for by our Cantonment Magistrate as a Judge of the High Court. Mind evidently unhinged by sun or misfortune. Now in charge Civil Surgeon, Central Asylum. No mention of any missing Judge in Presidency papers; but have communicated to you direct to save scandal. Inform family and arrange for his removal. He swears in the vernacular. Dreadfully.'

*V.A.S.* (*apologetically*): — 'Awful mistake as you say; but we'll try to hush it up for your sake. Hand over command at once and go to Pachmarri. Judge spoke truth. Block of promotion in Civil Service; shifting 'em into cognate branches y'know. He has been a Major of Volunteers and knows more about the Tantrik Mysteries than any living man. Better apologize to him. It's a bad business, but we'll back you up with a Resolution if necessary. Issue G.O. notifying transfer tonight.'

*I.G.* — 'D— your Tantrik Mysteries! G.O. has been issued and garrison is now running Judge over parade-ground to see how he manoeuvres. Better shove him into non-official berth. Mutiny here.'

*Pathetic and Overcome Shipping Company to V.S.A.* — 'Our Agents give us to understand that any Civilian is *ipso facto* Master Mariner, holding Captain's and Engineer's certificate and has been used as such, on our steamers by your authority. Unaccountable delay of two last mail-steamers leads us to believe this; but kindly confirm and relieve. Yours, etc., etc.'

*V.S.A.* — 'Of course. Not a man in our service but could give your Captain points in *Aristophanes*, and Indian Law of Torts. Please don't bother. It's bad form.'

*A year later.*

*V.S.A.* — 'Curious how these non-official classes swear and throw brick-bats at us when we appear in the streets. Must be want of education. They say they can manage their own affairs best. Of all the indecent impertinence! . . . . But we've got rid of that block in the Service anyhow and now for a comprehensive Resolution: —

WHEREAS, it has of late been abundantly made manifest to

us that our trusty and well-beloved Civil Servants have suffered from an undue and unnecessary stagnation in regard equally to pay and emolument, and WHEREAS we by our own distinguished exertions have, for the time being, circumvented and in divers manners walked round, underneath, through, and over that difficulty,

BE IT THEREFORE ENACTED that, to guard against such stagnation, block or jam in the future immediate or remote, the common or Covenanted Civilian shall be held, *caeteris imparibus, facile princeps, multum in parvo, otium cum dig et alia* as by previous enactments set forth and provided, to be equal, fit, imperatively necessary and supremely desirable, to and for, any and every service or services, craft or crafts, trade or trades, profession or professions, art or mystery covenanted or uncovenanted, special or general, private or public, vested or divested, literary, legal, financial, medical, mercantile, dramatic, obstetric, veterinary, administrative, technical, *or otherwise,* under the canopy of Heaven.

## The Private Services Commission

*Civil and Military Gazette, 29 June 1887*

**Attribution: Sussex Scrapbooks 28/3, pp. 128–9.**

A public services commission had been travelling from administrative town to adminstrative town up and down India for some months past, hearing testimony on the subject of the employment and treatment of natives in the administration of India. Kipling's paper tended to regard the business without sympathy, on the grounds that the jealousies, cliques, and intrigues of native servants – public or private – made any attempt at rational inquiry and just reform quite impossible. As Kipling wrote of the Commission, after it had been largely neglected by the officials in Calcutta:

this side-show which is performing up and down the country,

is a native side-show for the benefit of Anjuman-i-Sabahs, Associations, native newspapers, Subordinate Judges, Munsiffs and so on. The Great Indian Nation clamoured for and got it; and now the very metropolis of the Nation seems to have left it severely alone. The Civilian never had any connection with it from the beginning, because his hands were full of work, and unless he had a 'fad' to ventilate, or a mark to make, he did not trouble his head about the business. No man can help to govern a country and help to show how that country should be governed, at one and the same time (*CMG*, 29 January 1887).

The situation that Kipling develops in this satiric reduction of the Commission suggested further possibilities to him. Between 15 July 1887 and 9 January 1888 he published six stories about a man named Smith and his administration of his own household which grew out of 'The Private Services Commission'. One of these Smith stories, 'The Serai Cabal', reworks some of the material in 'The Private Services Commission'; the whole series was collected in *The Smith Administration.*

It owed its origin to a fortuitous combination of accidental circumstances; and its birth-place was the back-verandah where the ferash trees shut out the road. The *khansamah* had insulted the *bhisti's* mother, and I was called upon to arbitrate.

I was all the Commission, for Absalom, my long haired Skye, wouldn't attend to his duties as Recorder. He sat in the *mehter's* lap throughout; and I regret to record that the levity of his behaviour was only equalled by his shameless and glaring partiality. There were present, the *khansamah*, my bearer, and the cook, as representing the educated classes; the *khansamah's* son, the bearer's sons, the cook's nephew, and the *mussalchi* who was an orphan. These stood for the sons of the educated classes who hoped for employment. They were full of ungratified ambition, and wore their turbans fantastically. Apart from these were, the *bhisti* and the *bhistis bhai*, the *mallee*, and his mate, the *ayah* and the *ayah's* children — some hundreds — both *saises*, the coachman, and the two grass-cutters, besides a person who did grass cutters' work when the regular ones were sick.

BHISTI, OR WATER-CARRIER

(Copyright 1891, by J. Lockwood Kipling)

Last of all came the *mehter* and his broom. I was the State and I had the chair with the leg-rests. The *khansamah* filled my pipe, in order to show that he identified his interests with mine; and the bearer brought the matches for the same reason.

The charge against the *khansamah* was disposed of in a few minutes. The *bhisti's* mamma had called him a black lizard without a back-bone, and he had retaliated by comparing her to a toad before the rains break. Both comparisons were absolutely accurate; so both parties were dismissed with a warning.

But the evening was pleasantly cool, and no one had much to do, or showed any desire to get off the grass. So I declared myself a Commission and announced my willingness to hear everybody's grievances. No one spoke, for a long time; the witnesses began plucking the grass blade by blade, and smiling dubiously.

Then I said: — 'What sort of *nokri* is this your *nokri* and what is your opinion of the *nokri*?' Then they all shouted: — '*Hazur-ki-parwashti*' or words to that effect, and I felt that the Commission was going to be a sham.

But the *bhisti's* mother saved me. She drew the chudder over her nose, and growled: — 'The coachman is a liar, Protector of the Poor.' I had often suspected this and had hinted as much to the coachman, but I did not see that it was evidence exactly. The coachman had said '*choop*' to the *bhisti's* mamma, but the *bhisti* said: — 'That is truth. I water the horses, and he should give me two annas and nine pie a month but he only gives me two annas.' Now I pay the *bhisti* seven rupees a month, and his duties are not heavy. He has no right to perquisites. But I felt that this was [not] evidence. The coachman got angry and abused the *bhisti*, but the horse *sais* — not the *sais* attached to the carriage — said to the *bhisti* 'That is true. But who gives you the double handful of gram weekly from the *sahib's* bin?' Now the *ayah* had a *tendresse* for that *sais*, and she had quarrelled with the coachman on the same gram question. She screamed: — 'And who gives the grass short weight, and takes five annas dustoorie on each shoeing, O base born and rat-hearted, inadequate one?' That fetched the *mehter*, whose wife the *ayah* was, and he said nasty things about her, till she wept, vowing that he had never swept out the drawing-room to her own certain knowledge for three weeks.

You see the *bhisti* had quarrelled with the coachman, who was hated by one of the *saises* who again was beloved by the *ayah*, who backed his accusation against the coachman, she being the wedded wife of the *mehter* who naturally did not approve of her weakness for a *chumar*. That is clear enough isn't it?

From this point onward things began to get complicated. There is an enormous amount of subordinate administration about a *serai*, if you really go into it.

When the *mehter* was accused of neglect of his official duties, the evil spirit prompted the leader of the educated classes, the *khansamah*, who, up to this point, had been ostentatiously impartial, to wag his head slowly and tell me that the *mehter* was, without doubt, a careless servant. Now the *ayah* allowed no one but herself to abuse her husband. She came to the *mehter's* rescue and the two lifted up their voices and accused the *khansa-*

*mah* of brandy and sugar stealing from the almirah, and called upon the *mussalchi* to confirm their statements. Now the *mussalchi* was an orphan, owing nothing to any man, and he made answer that he was so busy doing all the *khansamah's* work that he had no time to watch his superior's thefts.

Here the cook, who wanted his own nephew to be the *mussalchi*, called the Orphan a black-mouthed gambler, a waster of time and pice in the Sudder Bazar, a thief and a vagabond. The Orphan was fighting for his own hand with none to help him. He answered sweetly that, whatever his vices might be he did not go shares in the rupees which the bearer stole from the *Sahib's* pockets of a morning. He stole from the *kala admi* when any theft was necessary. I admired the Orphan's freedom from fear. It provoked a high-pitched catalogue of his crimes at the mouths of the cook's nephew and the bearer's two sons. The bearer retired about this point. He tendered no evidence, but said that my *kamra* wanted *saf-haro*-ing. His sons were his delegates.

My *mallee* is a man of few words. He had no special views or grievances. He only knew that the *Sahib* had given strict orders that neither the cook's nephew nor the *khansamah's* son nor the bearer's sons should be allowed to live in the *serai*. He was a childless widower himself, and, besides, those young devils stole his onions. He did not recognize their right to speak at all. He was a poor man and raised onions —

'And stole vegetables from Esmit *Sahib* for the *Sahib's* dinner table' said the *khansamah*. 'All these *Arains* are one'. The *mallee* grunted, but the *mallee's* mate, who is evidently a man of culture and extensive reading, murmured abstractedly a proverb, which gives the chemical formulae of *khitmatgars* and *khansamahs*. Everyone tittered; the *ayah* loudest of all. Which was a pity, for there is another proverb giving the formulae of an *ayah's* composition, and this the cook's nephew made use of. The *ayah* wept copiously. Heaven was her witness she had served the *memsahib* for three years without an increase of pay, and the cook's nephew should never have been allowed in the *serai*.

Then the uneducated classes shouted that this was incontrovertible fact, and the *serai* was full beyond proper limits. The *khansamah's* son and the bearer's son put their hands upon my boots and asserted I was unique among *Sahibs*. The Orphan had

no partialities. He knew that the *serai* was full because the
*saises*, all of them, took in their *bhai-bund*, all of them; and
there was a lady in a pink *saree*, about whom the less said the
better. He was not surprised to learn that the *serai* was full.
The Orphan gets kicked by the other servants and sleeps, like
a dog, curled up in the dust of the garden. He is an Ishmael
among *mussalchies* and therefore a firebrand; though his light
be hidden under the *degchies*. The *khansamah* professed virtuous
indignation. The lady in question was the maternal aunt of one
of the punkah coolies. He regretted that all the coolies had gone
away to get a drink or water just then but. . . .

I don't quite understand the dialect of the villages. A pigeon-
breasted old man in a blue cloth broke into the circle of the
witnesses, saying that by my favour he was permitted to pull
my honoured punkah. I understood him to observe that the
crops had failed in his parts, but even in the wildest accesses of
frivolity, his co-villages never recognized the existence of ladies
in pink *sarees*, and, further, the *khansamah*, though a Mohammedan, was a thief; which is a money-lender. Also, that that
same well-scoop of abomination financed every pie of money
that passed through his evil hands. The old man was a poor
man and his crops had failed but he was still virtuous, and the
*khansamah* was not.

Then the rest of the witnesses made common cause against
the *khansamah* not because of his lack of virtue, but because he
did not pay away fairly the money entrusted to him. You must
know all my household accounts pass through the Khansamah's
hand and he seems to grow fat on the process.

I heard nine different anecdotes of the perfidy of the *Khansamah*, and a great deal of mixed bad language.

This seemed to prove the mistake of administering the bulk
of the population through the educated classes; but I remembered that my subjects had desired me to do this thing.

Then I rose up out of my long chair and said: — 'I am an
Englishman and incorruptible; caring neither for the frowns of
the *khansamah* nor the flatteries of the cook, nor the favour of
the *ayah*. I will administer you personally, paying to each into
his own hands his just dues and no more, and visiting with a
bamboo all who would prey upon their fellows, or encroach
upon their neighbour's string and grass fence, or illegally fill the
*serai* with their *bhai-bund*. I will extendedly employ myself

among you and your belongings and will see to your well-fare, and when your wives and children are sick I will doctor them.'

My subjects said: — '*Hazur ki parwashti*' in tones of very subdued delight and whispered to one another. They did not put garlands round my neck as I had expected. On the contrary, they scowled at me. Even the promise to look after the well-fare of their women-kind was not appreciated.

Then still sitting on the grass and whispering they told stories — interminable stories — of two anna oppression, and one anna wrong, and infinitely tiny intrigue. There was the *bhisti's* clique, which included the *malli* and his mate who fought against the coachman, but also against the *ayah* and her following, who further hated the coachman and liked the other *sais* before mentioned, who, occasionally and to serve his ends against the *chowkidar*, was a friend of the coachman. But the *chowkidar's* faction, which included the punkah coolies, was in the hands of the cook, as was the *mehter's* following, — which must by no means be confounded with that of the *ayah*, — by reason of the broken meats they received from the cook's hands, and to which they had no rights. The cook was a friend of the *bhisti* for obvious reasons, and this brought the cook, *mehter*, *chowkidar*, and *bhisti* and *mallee* against the coachman and the *khansamah*, and, semi occasionally, the other *sais*.

This statement, simple as it seems, was further complicated by some indirect relations between the bearer's son and the *ayah's* eldest daughter, and a gambling debt to the *goalla*. Behind all, was the lady in the pink *saree*, who had turned the *khansamah's* mind from the paths of legitimate *dustoorie* to theft.

These things, and may others I learned while the witnesses were sitting whispering among themselves, and from what I heard I evolved a plan of Government.

Selecting the Orphan whose voice is of a peculiar and rasping *timbre*, I bade him retire into the belly of the *serai* and there scream as though the bearer were beating him. When his yells were softened by distance to a merely melodious wail, I walked to where he stood, and with the tennis-court brush, drew a white line across the *serai*.

Then I spoke: —

'Oh people! On the side of this line which is furthest from my house you may scream and fight and bully and intrigue as you will, for at this distance your voices cannot reach me. But if I hear noises — unseemly noises — which break my rest, I shall know that you have crossed the line and evil will follow. The *khansamah* through whose hands my money passes has cheated the punkah coolies, who are rustic folk unable to protect themselves. These therefore I shall myself pay. The *khansamah* has also cheated you as you cheat one another, and all collectively rob me. Therefore I shall not now dismiss the *khansamah*, nor shall I dismiss you. Once a week because the weather is warm, I shall sprinkle *phenyle-ke-diwai* in and about the *serai* and shall severely punish all uncleanliness; because this is a danger to me. I shall accept no complaints. The horses must be fat, the harness must be clean, and for these things the *khansamah* is responsible.'

All this happened eight weeks ago and, since that day, great peace has fallen on my *serai*.

Next month I dismiss my *khansamah*, and his successor only holds office for a year. For six months of that time the servants will cheat him and, for the other six, he will defraud them. The phenyle sanitation arrangement was temporarily checked by a subsidized *Sunnyasi* who said that it was unclean. I however have more funds at my disposal than a syndicate of *chumars* and the phenyle is now accepted as a rare and precious balsam. I am only afraid of some one drinking it.

Beyond painting the white line in the *serai* from time to time, and docking without reason given, certain rupees from the *khansamah's* account, my domestic administration costs me neither time nor trouble. Curiously enough, my people are happy. I think this must be because they are allowed free scope to develop their national characteristics, and never know, when I descend into the *serai*, whether I shall give four annas to a *sais's* baby, or order the demolition of the *chupper* hut wherein the bearer strives to imprison an aged lowcaste female, declared by him to be a *pardah-nishin*.

They understand an administration which they can't understand, you see.

Smith

# Our Change. By 'Us'

*Civil and Military Gazette, 1 August 1887*

**Attribution: Sussex Scrapbooks 28/3, p. 137**

In this article Kipling explains to the readership of the *CMG* the paper's new appearance (see Introduction pp. 10–11). The subject, he at once concedes, is not one of general interest, but he manages to give a vivid sketch of the conditions under which the paper operated. In his autobiography Kipling remembered the hard work that the change required.

> In the joyous reign of Kay Robinson, my second Chief, our paper changed its shape and type. This took up for a week or so all hours of the twenty-four and cost me a breakdown due to lack of sleep. But we two were proud of the results (*Something of Myself*, p. 66).

The 'Miss Cass' referred to at the end of the article was a respectable young working woman who had been wrongly arrested late in July as a prostitute in Regent Street; the affair created a minor political crisis.

It is possible that, to-day, a few of our readers may notice certain alterations in this paper; may find that the advertisements begin at the wrong end; that the leading article has withdrawn itself to other pages, and that the telegrams flower aggressively in a new bed. To ninety-nine men out of a hundred, these things will be of the smallest possible importance. The Hundredth may wonder for a moment how they came about. It is to the Hundredth Man that we would tell our tale of trouble and sorrow — of sin and woe.

This Change is the outcome of a striving after perfection, and, from our point of view, the most important event that has taken place in the Empire during the last twenty-four hours. Several scores of intelligent native persons are of the same opinion; but their utterances do not reach the outer air. The Change had been impending for many weeks, and came at last in the form of two truck-loads of type of the newest. That is to say, the second truck full of the subtler and more frivolous varieties of print, wholly useless for the gravity of a daily journal, came first, while the other which contained the necessaries of the new issue disported itself in the Indus Valley. Not long ago, a journal entitled the *Rocky Mountain Cyclone* essayed a change similar to ours. There are but few trains in the Rocky Mountains, and the mules died on the way to the *Cyclone*'s door, before all the c's, f's and g's had been delivered. Then the Syklone akquainted its konstituents with the phakt in languadje more pekuliar than prophessional, and phor several weeks phoudijht with phate, as it were with krippled plumadje. Having this awful example in our minds, the agony caused by the missing truck was distracting; doubly distracting, inasmuch as a specious air of unconcern had to be preserved towards an unsympathetic public, in the daily issues. After continous telegraphing, the missing waggon was discovered, hidden in a siding where it sat down to rest, and conveyed safely to this place.

Followed, next, a weary period of consultation as to the best use to be made of the contents of the trucks. The secrets of that *sederunt* it would be unprofitable to reveal. Imagine half a dozen persons all playing the Fifteen-Thirty-two game on one board, and all wanting to play it their own way. Above the clamour of conflicting opinions and the rustle of sample sheets turned out to see 'how they would look', rose the still small voice of the Punjabi compositor, mourning that he had been ousted from the paths of customs and use. Semi-nude and laborious, the Punjabi was, after all the last Court of Appeal and the stumbling-block in the path of evolution; for the instincts of the Oriental lead him, if unchecked, to revert to the primitive type — in this particular case, the bleared and blackened pieces of metal that he had battered for so long.

Finally, after enormous discussion, all to please a public which really does not care much how a paper looks so long as it is moderately legible and contains criticism of Hill theatricals, the New Paper evolved itself 'from the title page to closing line' and the contending artists were unanimous that everything might have been ten times better had their own unmodified suggestions been carried out. Then the real difficulties opened themselves. They were not so much pitched battles with the conservative compositors, as the harassing duties of an under-handed Preventive Service. The Old Paper stopped the day before the New began, but the interval between the death of one and the birth of the next could be measured in minutes.

The Hundredth Man will understand that there was no time to remove the old type; new and old lay within a short arm's length of each other, and, between the two, stood the Patient East — composing-stick in his fist and bewilderment in his heart. The East did not intentionally and of evil ingrained weave into the new and shining metal, streaks of the dirty black stuff he should have quitted for ever. On the contrary, he did his best, but he became mixed. The accustomed hand strayed to the well-known trays, the habituated eye turned to the recognised print, and, gently and wearily, the Impatient West caught the East by the wrist, and, as when a mother forces her child to loose its hold of the broken medicine-glass, the old type fell from the unwilling fingers.

The delay of the trucks was sad and wearing, the conference on the future form of the paper, profanely called the 'puzzle-party', was lively and more wearing; but saddest, liveliest and most wearing of all was the watch over the compositor to prevent an unseemly mixture of letters and the consequent scorn of the public which does not care how its newspaper looks, so long as it comes forth regularly and contains sufficient names of the public's acquaintances. It was not the compositor's fault. He explained that things were otherwise in the days when he first constructed newspapers, and he was a *poor* man. Besides which, it would be much better to work these changes to-morrow, and, if little accidents had occurred, it was an incontrovertible fact that *he* was a poor man; and so on, after the fashion of *Patience*.

Lastly, as night sank upon the earth, the work was completed, and those who for years past had held the paper as part of themselves, on whose heart the three thousand two hundred and eighty-two impressions, with all their faults, had been stamped, gazed blankly on a new and strange Thing — their child and not their child — an alien in painfully clean garb. But, as they looked for the last time ere sending the New Paper into the world, there twinkled in the unfamiliar waste, as a friend's face shines in foreign land, a star — a fixed undying star. Which was the Inevitable Misprint. The compositor saw it also, but it was too late to make a correction. 'Without doubt,' said the

compositor in sober glee, 'a fault has befallen.' And his mind
was at peace again. Papers may 'shift and bedeck and bedrape
them In pica, burgeois and antique' as Swinburne sings, but the
Misprint is eternal.

With these cheerful reflections, the old type was put into the
melting-pot, and the New Issue went out to catch the eye of the
public which has not the faintest interest in the appearance of a
paper so long as the all the 'leaves' are gazetted, and it knows
who Miss Cass is.

# The House of Shadows

*Civil and Military Gazette, 4 August 1887*

**Attribution: Sussex Scrapbooks 28/3, p. 138**

This is the first fiction by Kipling to appear in the new 'turnover'
space of the remodelled *CMG* (see Introduction p. 10).

### By its Occupant

A woman has died and a child has been born in it, but these are
accidents which may overtake the most respectable establishments. No sensible man would think of regarding them. Indeed,
so sound is my common sense, that I sleep in the room of the
death and do my work in the room of the birth; and have no
fault to find with either apartment. My complaint is against the
whole house; and my grievance, so far as I can explain it in
writing, is that there are far too many tenants in the eight, lime-
washed rooms for which I pay seventy-five rupees a month.

They trooped in after the great heats of May as snakes seek
bathrooms through drought. Personally I should prefer the
snakes, the visible, smashable snakes, to the persons who have
quartered themselves upon me for the past ten weeks. They
take up no space and are almost noiseless, like the Otto Gas
Engines — but they are there and they trouble me. In the very

early morning when I climb on to the roof to catch what less heated breeze may be abroad, I am conscious that someone has preceded me up the narrow steps, and that there is some one at my heels. You will concede, will you not, that this is annoying, particularly when I know that I am officially the sole tenant. No man, visible or invisible, has a right to spy upon my outgoings or incomings. At breakfast, in the full fresh daylight, I am conscious that some one who is not the *khitmutgar* is watching the back of my head from the door that leads into my bedroom; when I turn sharply, the *purdah* is dropped and I only see it waving gently as though shaken by the wind. Quitting the house to go to office, I am sure — sure as I am of my own existence — that it is at once taken possession of by the people who follow me about, and that they hold who knows what mad noiseless revels in the room when the bearer has done his duster-flapping and the servants have withdrawn to their own quarters.

Indeed, once returning from office at an unexpected hour, I surprised the house, rushed in and found. . . . nothing. My foot-fall rang through the barn-like rooms, and as the noise ceased, I felt that the people who had been crowding the floor were rushing away — pouring out into the garden and the verandahs, and I could not see them. But I knew they had been there. The air was full of the rustle of their garments.

Still an assembly is preferable to the one man — he must be a man; he is so restless — who comes in to spend the evening and roams through the house. His feet make no noise, but I can hear in the hot, still night the jar of the *chik* as he comes into the verandah, and the lifting of the *purdah* over the drawing-room door. Then he touches a book in the drawing-room, for I hear it fall, or he thrums the Burmese gong ever so lightly, for I catch the faint ring of the smitten metal, and passes on, shifting things, scratching things, tapping things, till I could shriek aloud with irritation. When he comes to the room I am in he stops, puts the *purdah* aside and looks at me. I am sure of it, for when I turn the *purdah* has always just fallen. He must be the man who takes so impertinent an interest in my breakfast. But he will never face me and tell me what he wants. He is always in the next room. Though I have hunted him through the house again and again, he is always in the next room.

When I enter, I know that he has just gone out. The *purdah* betrays him. And when I go out I know that he is waiting, always waiting, to slip into the room I have vacated, and begin his aimless stroll among the knicknacks. If I go into the verandah, I know that he is watching me from the drawing-room. I can hear him sitting down on one of the wicker-work chairs that creaks under his weight.

On Sundays, the long, hot pitiless Sundays, when the consciousness of arrears of work prevents their clearance, he comes to spend the day in my house from ten in the morning till the hour of the evening drive. I can offer him no amusement. He cannot find me cheering company. *Why* does he hang about the house? He should have learnt by this time not to touch a *punkha* fringe with his head or to leave a door on the swing, I can track him then and prevent him from sitting down on the chairs in the next room.

I would endure the people who hide in the corners of the lamproom and rush out when my back is turned, the persons who get between the almirah and the wall when I come into my dressing-room hastily at dusk, or even the person in the garden who slides in and out of the *ferash* trees when I walk there, if I could only get rid of the Man in the Next room. There is no sense in him, and he interferes sadly with one's work. I believe now that if he dared he would come out from the other side of the *purdah* and peep over my shoulder to see what I am writing. But he is afraid and is now twitching the cord that works the ventilating window. I can hear it beating against the wall. What pleasure can he find in prowling thus about another man's premises? I asked him the question last Sunday, but my voice came back to me from the high ceiling of the empty room next my bedroom, and that was all my answer.

One of these days, perhaps, if I enter my own house very, very silently, with bare feet, crawling through a window, I may be able to catch him and wring from him some sort of explanation; for it is manifestly absurd that a man paying seventy-five rupees a month should be compelled to live with so unsatisfactory a chum as the man in the next room.

On second thoughts, and after a plain statement of facts to the doctor, I think it would be better to go the Hills for a while and leave him to maunder about the empty house till he is tired. The doctor says he will be gone when I return; taking all the other persons with him.

# A Break on the Line

*Civil and Military Gazette, 6 August 1887*

**Attribution: Sussex Scrapbooks 28/3, p. 139**

Gujrat, where the break occurred, is about fifty miles north of
Lahore, on the North Western Railway running to Rawalpindi.

The 'ticket collector's poetry' referred to in the third paragraph was the work of a native on the East Indian Railway
noticed by Kipling in the *CMG* on 14 June 1887. The ticket
collector had devised a language in which English words were
arbitrarily abbreviated, with strange results, as in these sample
lines from the poet's verses on the Jubilee:

'A grand J'lee conv'ntion to c'rem'nize that grand 'cess'n day';

and

'Ye No'le Go'rnors and Go'rnor Gen'rals of Ind vast.'

**(From our own Correspondent)**

Lahore, August 3rd

As a sensation, the first telegram that found its way into Lahore
on Tuesday was a success. It said: — 'Line washed as far as the
eye can reach', and bore every evidence of having been compiled
by some agitated Aryan. Later on in the day, came the news
that there were 'gaps at mile 76–77 between Gujrat and Lala
Musa', on the way to Pindi that is to say. The nature and extent of the gaps was not specified, but the telegram alluded to
arrangements for transhipping passengers and bringing up
material-trains.

Now a break in a railway system produces much the same
effect as a break in a worm or a lizard. The two sundered
sections grow exceedingly lively.

On Tuesday fore-and-afternoon, the Gap set up a local irritation on its own account, and sent down to Lahore sheaves of little hieroglyphical telegrams which read remarkably like your ticket collector's poetry. Lahore, in return, sent up men — Heads of Departments and the like — to soothe the Gap and put things straight.

In the mixed train which left Lahore at 10.50 P.M., on Tuesday night for Pindi, if possible, was one of these Heads, and, by singular favour, a Perfectly Disinterested Observer, whose only use in life for the time being, was to look at the Gap. The pleasure, the keen artistic delight, with which one sets out to study an accident that does *not* block the road to Simla, but merely prevents two or three families from getting up to an inferior place called Murree, must be felt to be understood. The observer, more especially if he be sumptuously entertained in the Inspection Carriage of a Departmental Head, comforted with a big arm-chair and a broad and stately bunk, feels so good, so impartial, so calm — so secretariatish and administrative, in fact. Then, and only then, can he watch 'another man's break' with satisfaction.

After the train had cleared the Shadera Bridge, the Ravee growling angrily among the piers in the watery moonlight, it seemed suddenly and without warning to shoot forth into the deep still sea. Never was transformation more complete. Lahore up till Sunday at least, had been suffering sadly from want of rain: but here was the explanation. All the heavy clouds that for weeks past had come up from the South, circled over our heads and departed, must have spent themselves from Muridki onwards, for the country-side was swamped. The first telegram from the Gap had been perfectly correct, for the railway was 'washed as far as the eye could reach'. The leaden levels of water were broken only by the line of embankment and, in the uncertain distance, by island-like clumps of trees.

Here the warm rain began to fall and the rest of the journey till dawn was as a journey in a dream. On both sides lay nothing but water — flush it seemed with the culverts and the top of the wire-fencing; when the train stopped, was heard nothing but the noise of a hundred waters — the murmur of the rain on the carriage-roof — the lap, lap, lap of water by the side of the line, the gurgle of tiny streams running down to the borrow-pits — and the sullen splashing from the eaves of the carriage. At the stations, very wet gentlemen in white uniforms, with lanterns, talked about the Gap. There was a certain 'Bill' supposed, like 'Bill the Lizard' in *Alice in Wonderland,* to have done or left undone everything that was possible. The wet gentlemen would talk of and at him, and the luckless Bill, very wet, would strive huskily to defend himself. His voice seemed to come from under the carriages for the most part.

Then the train would stand out to sea, and in a moment, all trace of dry earth would vanish. It was a nightmare of a journey, for the Disinterested Observer's mind was vexed by the notion that the train might find out yet another Gap through the simple process of falling into it. There seemed to be water enough on the premises generally to drown the whole North-Western Railway. But the Departmental Head was asleep, and there was comfort in the knowledge that, if any thing happened, he would be washed away with the rest. The Chenab was 'up' — so much so, that it seemed nearly level with the girders of the Alexandra Bridge, and the wash of the waves — real waves — among the piers was unpleasant to listen to. Especially when the Observer remembered that on the previous night the Chenab had beaten and chopped like the Channel — the Channel full of yellow mud.

Lastly came Gujrat and the drenched and draggled dawn, showing the indigo-blue Jummoo hills on the East, with black cloud above them and stretches of water almost up to their feet. The Gap was, as nearly as possible, midway between Gujrat and Lala Musa, and at Gujrat the train stayed pending developments. This was at 6 A.M.

During the night, many passengers from Sialkot, bound for Murree, had entered the train at Wazirabad. They appeared depressed and inclined to grumble. To be sure they had not spent the night in an Inspection Carriage with 'every thing handsome about them' and their leaves might have been limited, but they were surely needlessly concerned. They did not turn to admire the hundred tints of grey — from almost black to pearly blue — that made up the landscape; nor did they trouble the engine-driver with questions as to how Gaps were found out; whether by stumbling headlight first on to the cow-catcher or otherwise. On the contrary, they wanted to know: — 'When are we going forward?' Decidedly, they were a narrow-minded, selfish people on whom it was so easy to look down. Another train, which had preceded the '10—50 mixed' had been stopped, and all the native inhabitants put into the latter. They bought sweetmeats — terrible sugar flap-jacks — and talked of their family affairs. The line they explained had been smashed by reason of too much water, but a "raport" had been made, and a *bundobust* was even now in course of construction.

After a time, a long time, appeared an engine manned by an Assistant Engineer — white, wet, and muddy. He had come from the Gap and, by the earth-works with which he was adorned was it possible to judge of the state of the Gap. This engine brought the news that two Heads of Departments with coolies and a material-train had come down overnight and were 'packing the bad bits as fast as they could'. In the mean time, the Lahore train was to advance as near as might be to the Pindi train from Lala Musa, and the passengers would then be transhipped. The next train would be got over the Gap which had showed itself more important than had been at first estimated.

Then everybody in authority gave orders at once to the engine-driver of the Lahore train. He drank tea stolidly till the tyranny was overpast, took out his engine and executed manoeuvres in and about a siding — apparently to show that his charge had not suffered from the damp journey.

The procession formed itself, and the train was taken out gingerly to the Gap — six or seven miles away. Men said that the Bhimbar river, which comes from the Jummoo hills and runs more or less parallel with the track, was the real cause of the Gap. Whatever it was, the rush of the water when the flood was at its fiercest must have been a grand sight.

The posts of the wire-fencing were wreathed with the raffle brought down by the flood, till they looked like so many haycocks; weeds were piled on the sleepers, on the piers of the culverts, through which rushed an angry yellow flood, and the pure green tussocks of jungle-grass had been beaten flat and most ingloriously crowned with mud. It seemed as if miles of the line had been under water since 11 o'clock on Tuesday forenoon when the first spate began. Now the waters were abating off the surface of the earth, and the desolation of the scene was complete. The fields were under water; only a ripple-mark showing where each boundary ridge ran. The trees were out of water and so was the Grand Trunk Road; there was little else clear so far. But in every direction the water was slipping down to a lower level — from the village-gates to the well outside, from the well to the fields and from the fields, in a thousand mud-cut channels, into the borrow-pits.

Half an hour brought the train to a halt amid gangs of muddy coolies, and here the passengers were ordered to disembark. It was now possible to see what the flood had done. From a flood's point of view it was not much. The water had merely formed on the embankment, as on a dam, and, when the pressure was sufficient, gone through — and out the other side. The red brick of the ballast lay scattered far across the fields as if it had been puffed out from under the rails. Elsewhere the metals were bowed sideways and sleepers tilted. These amateur alterations had been carried out in a few hours, at various places over a distance of half a mile.

The coolies with crowbars, pickaxes, and lumps of Tarakhi stone were busy packing the line. Already, during the hours of our detention at Gujrat, much had been done but there were places where the metals waggled when a hand was laid on them. In the middle of the 'slurry' — the wet sand, earth and stone — were two Heads of Departments who, at that hour, it would have been gross flattery to have called 'loafers'. The Assistant Engineer before mentioned was a speckless cherub compared to these gentlemen. They were girdled with prickly heat as with a garment; up to their knees was solid mud laid on with a palette-knife; they were hot, flannel-shirted, ammunition-booted, damp-haired, mucked, mired and laborious. When they were not platelaying, they were showing the coolies how to fit the jagged blocks of stone between the sleepers. This was a revelation. If gentlemen who have secured the thanks of Government, and command of Divisions, are forced, at a moment's notice, to quit the decencies of the Punjab Club to labour after the fashion of navvies, Railway service must be a highly dangerous and exhausting department. Up till that time, the Disinterested Observer had believed that breaks were mended by telegrams and written orders from an Office with a punkah in it. This impression is now dead. One of the two gentlemen owned an engine with which he was exceedingly anxious to test the other's packing, and neither seemed to object to laying their heads along the rails to see if the metals were coming back into position. While the Disinterested Observer sat on a pile of stones and felt how truly great is the dignity of labour, when some one else is working, the passengers were being transhipped and were walking over to the Lala Musa train. Yet another Departmental Head was superintending this; and, since a lady, even with both hands free, cannot walk comfortably in inch-deep slime over the tails of sleepers, took, as if it were the most natural thing in the world, a certain small and very much astonished baby from her arms, and bore it half a mile, issuing orders meantime. The quaint little face among the turmoil of hissing engines, clanking crowbars, and pickaxes, grunting coolies, rattling stone and all the hard realities of labour was a pretty touch. 'It took to me', said the Head of the Department gravely and solemnly, as he came back with a few hundred of the passengers from the Lala Musa train at his heels.

A new and peculiarly venemous variety of prickly heat grows by the side of lines. Also, Tarakhi stone cuts boots very badly. Gaps are not nice things to linger over, unless one is working on them.

The passengers had been all transhipped, and it was time to return to Lahore, and leave the Heads of Departments to their toil which they seemed to enjoy. The gentleman with the engine announced his intention of testing the next few yards of packed track; but before this was done the train went away to Lahore.

At 11 o'clock on Tuesday morning the waters were up, and doing damage; at 4 in the afternoon they were down. At 3 A.M. on Tuesday night in the rain, when all men hoped for a moon-light night, the work of packing began, and by 10 A.M. on Wednesday the Gap was practically repaired; though the rails had been left hanging in twenty-yard lengths.

Let us all be deeply thankful, therefore, that our share in Railway work is limited to travelling over the line, and writing furious letters to the papers when a break occurs.

# An Important Discovery

*Civil and Military Gazette, 17 August 1887*

**Attribution: Sussex Scrapbooks 28/3, p. 144**

Kipling admired Lewis Carroll from an early age and knew his work in intimate detail. The record of that admiration is scattered throughout his work; this article is one of the fullest and most explicit parts of that record, even though in comic form.

'The Poligs of the Oern Vent in dugard to the Brounincinl Coutrick is the colic of the unscrifulouse Gawler.' So ran the printed slip technically known as a 'rough proof'. The Aryan had surpassed himself; but, as he read, light filled the mind of the Reader. He had written — 'The policy of the Government in regard to the Provincial Contract is the policy of the unscrupulous lawyer', and, behold, with a mere turn of his wrist, the Aryan had glorified, and enriched with the wealth of an exuberant Orientalism that simple sentence, till it stood forth a gem, or rather a collection of gems! 'The Poligs of the Oern Vent' — George Meredith might have woven those words into the *Shaving of Shagpat*, and so made that dazzling piece of broidery yet more gorgeous. 'Brounincinl Coutrick' would suit admirably the manager of a travelling-circus. Conceive the effect, on white and red posters of: — 'To-night! To-night!! To-night!!! The Brounincinl Coutrick!' The words would draw thousands — millions. 'Unscrifulouse Gawler' again would furnish an absolutely unique and startling title for a semi-humourous, semi-grotesque, wholly-horrible story, of the American school, let us say. Think for a moment what fashion of ghoulo-demoniacal, triple-Quilpian, Jekyll-and-Hydeous character, the 'unscrifulouse Gawler' would be. Out of the incult wantonings of a Punjabi Mahommedan with a box of type, had been born the suggestions of three Brilliant Notions, did any man care to use them, exactly as ideas for patterns are conveyed to the designer by the chance-ruled twists of the Kaleidescope.

As the Reader was pondering these things, the Revelation smote him between the eyes. The world is very old, and men have been misprinting for more than four hundred years. Who then was the man who, greatly daring, had already utilized misprints. Who but the author of *'Through the Looking glass'*? The Reader turned hastily to the book and read slowly, aloud to himself, the opening verse of that coruscation of genius — *Jabberwocky*.

'This thing,' argued the Reader, full of the new light, 'was not made by Lewis Carroll. Else would a humble fellow-craftsman hear faintly but none the less clearly, the creaking of the machinery. This thing must have been *found* by him — a diamond all but clear, and needing only a few polishings, to sparkle on the band on the Crown of Absurdity for ever.' The Reader consulted the rough-proof in his hand, and thought of the ideas that had been suggested to him thereby. 'Had Lewis Carroll not been first in the field in that line, I could have made something good of the Oern Vent — an epic perhaps — and all from the first sentence of an ordinary newspaper-article. What Lewis Carroll did must have been this. He must have seen the rough proof of a very vilely written poem and — used it bodily for *Jabberwocky*. Perhaps, knowing the value of misprints, he made the printer drunk beforehand. The question therefore is, what is the poem that underlies the *Jabberwocky*?' The Reader addressed himself to finding it, and his patience was rewarded. His business was to discover the foundation, the bed-rock, whereon the supremely crazy structure had been built — the matrix whence the diamond had been drawn — the writing of the palimpsest. There are certain rules which regulate the incidence and nature of misprints. These rules, which vary with every type of calligraphy, had first to be discovered and then applied by the Reader to a poem written out in all varieties of hand-writing. Word by word and line by line, came to the surface, as a dead man's face rises through dark water, the original poem. Lo! Under the cap and bells of Folly, lay the drawn face of human woe, the oldest sorrow of all time. The Reader was filled with remorse for his impertinent curiosity. See now, how the first verse of the reconstructed poem runs, and you will admit that he had reason for his shame. But first let me give the opening stanza of *Jabberwocky*: —

> 'T was brillig and the slithy toves
>   Did gyre and gimble in the wabe.
> All mimsy were the borrow-groves
>   And the mome-raths out-grabe.

Bearing that in mind, read this: —

> 'T is fitting Arthur slight thy love,
>   Did gyve and gin bind in thy mate?"
> Ah! Memory wreathes the barren groves
>   And the worn paths of fate!

A word of explanation is necessary. The first two lines, you will
see, are addressed by some happy girl, rich in Arthur's love, to a
proud and passionate woman with a past, a widow, or a mistress
betrayed if the allusion to 'gyve and gin' have any meaning.
Hear the latter's wailing protest against the hardships of Destiny
that fills the last two lines. The memory of those fair days when
yet she was all in all to Arthur drives her to meet inevitable
scorn, bitter woman's scorn from Arthur's bride. On this
splendidly dramatic situation the key-note of the verses is
struck, and the pitch of passion is sustained throughout. You
may, as the Reader did, reconstruct it for yourself.

Yes, the whole of *Jabberwocky* hides a priceless poem, the
record of a soul's tragedy mangled in the first instance by a
drunken printer and, in its mutilated form, used with the insight
of genius, by Mr Lewis Carroll.

Great Literature! What would he not have produced from
the errors of a Punjabi compositor?

# The Longest Way Round

*Civil and Military Gazette, 30 September 1887*

**Attribution: Sussex Scrapbooks 28/3, pp. 146—7**

Kipling had been at Simla since late August and had now to
return — with what reluctance this article makes clear. The
floods down in the flatlands had caused a railway accident
near Rajpura, on the Umballa—Lhudiana line, on 18 September,
and the disruption meant that Kipling had now to make his way
back to his station, not exactly by 'the longest way round', but
by tedious conveyance over the break in the line.

Kipling's reference to the days when he travelled in the 'wake
of Ripons and Aitchisons' is to his visit to Patiala in March 1884,
when he attended the opening of the Mohindar College.

Trouville-sur-Khud looks its loveliest asleep in the very early morning; its beauty is most heart-renderingly apparent when the loaded-up tonga bugles furiously from the Mall below, and the driver announces that he will reach Kalka — for a consideration — in five hours. To go down by tonga it is necessary to sit up all night, still more necessary to dance, and most necessary of all to drown the sorrow of the coming morning, in any brew that seems good. About five A.M. arrives the Judgment, in the shape of a crisp and creeping 'headache in the hair', vain regrets for time misspent, cobwebs spun and broken, and irritability intensified by the scorn and the silence of the hills. Decidedly, the Himalayas are unsympathetic companions for a sixty-mile ride. They say so little and they imply so much. A few days before this most uncomfortable journey was undertaken, heavy rain had distinctly enlivened the route to the Plains, and the evidences of its work remained in slips of rather respectable size. Also rumours had reached Trouville-sur-Khud of an accident near Umballa and a breach of the Grand Trunk Road — unbreached for seventeen years. Having many rumours of its own, Trouville-sur-Khud paid but little attention to the news from below; and it was only when the tonga-driver announced at Kalka that there was no more work for the Gugger elephants and the Sahib might go his way dry-foot, that the traveller came out of his own thoughts, and began to concern himself with the Plains, so far as these affected his own comfort. In spite of the dust, born of four days' fierce sunshine, it was easy to see that the Kalka-Umballa road had been water-swept to the bone, and the white tide-marks on the tree trunks showed how high the flood has risen over the face of the land. An Irish bridge over which, six short weeks before, the torrent-driven boulders had been leaping like trout in fly-time was reduced to a dusty causeway; but the wash of the stones showed that a stream had but lately flowed that way. As a general rule, the Gugger, except when Viceroys pass over like the Israelites, may be trusted to make itself as objectionable as it can. Three yoke of bullocks were necessary to drag the lumbering dak-gharri across; for there was more water in the pestilent runnel than was right or proper at the end of the Rains.

Then sprang out of the earth a nomad khansamah who supplied soda-water to wayfarers on the banks of the stream, and demanded conveyance into Umballa; his day's work being done. He was prepared to give two bottles of soda-water— real Umballa soda-water — in payment of his fare; but, later on, he cheated, explaining that one bottle was empty and borrowing as much of the Sahib's smoking-tobacco as he could. After all, the Sahib should have known that a khansamah who makes his own cigarettes out of old *Civil and Military Gazettes*, and talks English, is not the sort of man to be worsted in a bargain.

At Umballa, the waste water hung about in larger patches and there was a faint unwholesome smell of rank greenery in the air.

The Station-Master, throned in a comfortable chair, explained that the North Western Railway had ceased booking northwards beyond Rajpura, and that it would take three days, more or less, to go round *via* Delhi, Rewari, and Ferozepore. There was a break beyond Rajpura of miles, but there were ekkas waiting at the break and, possibly, *dak gharris*. The length of the break he did not exactly know, but it was of several miles. A train would arrive at 10 P.M. in which the traveller might, if he felt so disposed, journey.

Allowing ten minutes for finished and encyclopaedic abuse of the Government, the North West Railway, and everyone connected with it, and twenty minutes for dinner, there still remained two and half hours' of waiting between seven and ten. Most opportunely, Thomas, snow-white as to his clothes, brass-badged, and heavy-footed, came by on duty — and the rest was easy, for Thomas is a cosmopolitan. The traveller saw what might or might not have been the beginning of a tragedy. A passenger missed, in some curious way, a down-country train and was stranded on Umballa platform, declaring that all his kit was in the carriage. Thomas — there were two of him — watched the man as cats watch a mouse, and the outcome of their investigation, under bent eye-brows, was: — ' 'E's no civilian'. Indeed, he looked miserably poor and dejected, and hung about the station watching Thomas as intently as Thomas watched him. For half an hour, the two Thomases talked, never taking their eyes off the stranger, of such things as they conceived would interest the traveller. But their minds were on the man who had been left behind. He presently lit a pipe and, with ostentatious free and easiness, came to join the little circle on the bench. Thomas fell into a deep and frozen silence. The man put down his pipe, and jerking his thumb over his shoulder at another Thomas further up the platform said: — ' 'E sez 'e's seen me before. I should like to know *where* 'e 'as seen me'. Thomas held his peace. 'I'll lay 'e asn't seen me any wheres.' 'I never said 'e 'ad,' said Thomas 'but 'ow did you come to know 'is name?' 'I called 'im that on chanst' said the man 'same as I might call you anything on chanst.' Thomas turned to his cheroot and his fixed stare at the man without collar or tie. The night was a reasonably cool one, but the man began to perspire gently, till his face shone under the lamplight, 'All my kit's in that carriage' he said at last, but the attempt to break the ice failed. He rose and went his way up the platform whistling. Then said the second Thomas, who had, up to that time, held his peace, in the tones of a brooding dove: —' 'E's got regimental socks on. I seed 'em.' Thomas the first shook his head: — 'Ay! But 'e asn't been showed yet. They'll get 'im at Ghazerabad or Sharanpur if they wants 'im.' The conversation was not intended for 'civilian' ears, any more than was the expression of grief at the possible loss of thirty rupees, or the prophecy that the man 'would come an' 'ang about barricks tomorrer'. Over beer, Thomas became more communicative, and, in a perfectly abstract light be it understood, discussed the theory and practice of desertion — up-country and at Calcutta — 'where a man can make friends with the ships'.

Thomas the first had been eight years a Servant of the Queen, and had no fault to find with the army. Thomas, the Second, explained that desertion 'didn't mean much more than twenty-eight days any 'ow, an' at 'Ome boys was always runnin' off to see their mammy'. 'If a boy gets checked too much, sometimes 'e can't stand it an' then 'e goes. But that is because of a man and not of a service,' said Thomas the first. Outside the refreshment room stood the man, and he peered in thirstily. It was the fable of the Wolf and Watch-dog dressed in human clothes, and Thomas the first saw it in this light. ' 'E's a civilian,' said he nodding his head towards the door. '*An*' a free man' said Thomas the second, who had seen the regimental socks. 'Well! 'Ere's luck.' They went out and grouped themselves in picturesque attitudes near the man, and the lamp-light glinted on the brass letterings on their shoulders.

The up-train came in and with it passengers who had been

personally acquainted with the break near Umballa. They had been forced to deal with it in the way of business — which means, in these matters, to risk their lives over it. From their words it was possible to see how big an affair the break had been, and how narrowly the accident of Sunday the 18th instant had escaped ranking as a champion butchery. But of these things Trouville-sur-Khud knew and cared but little, and the sudden change almost from the threshold of the music-filled, dance-throbbing Town Hall to the grim pithy talk on the platform, was like stepping from a Turkish to a cold shower bath.

Fifteen miles of line, men said, had been rendered unusable by the biggest flood within the last twenty years. A stationhouse had been swamped; there were two and twenty breaks in two miles of the Rajpura-Patiala line; most of Patialla city had been cleared out; the Gugger had nearly carried away its bridge; dead cattle and black-buck had been washed on to the line, and at Serai Bunjara a Huge Stink from a cemetery of bullocks awaited the traveller. This was cheering. The account of the actual accident, the smashing up and carrying of help to the train, told after the manner of Herodotus, was a small epic. The train was under charge of one of the most careful drivers on the line. He had got down on to the footplate to look at the permanent way with a lantern, for it was raining in torrents, and, even as he looked, something happened and the wreck began. The generally received opinion among experts seems to be that a rail sunk into the soft slush as the train passed. . . . and the rest was confusion. The actual number of deaths accounted for is three, but as the train turned over into water it is possible that some people may have been killed and washed away. This however cannot be lightly said. Still it seems certain that the loss of life was very small indeed. If compensation be given to the relatives of the dead, the chances are very much in favour of every poor wandering corpse that has been whelmed by the flood being faithfully credited to the Government. After the accident occurred, the guard walked back, it seemed, to the last Station which the train had left as sound and safe as any way-side station need be. When he reached it it was flooded out, so quickly had the flood come down. The Gugger — that stream which is not worth bridging — is credited with having done a good deal of damage, as the reports from the districts will doubtless show.

Leaving Umballa and listening to the story of the break at

the same time the traveller presently arrived at Simbul station, or rather what was left of it, for the station-house was roofless, windowless and doorless and, in the light of the half-moon, seemed as though gutted by fire. The flood here must have been six or eight feet deep. At Rajpura, ten miles from Umballa, the train stopped for the night; there being three thousand coolies working on the line just ahead. It was necessary to take an ekka from Rajpura to Sirhind, a distance of eighteen miles, to catch a train that would come in at three in the morning and go northward at eight.

One of the least respect-worthy of the characters in *Ten Thousand a Year*, weeps copiously after his fortune has passed into the hands of a counter-jumper, remembering, as the shades of even fall, that he was once accustomed to dine, sumptuously, at seven o'clock. In like manner, as the traveller went out of Rajpura station and was attacked by a crowd of unwashed ekka-men, he groaned, remembering that he had, in years past, been wont to quit that station in the wake of Ripons and Aitchisons behind four prancing steeds, silver-studded as to their harness, and scarlet as to the raiment of their drivers. Then he fell over the hinder parts of an ekka where the shafts cross like swallow-wings, and thought hard things of the Empire and its Rulers. The third-class passengers meantime had got out, and were cheerfully tramping towards Sirhind.

An ekka is a bundle of tortures, being made up of Ixion's wheel, in duplicate and triangular, St Lawrence's gridiron, of country string which covers the body with patterns, and the shirt of Nessus, worn by many Nessuses, spread over all. It allows for no dignity, it is destruction to the liver, its motions are unseemly, and its pony — smells. No man who habitually rides in an ekka can be clean, or moral, self respecting or sturdily fashioned in his bones. An Englishman in an ekka is a racial anomaly, and it is well for him if he does not become the 'pasture-ground of thousands', in ten minutes. A mournful procession of three ekkas set out to Sirhind, as the moon began to go down, along the Grand Trunk Road which was being mended in places. The ponies made their own pace — a trot of 'not less than four, or more than six miles an hour' — and that trot they maintained without a break till the end.

At first — for three minutes, at least — the novelty of an ekka's motion is attractive, Afterwards, the passenger would

SIX PRECIOUS SOULS      TO DASH THROUGH

AND ALL      THICK AND

A GOG      THIN

Cowper

THE EKKA      NORTHERN INDIA

Copyright 1891]      [by J. Lockwood Kipling

*The ekka, a tea-tray on wheels, dear,*
*Flies past as its occupants sit,*
*—For a pony you know never feels, dear—*
*All five pulling hard at one bit.*

fain alight. Later still, he would sell his soul for sleep, and all the while he is only restrained from murdering the driver because of his own inability to drive the car. In time, the ekkas fell violently down a steep place off the road and the passengers had to alight and walk over soft and smelling ground, facetiously called the 'diversion' of the Grand Trunk, here broken for the length of two railway carriages. The water had taken out, as one drives a cheese-scoop through cheese, as much of a twelve-foot embankment as it required for its own purposes; and this breach was the direct cause of the break on the railway hard by. So long as the water was still and dammed no great harm arose, but, when the flood raced through the breach, the set of the rush tore up the line to the right of the Trunk road and scattered the ballast across the country. The sides of the breach in the road were sheer, and the low moon looked through the opening and grinned. It was an unpleasant picture-frame. Once more on the Grand Trunk, the ekkas settled steadily to their work and the beauty of the journey began to declare itself. On either side, half veiled behind the shadows of the fringing trees, lay great pools of water, and in some of the pools floated black blobs which commended themselves to the nose as deceased cattle.

The air was full of a marshy smell, and the night began to grow chilly. Then, while the driver was adjusting a foul rag that he called a purdah, the pony ran away and into another ekka. This it did twice, till the purdah fell down and was used as a wrap. There were — call them drawing-pins, or Norfolk-Howards in that purdah, and its *esprit de corps*, horse for the most part, was indescribable and unequalled, until the night-wind blew across the fields some small portion of the Huge Stink promised at Umballa. The purdah then became a sweet and desirable thing — a wrap to wrap the head in and wind round the nostrils.

For three hours and fifty minutes the ponies trotted through what appeared to be the length and breadth of the Indian Empire. The moon went out and only the star-light showed the white road and the trees and the waste of land on either side. Once, a man came out of the dark and demanded if the ekka plied for hire. He was going to Sirhind and had a child with him. He was taken up and wished to flee, being presumably unaccustomed to Sahibs who sub-let ekkas; but was presently comforted and began to haggle about the fare. One pice, picked out of the corner of a waist-cloth carried him nine English miles. The unclean little coin will be preserved as a memento of a most genial companion and a very wicked little boy who wept continuously and, when not watched, tried to fall out upon the road.

So the child cried, and the man babbled of the weather at Mustaphabad, and the driver beat the pony, and the crying and the speech and the jolt of the ekka, wove themselves into an uneasy dream of a waltz that *would* change to a polka where the dancers bumped horrible, and of an 'extra' that was always being promised and never given, and of a supper that rotted on the tables as it stood, because all the merry-makers had been washed away in a flood, and Simla Town Hall was filled with deserters hiding in corners. . . . Here the leading ekka dropped a wheel and came down with a crash, while the second ekka nearly fell over it, for horse and man were asleep. Half an hour later, the funeral reached Sirhind and the break had been crossed.

But mark the astuteness of the Oriental! The man from Mustaphabad, who had honestly paid a pice for his ride, demanded *bakshish*, and got it. Just before falling asleep in the train, it struck the donor that the man from Mustaphabad must have travelled in an *ekka* before, and that the journey could not have damaged him greatly.

To an Englishman, jolted, contused, filled with little bamboo splinters, stiff, sore, dusty and bitten, a hundred rupees would have been no sort of consolation.

# 'The City of the Two Creeds'

*Civil and Military Gazette, 1 October 1887*

**Attribution: Sussex Scrapbooks 28/3, p. 148**

This article must be distinguished from the two-part article that Kipling published in the *CMG* in 1885 as 'The City of Two Creeds' (19 and 22 October, reprinted as one of the unauthorised Ballard-Martindell pamphlets, and in Harbord's *Reader's Guide to Rudyard Kipling's Work*, I, 1961). The earlier article, like the later, describes the Mohurrum festival in Lahore, the 'small Mohurrum fight' alluded to at the beginning of the later article; it is perhaps by way of allusion to the earlier item that Kipling puts the title of this one in quotation marks (note also that an extra 'the' has been added to the title).

Mohurrum (or Moharram) is the festival commemorating the deaths of the Imams Hassan and Hussein, when replicas of the Imams' tombs, called *tazias*, are carried in procession; it was frequently the occasion for fighting between Muslim and Hindu.

The novel that Kipling mentions, *The City of Sunshine*, was written by Alexander Allardyce and published in 1877.

(From a Correspondent)

Two years ago, Lahore at the end of the hot weather was enlivened by a small Mohurrum fight in the City, and the outcries
of many bunniahs. A British regiment, to the extent of four
companies, was dug out of its bed at Mian Mir, the 14th B[engal].
L[ancers]. smote with their lance-butts on the toes of the peace-
breakers and Lahore Fort was crowded with riotous subalterns,
while most of the high officials in the station mounted horses
and ran hither and thither. In the dearth of other news, down-
country papers called the scuffle 'Riots' and the 'Lahore Riots'
it has remained in the memory of man ever since. Forty-one
years ago, it may be mentioned incidentally, when an overzealous sword-maker was hanged outside the Delhi gate in the
early morning, the night's work in which he had taken a leading
part was dignified with no loftier title than that of 'a disturbance'.
    This year's Mohurrum has passed with a peace that was al-
most dullness. No one threw bricks into the tinselled *tazias*, and
none except the police excited their neighbours with *lathis*. A
'processional' conflict in one of the narrow gullies, when all
are so tightly packed that they can do nothing save shout abuse,
is worth seeing, and still more impressive is the rush that follows,
on a rumour that the *gorah-log* are coming. But Lahore has
given up these dissipations under the benign influence of a
native municipality and the education of the University. Because many hundreds of years ago Yezid, son of Mowwajib, first
of the Ommeiad Caliphs of Damascus, met, on the plains of
Kerbela, west of the Euphrates, and slew Hossain and Hussan,
sons of Ali, First or Fourth (as you are Shiah or Sunni) of the
Caliphs, and of Fatima, his wife, it is now necessary for every
Deputy Commissioner in the Province, once a year, to spend half
the night in a native city while the representations of the tombs
of the butchered and Blessed Imams stagger up and down the
ways. The consequences of any act, some moralists hold, are
infinite and eternal; and this instance backs the theory.
    On Wednesday as soon as the darkness fell, the drums began
throbbing in the heart of the city though the three and twenty
*tazias* were not to begin moving till half-past eleven. This year
as in previous ones, there did not seem to be the slightest
attempt towards a massing of spectacular effect. As in the
famous Caucus race, witnessed by 'Alice in Wonderland', the
*tazias* began where they liked and left off as seemed good to

them. A little trouble on the part of the owners, a little fore-
sight and a careful disposition of torches would have done great
things. The City by night, and by moonlight more particularly,
supplies one of the most fascinating, if least savoury, walks in
the station. The yard-wide gullies into which the moonlight
cannot struggle are full of mystery, stories of life and death and
intrigue of which we, the Mall abiding, open-windowed, purdah-
less English know nothing and believe less. The open square,
under the great front of Wazir Khan's mosque where any man
may find a bed and remarkably good *kababs*, if he knows where
to go, is full of beauty even when the noonday heat silences
the voices of men and puts the pigeons of the mosque to sleep.
Properly exploited, our City, from the Taksali to the Delhi
Gate, and from the wrestling-ground to the Badami Bagh would
yield a store of novels to which the *City of Sunshine* would be
as 'water unto wine'. However, until some one lifts its name
into the light of a new fame Lahore is only a fraction of a
Deputy Commissioner's charge, to be watched, drained, coaxed
and scolded as such. From the Delhi Gate to the Soneri Musjid —
was it the founder or the architect of this mosque who, ignoble
end, was slippered to death by a too powerful mistress? — runs
the main artery of the city, the Road of Globe Trotters and
inferior folk of their kidney. At the Golden Musjid, a little
beyond the cloth-seller's shops, the first *tazia*, a gorgeous
arrangement in tin and tinselry was reeling and plunging like
a ship in a heavy sea. It is the proud privilege of all the little
boys who can, by any means, lay hands upon them to carry
the torches of rolled rag dipped in oil. The boys were prancing
and squealing with impatience, occasionally chasing each other
across the road, and under the legs of the mounted policeman's
horse who was a patient beast and went to sleep when the drums
were beating under his venerable nose. As the hour of the
general move forward to the Shalmi Gate drew nearer, the din
increased; *tazia* answering *tazia* and the gullies holding the roll
of the drums as the hills hold thunder.

The Mochi Darwaza *tazias* were some four or five in number
and had packed themselves into an especially narrow street which
they did their best to choke. Seen from the safe shelter of a well-
curb the movement was picturesque; but after a few years the
eye of the dweller in this country becomes scared and his heart
hardens, so that the finest effects of red light and black shadow,
seas of turbans, upturned faces and arms tossed aloft, fail to

impress him as anything new or startling. The heat, and the heat in the City even on a September night was inconvenient, the smells and the noise touch him as keenly as ever; but it is impossible to wax enthusiastic over these things.

A *tazia* advanced, swayed, shook, retreated, was driven back, dived forward and passed with a yell, a shout, a patter of hundreds of feet, a blaze of torches and a rain of lighted tow, to be succeeded by another *tazia*, another mob and occasionally a brass band of terrible quality. In the pauses of the processions the *gutkas* leapt into the middle of the way and fought with lath swords carrying arm guards to the elbow. With the best will in the world, and all possible desire to recover 'the first fine careless rapture' of the griffin who gazes on the gaudier aspects of the East, the attention wandered from the crowd to the watch, and interest was swallowed up in a yawn. There had been no trouble, the City was quiet and another Mohurrum had been safely tided over. Beyond the city walls lay civilization in the shape of iced drinks and spacious roads.

But one feature of the last night of the Mohurrum cannot be overlooked. In the broader streets, surrounded by the faithful, sat Maulvis reading the story of the death of the Blessed Imams. Their *mimbars* were of the rudest, but the walls behind them were in most cases gay, with glass lamps, cuckoo-clocks, vile 'export' trinketry, wax flowers and kindred atrocities. A Normandy shrine could hardly have been in worse taste, but, looking at the men who listened, one forgot the surroundings. They seemed so desperately in earnest, as they rocked to and fro, and lamented. The manner of the Maulvis' preaching varied as much as their audiences. One man, austere, rugged-featured, and filthily clad, had sat down upon a shop-board in a side-alley and his small congregation were almost entirely provincial. He preached literally, as the spirit moved him, and whatever Power may have come upon him held, and shook his body. The *jats* made no sign. Only one small child ran up and put his hand upon the preacher's knee, unterrified by the working face and the torrent of words.

Elsewhere, five massive wooden bedsteads had been piled one above the other to make a *mimbar* for one who read from a book. He was a strikingly handsome man, level in his speech and philosophical, it seemed, in his arguments. A dirty sheet had been thrown over the uppermost bedstead and by some sport of chance had draped itself 'into great laps and folds of sculptor's work' perfect and solid, so that the preacher looked as though he had been newly taken out of a fresco in a certain palace by the water. In the lowest bedstead several children wearied with the weight of their turbans and ornaments slept peacefully, turning a little in their sleep as the voice of the preacher rose above its normal pitch.

Yet another *chabil* was filled by quite a different sort of person – a smiling, smooth-featured *Hajii* who moved his hands gently and persuasively, to beckon people up the path of good living. He was evidently the local Talmage. He sat in a flower and pot-plant decorated verandah, on a handsome carpet, with stretched cloths above his head. All classes had come to hear him, from the chaprassi to the native gentlemen who owned a horse. Just across the road, Jezebel, in all the insolent affluence of beauty bedecked with *lon* and *tikkah* looked out of the window to listen, and into a recess below the window the chaprassi hoisted his blear-eyed shrivelled mother, old and hideous as Gagool, that she might be clear of the crowd. Jezebel dropped the hand that supported her chin and as it fell, it touched the head of the chaprassi's mother and there rested.

It was a curious picture, one that remained longest in the mind after the crush and smother and blaze of the last night of the Mohurrum.

# To Kabul and Back: Mr O'Meara's Experiences

*Civil and Military Gazette, 27 October 1887*

Attribution: Sussex Scrapbooks 28/4, pp. 6–7

A rare instance of Kipling's conducting an interview. It may have furnished some hints for 'The Ballad of the King's Mercy'.

The Mr Pyne mentioned in the article had joined the Amir's service in 1885; in 1893 he served as the Amir's ambassador to the Viceroy of India, and was knighted.

A great many people have seen His Highness Abdur Rahman, Amir of Afghanistan, ally of the British Government, and very strong ruler, at close quarters. But few men have been permitted to see him as he appears in the midst of his own people, in the full swing of his daily and royal office-work and the government of such turbulent territories as those of Afghanistan. A chance which, since times are troublous and the lives of monarchs in the East uncertain, may never occur again, has fallen in the way of Dr A. O'Meara, the well-known Dental Surgeon of Upper India, and that gentleman has much to tell about it.

Some few months ago, it will be remembered, the Amir demanded the services of a dentist, for reasons which we may presume appealed to him strongly at the time. In response to that demand Dr O'Meara, taking the word of the Amir for a sufficient guarantee for the safety of his life, went to Cabul on August 15th. As the telegram has already informed us, he returned to British territory a few days ago, and is now staying in Lahore.

Some portions of the story of his travels and impressions, as told by himself in the course of conversations, are likely to be of interest to our readers. It must be premised that Dr O'Meara went into the country, as he himself says, strictly for business-purposes; to get to Cabul, to see the Amir and to return as soon as might be. It was not his intention to concern himself with the tangled web of political intrigue in the country in any way whatever.

'I went into Afghanistan,' said Dr O'Meara quietly, 'under the impression that I was not at all likely to return. I fancied that this would be my last and longest holiday.' And so far as the journey from Peshawar to Cabul was concerned, he had some justification for his belief. Six of the Amir's men took possession of him on the Border, and escorted him to Cabul with all speed. They took the worthy doctor up-hill and down-dale, across country, and, in a manner, smuggled him through. 'I think some of the Shinwaris had burnt a caravan somewhere and my escort did not want to meet them. They kept off the regular road altogether, took me up the beds of rivers and passes and over hills, and goodness knows where.' This in itself was not cheering, but the most trying episode of the march came last. Perplexed by fear of the Shinwaris, or desiring to introduce their charge as swiftly as might be into the presence of the Amir, Dr O'Meara's sturdy caterans took him over the last three marches in one day. He was thirteen hours in the saddle under a blazing sun, and his feelings towards his guides was that of unmixed hatred; for a ride from Jugdullack to Butkhak, ten miles from Cabul, in August, is not soothing.

At Butkhak he was met by an Englishman, Mr Pyne, Engineer of Afghanistan generally, and Superintendent of the Amir's workshops in particular. He had ridden from Peshawar to Cabul by *pagdundies* in eleven days; and the fame of his coming had preceded him. The populace of Cabul understood that an Englishman one hundred years old had come in to attend to their ruler, and were somewhat astonished to find Dr O'Meara below their estimate. However, they said that he was sixty years old, and from that day forward to the hour of his departure seem to have taken no interest in him whatever. 'The people don't take the faintest notice of you. You might be a fly, for any sign they make,' said Dr O'Meara thankfully. Cabul was reached on the 26th day of August, the Amir being then at Paghman, his summer residence, eighteen miles beyond and at a much higher elevation than the city, which is a remarkably evil-smelling place worse than any Indian city. To Paghman accordingly Dr O'Meara went to pay the Amir a first visit. He was a good deal knocked up by his ride, and rather doubtful as to the possibilities of return. 'I was wondering how in the world I should get back again, or whether I should be allowed to get back at all.' It will be conceded that this feeling was, considering the nature of [the] good folk of Afghanistan, perfectly justifiable.

The first interview with the Amir took place, as did all the others, in daily durbar. 'He was at work in the Paghman gardens, with some of his officials round him. He was working when I first saw him, and he is always at work.' 'My opinion is,' said Dr O'Meara, 'that he is overworking himself. He holds a durbar wherever he happens to be, and he shifts his quarters a good deal from Paghman to the Baber gardens, about half a mile from the city, and back again. Of course all my conversation with him had to be through an interpreter, so I could only see what was going on. As often as not, the durbar was in the open air — anywhere; or sometimes at Paghman it was held in huge durbar buildings — sheds you may call them, supported by wooden pillars with white roofs. But wherever he went the work always seemed the same. He received letters all day long, from all parts of the country, wrote his remarks at the bottom of the paper, and passed the letter on to the official who recorded it. His courtiers formed a rough sort of semicircle

near him, and any living man in the kingdom, so far as I could
see or learn, could make his way to the Durbar, get within
about three or four yards of the Amir, hand in his petition, or
speak to him personally. The manner of the petitioners was
cringing – abjectly fawning; but they could all speak to him,
and he listened to them.'

'Could you guess what was going forward?' 'Not I – nor
could anyone I think. There was nothing in the Amir's face to
show what he was feeling, either when he read the letters or
spoke to the men. He is a. very quiet man. I have seen men
taken away somewhere, outside gardens; and I suppose . . .
but I could tell nothing from the Amir's face. Justice isn't
executed in his presence, you know. There was no visible
emotion on the faces of the men round him. If he said anything
directly to them, they said that it was good and right; but you
could never judge of anything by looking at the Durbar.'

'Yes, but when you got the Amir in private – ' 'I saw him
always when he was at work.' 'Then do you mean to say he
– ' 'I mean to say that I did whatever I had to do to him in
Durbar, on the spot. When I first saw him he was in a little
low chair, and did not seem anxious to be treated at once. I
explained that I only wanted to look at his mouth first, and
I looked and gave him my opinion. He said through the interpreter: – "Yes! I think myself that is what is wanted" and from
that time he put himself entirely in my hands.' 'What sort of
patient was he?' 'Well, I only wish all my patients were as
manageable as he was.' 'And what did you have to do?' 'Oh!
A lot of things that only concern him; but whatever I did was
done before all the crowd so to speak. He said that he was very
comfortable where he was, in his seat, and if he did not mind
his ministers looking on, I had no reason to object.' 'How did
they regard the operations?' 'They made no sign; when he spoke
they said the equivalent of *bahut accha*. That was all.' 'And you
actually had to draw one of the Amir's teeth *coram publico*?'
'That was one of the things for which I had left India. But you
don't suppose that he would chop my head off in durbar if
he was hurt. My business was to cure him, and he is a perfectly
rational man.' Dr O'Meara laughed, and the conversation turned
to Abdur Rahman as a man and a King. 'He is a grand man,' said
Dr O'Meara, 'and he is feared. I don't suppose rulers with his
powers can be popular, but he is feared. They said in Cabul that
he knows everything that is going on. I know myself that every-

thing I did, and every walk and ride I took, were reported to him. And the same system seems to exist all over the country. I suppose he is feared as much as any man in the world, within his own jurisdiction. But here is another side of the picture. When I was at Paghman — Paghman was my headquarters till the 16th of September, and then the Baber Gardens — I rode into Cabul one morning an hour or so behind the Amir; thinking I had given him and all the cavalry with him ample time to get on. There were about three thousand horses of sorts with him and presently I caught up to the cavalcade. The Amir was riding a little way ahead, and, now and again, he would stop to take a petition from some ragged ruffian on the roadside. In one instance a dirty old woman delayed the march. The Amir stopped, read her petition, on a little scrap of paper, said something and passed on. This sort of thing was happening along the entire route to Cabul, and seemed to be part of the regular routine. The Amir is not in the habit of laughing. He may be a humourous man, but he seemed weighed down with work; for he trusts nothing to underlings. My opinion, so far as I could form one, was that the Amir really does work for his people. I don't say he does it in a kind or a civilized way, for the country does not admit of civilized government, but none the less all his thoughts are for his people. It seems to me, from what I saw of him, that he is a man a good deal in advance of his age, and that his people don't understand it. Sooner or later, if he lives, he will have a railway running from Cabul to Paghman. Perhaps it will be only a royal freak to save himself. At least, though he showed me all hospitability, there was no show of magnificence in his surroundings. He said the other day in Durbar, *apropos* of the difficulty of getting in his revenues: — "One quarter of the money that is mine rightly I get; one quarter I get by fighting for; one quarter I do not get at all; and those who should pay the fourth quarter do not know in whose hands to place it." ' 'Did you see the gun-factories by any chance?' 'Well, I took up an English Martini-Henri carbine, and when I was in Cabul was shown and offered, for one-third of my weapon's price, a Cabul-made article which, to look at, seemed just as good as mine. Of course, it had been hand-rifled, and I don't think it could have shot absolutely true, but still it was surprisingly well made for a thing made by hand. If they can get English machinery into the workshops, I should think that they could make really first-class rifles. The Cabuli workmen are very clever and very quick to take a hint. I had a man out of the Amir's workships put under me in order that I might give him some rough knowledge of my profession; and he was very quick at picking up things.

'I fancy he will do his best too. When I was in Cabul the Amir seemed to think that I had better stay and "make teeth" as they called it, for all the people in the country. However, I had his promise that I was to go back; but I made teeth for some of the ministers, and there should be a demand for my pupil's services. Sufi Haq Khan is an Afghan about forty-five years old. I left him "making teeth" for the Governor of Cabul, who has almost as much power as the Amir in matters of life and death. Sufi Haq Khan is not likely to bungle his work.'

Again Dr O'Meara laughed, and the laugh suggested an enquiry. 'Did you see anything startling in or about Cabul?' 'Never mind what I saw beyond what I am telling you. You cannot govern Afghanistan like India. I went up, as I have told you, anything but hopeful about coming back and I have returned rather in love with the place. Cabul is a nice spot to spend a holiday in. The climate, when I was there, up to the 11th of October, was delightful — like Simla — and I enjoyed myself thoroughly as soon as I had picked up my health. There was little or no rain at Cabul, and only three showers fell at Paghman, and life under canvas — for I was in tents the whole time, in order to follow the Amir better — was exceeding pleasant. The Amir wants me to come again, and I should like to go. Mr Pyne and I rode wherever we liked, not only in the main streets but up the allies of Cabul city, and there was not the slightest attempt made to interfere with us. As I have said, the people took no notice whatever of us. There were a couple of Usbegs behind us; but on one occasion we got rid of them and went all round the city; and nothing happened.'

A little later Dr O'Meara showed the Medal of Honour with which he been invested. This was a heavy gold medaillon about twice the size of a spade-guinea, and thrice as thick stamped on the face with the sun in its splendour, enclosing a conventional wreath, within which was an inscription in Persian, which translated read: — 'For Honour'. The back of the medal was blank, and the whole was suspended by a clasp from a narrow loop of green silk, worked with a curious pattern in purple. 'It is a pretty memento of a very interesting visit,' said Dr O'Meara.

'Mr Pyne and I came away together. Mr Pyne is going home, by the way, for a time. He has been some months in the Amir's service, and he seems popular. They say in Cabul, that if he will only bring back an English *memsahib*, they will lay down a mall, a *pukka* English mall, three miles long, for the couple to drive up and down. That sounds like progress doesn't it? Well, Mr Pyne and I left together, but we had to wait first for ten days in hourly, not daily, expectation of the Amir's permission to go. This time I had the satisfaction of travelling on the regular road, and we had a mounted escort twenty-five strong. As soon as permission came, we did not wish to wait on the road; and I think we did fully half our journey at a canter. The Amir might have wanted me to come back, or the Governor of Cabul might have discovered that Sufi Haq Khan's "Made teeth" were deficient in some way. We did not care to give him the chance of stopping us; so we came through from Cabul to Peshawur in ten days, doing the nine miles from Jumrud to Peshawur at the end of the march in under the hour. 'All the same,' said Dr O'Meara reflectively, 'though I was in a hurry to come out, I should like to go again — or better still, to Kandahar. So far as I am concerned I found the Amir extremely pleasant.'

'But, one minute, Doctor, what will happen to Sufi Haq Kahn, if —

'Aha! You had better ask the Governor of Cabul. You want to know too much.'

And here Dr O'Meara declared the interview at an end.


# The Great Strike (A Tale of 1910)

*Civil and Military Gazette, 5 November 1887*


**Attribution: Sussex Scrapbooks 28/4, pp. 9—10**

The decline in the exchange value of the rupee was a standard grievance throughout Kipling's years in India. Everyone had a theory or a remedy, but the generally desperate character of

feeling in face of this mysterious loss of income is made clear
enough by Kipling's sketch.


The remedy was simple — so simple that, when all was over
and the rupee stood at *2s.—2d.* once more, every one wondered
why it had been overlooked so long. Men had devasted [*sic*] the
country with meetings to protest against the 'present serious
inconvenience arising out of the fall in silver' or the 'semi-
pauperised condition of the European population'; but no one
paid any special attention to their words, and subscriptions
in aid of the 'Cause' could not, when the rupee stood at 11¾d.,
be very large. There was an impression abroad that 'this state
of things could not continue much longer'; but no one dreamed
that it could ever be set right by juggling with the currency. All
had passed from the argumentatively philosophical frame of
mind to the irrationally determined — and this is the much
more dangerous mood. They had decided that something
*must* be done and that all the cheap production in the empire
did not console them for having to drive in bamboo-carts and
send their children to Hill-schools where they picked up curious
accents and learned a great deal too much of life. At Home,
when the Masses wanted anything new — a day's ration or the
stock of any tradesman's shop — they just assembled in their
might and hammered at the Lions in Trafalgar Square or threw
brickbats into the windows of the *Times* Office, and all their
wants were immediately gratified. This hurt the feelings of the
poor wretches in India, and they held a conference on their
grievances. The Army, of course, stood aloof, but it grinned
cheerfully, and said that it would be most happy to march
against the mutineers. Some of the more anchylosed spirits at
the conference said that the steps proposed would be absurd,
but others held that a mere hint of those steps would be enough
to bring the Secretary of State to his bearings. There would be a
stupendous novelty in the move. It was decided to exempt the
lower grades of society from taking any part in the campaign.
They were to attend to the railways and things of that kind
without heeding. The Army also was not to be mixed up in the
affair at all; but the Civil Engineers rallied round the standard
as one man.

There was a certain natural hesitation in being the first to begin; but a Deputy Commissioner leaped into the gap, and he was a bachelor — said that he was ready to sacrifice himself for the good of the community. He led off, alone and unaided, and when he informed his Assistant that there would be no more work done in the district, that young gentleman telegraphed into the capital that his chief was insane. Now the strike of a Deputy Commissioner being absolutely new in the annals of Indian administration, the Government at first wished to send him Home on Medical Certificate, but he declined. He wished it to be distinctly understood that he was sane but on strike till the rupee was nearer two shillings than one. He would be delighted to resume his executive duties when. . . . but at this point the Government 'broke' him in the *Gazette*, and he was ordered to go away. He went into the capital and was supported by his friends. The case appeared in the English papers and excited a certain amount of comment.

A few days later, an Executive Engineer in charge of about 230 miles of rather important railway, lost interest in his labours and went on a prolonged shooting-tour, picking up an Assistant Commissioner *en route*. There was no trace of soreness in their letters to Government. They thanked it for its uniform consideration and sent it some teal; but they intimated that the section of the line and the sub-division of the district had better be looked after; a few hundred thousand cubic feet of stone and a few tahsildars required supervision — at least that was their humble opinion. They were 'broke' promptly, and a wing of a British regiment despatched to bring them in as deserters. They were brought in in chairs on the shoulders of the officers — and this time the proceedings were telegraphed Home. The London journals were not facetious. They said that English gentlemen were not in the habit of striking for nothing. Then a Commissioner — camp, salute and all — went out on strike. He said that he had been sacrificing himself to the Empire for about half a century, and that it was getting monotonous. He admitted that his duty was to set an example, and he considered that this example would be largely followed. He went into the hills and lived on his prestige and the balance of his current-account, while the Government wrote agonizing letters to him.

*Then* the blaze broke out. A Border Deputy Commissioner

led off, by shutting up his *kutcherry* and smoking on the roof.
He said that he was the only human being who knew how to
soothe the Haramzada Kheyls, and that he would be most
happy to talk to that turbulent tribe when the rupee was one-
and-ten-pence, say: for he was a moderate man.

A Southern Deputy Commissioner followed suit, and the
whole country was pitted with districts in what the native papers
called 'the *status quo*', and the Persian Gulf telegraph broke
down under the strain of the telegrams from Simla to the India
Office — 'Urgent, State, Bearing'.

Now the beauty of the arrangement was that it was impossible
to send troops against a man in *pyjamas*, smoking on a housetop.
He always received them kindly and asked the officers to breakfast. The troops enjoyed those expeditions.

Another interesting feature of the case was the incompetence
of the substitutes for men on strike.

It takes twelve years to make an average Deputy Commissioner,
and the *badlis* were rather too raw from the hands of the Civil
Service Commissioners. The third strong point was that the
strike affected the very axle of the administration. A district
may struggle on without a Judge or a Forest Officer, or even a
District Engineer, but without a Deputy Commissioner it cannot work. After fifteen 'breakings' some one at the India Office
began to feel afraid, and suggested that enquiry be made into
the grievances of 'the gentlemen who have so summarily abro-
gated their Covenant'. The gentlemen in question stated that a
man would not live on paper, and they they would be very
pleased to see the rupee at two shillings. They had, for the last
twenty years, heard every conceivable and inconceivable scheme
for restoring its value. They now suggested that one, some, all,
any new scheme or schemes, be put to the test. They were not
in the least concerned as to the mechanism of the change. This
was their only answer; it was followed by renewed demonstra-
tions on most of the State Railways. Every strike was timed to
cost the Government lakhs in money and more than lakhs in
loss of confidence. The Army stood firm, but it grinned horribly, and when off duty sympathized with the strikers.

What measures were taken by the Secretary of State for
India will never be known. It is currently believed that he set
every 'silver scheme' he had ever heard of in action at the same
time, and caused a compact little army to smash its way into

China. Whether the schemes or the silver suction of the Chinese Empire, for the hole left by the Army was never again plugged, worked the rise, is an unfathomable mystery. The rupee rose steadily, and at 1s. 10d. the men on the strike began to come in; at 1s. 11d. they were once more dispensing justice as usual; and the curious thing is that all the 'breakings' were rescinded in the *Gazettes*.

No one knew where the business might stop, for no one had ever imagined it possible that English gentlemen should go on strike just like common labourers.

## 'The Biggest Liar in Asia' (by One Who Knows Him)

*Civil and Military Gazette, 7 November 1887*

**Attribution: Sussex Scrapbooks 28/4, p. 10**

For 'the feet of the young men without' see the story of Ananias, Acts 5: 5—9.

The title carries great honour and glory east of Suez and is much sought after. It is strictly personal; being neither hereditary nor transferrable. Unlike Knighthood, Orders and the like, it must be won through a man's unaided exertion, and, when attained, is by no means a secure possession, for another and a more fluent tongue may, at any moment, ravish it from the happy owner.

As virtue lost can never be recovered; so the proud name of 'The Biggest Liar in Asia' once forfeited is gone for ever. Men have essayed to regain it with fifteen years' mountainous mendacity, but they have failed. In the Illustrious and Most Dishonourable Order of the Bonnes Fortunes, the Grand Cordon is known and revered by all his associates. Equal honour is shown to 'The Biggest Liar in Asia' when he condescends to do battle in public places against all comers for the honour of his name. Men flock round him three deep, or slide their chairs towards him, and, when occasion serves, thrust forward some local liar, a bantam of yet unproven beak, to engage with the adversary. Such encounters are worth travelling across an Empire to hear. They occur but seldom.

Almost as much instruction may be gathered from a meeting between Presidential Liars — squires, as it were, striving towards the full glory of knighthood. Such a tourney these eyes have been privileged to witness. The honour of Bengal and Madras was concerned, and the betting ran high. The meeting was strictly private, and if ever man was brought to the post — the smoking-room after dinner — in fit condition, the Bengal Representative was that man. But his very fitness went near to be his ruin. He spoke too quickly, covered too much ground, and the effect of his epoch-marking inventions was in a measure lost. The Madras Man was tubby in person and slow of speech, but an artist in delivery and intonation. He capped his opponent's ancedotes with apparent effort and an assumed halting of memory; but his words sank one by one into our appalled ears, and the pauses between the sentences were devoted to listening for 'the feet of the young men without'. They never came, and the Madras Man continued the awful tenor of his way.

At the critical moment, after the twenty-seventh ancedote, when Bengal was beginning to show signs of exhaustion, the door opened and there entered 'The Biggest Liar in Asia'. No need to tell him what was going forward. His practised eye took in the situation without winking. On principle the Grand Master objected to any unauthorized lying, as tending to weaken his sovereignty. He struck and struck hard — this Abdur Rahman of Ananiases.

'What was that you were saying about a horse, you fellows? I remember when I was at Chittagong — ' and then and there, without an instant's hesitation or weakness, he delivered the most stupendous, complete, and colossal lie that has ever been told of anything carrying four legs since the Primitive Man saw the Three-Toed Horse, and attempted feebly to fabricate his first untruth. Observe the magnificent originality of the idea! Not a word had been said of horses; the conversation at the moment of his entry running on railway-collisions. He had taken, of design, the oldest theme in the world, and from it evolved a melody unapproachable and unique. Paganini playing overtures on the C string was a suckling compared to 'The Biggest Liar in Asia'.

There was a moment of silence that might have been weighed in the balance; then Madras and Bengal rose to their feet and saluted. It was their tender of submission, of admiration, and awe. The sovereignty of 'the Biggest Liar in Asia' was assured. The strain on his brain must have been tremendous, but he betrayed no emotion beyond asking for a 'peg'. This disposed of, he left the room amid thunders of applause — every inch a king. All bets were declared off, for public opinion felt that after such a display, any financial transaction would too closely resemble betting in a Church.

But a doom hangs over 'The Biggest Liar in Asia', and he knows it and trembles. In a far-away, desolate, by-white-men-forgotten district, the Government have locked up a little wizened man with a voice like the cleaning of a file. In his banishment, he has heard calls and dreamed dreams, and he feels that Destiny has designed him to supplant 'The Biggest Liar in Asia'. He has struck out a new gospel — one absolutely untramelled by facts of *any* kind. His stories will be unearthly in their mad prodigality of invention. A mystic and dreamer, he will presently descend upon India, and, in that day, 'The Biggest Liar in Asia' will go down. He feels it himself, for he has spent a week with the little man and sees in him his Wellington. So transitory, alas, is human fame, and so unstable the foundation upon which human glory is builded!

But when the two meet it will be a perfectly gorgeous fight.


# The Old Station (by the Visitor)

*Civil and Military Gazette, 8 May 1888*

**Attribution: Sussex Scrapbooks 28/4, pp. 60–1**

Kipling had left Lahore in November 1887, after five years of work on the *CMG*, to join the staff of the *Pioneer* in Allahabad, many hundreds of miles to the south and east. He had become the recognised special correspondent of the *Pioneer*, was in charge of its weekly supplement, *The Week's News*, had published the collected *Plain Tales from the Hills*, and was writing the stories that went into the volumes of the Indian Railway Library beginning with *Soldiers Three*. Already he was making plans to leave India for England to try his fortunes as a writer. It was therefore an abrupt change of direction that sent him back to Lahore for six weeks in May and June 1888, to take over the *CMG* in the absence of Kay Robinson.

No doubt there had been changes in the half-year that Kipling had been gone, but one may suppose that he is more interested in effect than in reporting. In his letters from Lahore at this time he stressed the familiarity of the scene rather more than the changes. As he wrote to Mrs Hill,

> I have returned to the old, wearying, Godless futile life at a club – same men, same talk, same billiards – all *connu* and triply *connu* and, except for what I carry in my heart, I could almost swear that I had never been away (9–11 May 1888: copy, Sussex).

It is Stevenson who writes on the pains of 'coming back'. But he understates the case – he understates the case. There is no small sorrow more grievous than that of returning to the Old Station after a season, seasons, and a season and a half.

To the eye, nothing has changed. The permanent grey dust-cloud dances over the unshifted umber brick-kiln; the venerable Church that is always being built and never finished by the scattered leaven of devout is as unadvanced as ever; the *gharris* at the Station boast no new paint, and their wheels are as 'wobblesome' as of yore; the sun is not dimmed – and the many and manifold stenches have lost nothing of their poignancy. The Old Station has assumed no new graces and discarded no blemishes. Here is the identical guard-post against which Timmins riotously ran his trap on that bleak November night, and then laughed futilely to see the spokes fly from the shattered wheel. Timmins laughs no more now; for six feet of rank Irrawaddy mud on mouth and chest do not predispose to merriment. Goyler was with Timmins and was nearly pitched into the road. By the way, where is Goyler? 'Oh! He exchanged,

ever so long ago, into a battery in Madras. D'you mean to say
that you didn't know that?' Old friends have an unpleasant air
of superiority about them when you ask questions after an
interval. I was in the third seat of the dogcart, and I gripped the
rails for dear life. . . . and now Timmins is dead and Goyler has
drifted into the *Ewigkeit* down South.

What has happened to the old Samundri Road that used to
run by the Canal? 'The Municipality changed it ages ago, and
it leads straight into Yallapetty now? You're awfully ignorant.'
Lead on, faithful friend who never left the Station, and let us
see what of new the land has to offer. The eye is keen to observe
after lengthened absence. 'Who cut down the big *dhak*-tree
at the Three Shrines?' The Municipality again. *Bless* their liberal
souls! The old lightning-stricken *dhak* was a landmark and a
trysting-place for miles about. Ponies that bore the fairest form
that ever graced a saddle have been hitched to the lower limb
of that confidential tree. And the Municipality cut it down, did
they? May their infamous octroi dues shrivel up to naught —
may they die in their own blocked drains, and may their bones
be buried without a Government Resolution to record the fact!
'Oh — er — hm! I say. Have you seen anything of Miss — Miss —
oh, what's her name — lately?' 'No, I haven't, seeing that she
has been Mrs Bunnion this year and more. If you call tomorrow
I daresay she'll let you look at the baby. It's cut its first tooth
or something remarkable a fortnight ago. She's wrapped up in
it!' Indeed! There *was* a time when she took a livelier interest
in that decayed *dhak* than in all the babes in all the nurseries
in Asia. But she must have changed with the Municipality. Shall
*she* be cursed, therefore? A thousand times no. What does Sarah
Bernhardt's play say? 'The justice of man is satisfied. Let us
await the justice of Heaven.' That baby will make life a sorrow
and sighing for Mrs Bunnion. It will be sick in the night, and it
will cut all its teeth at distressingly short intervals, complicated
by fits — Yes, and croup, and hooping-cough, and big blotches
of scarlatina. Happy Mrs Bunnion! After all, the Club is the best
place to go to. There are sure to be a score of old friends there.

'In the name of Auld Lang Syne, to whom do all these new
faces belong, and who is the unshaven scallawag who is scowling
at me for having taken my own proper and rightful chair in the
mouth of the thermantidote?' 'New faces! Ah! I see. Those
are the men of the old regiments. They are going to be relieved

in a little while; and I think you've got Deemster's pet chair.'
'Have I! Then Deemster may wait for it. He's an upstart, a
*parvenu*, without *locus standi*. Deemster be condemned!' The
snow of extreme age has fallen upon my temples, and I have
lived too long. My very chair, too! The one that I sat in when
the Club was young — before Deemster was ever born — much
less balloted for. Take me away to the Central Gathering Ground.
    'Old friend, I asked for the Old Station — not for a Sahara
of strangers. Who are these, and *these* and THESE? What has
become of the Babbleton children? Does the Raller–Daulsie
flirtation go on still? Where is old Bolster and the Brood?'
'The Babbleton kids went home last hot weather. Raller is
transferred to Assam and flirts with tigers on the Brahmaputra
now. Bolster has retired, taking the Brood with him. What a
chap you are for asking questions! Let me introduce you to — .'
    'If Friendship depend on anything more than Time and
Chance, and if you value my friendship, introduce me to no
one. Those irreverents are playing on the new tennis courts,
and when I left the courts were taboo.' 'They've been grassed
three times since then, and Romayne caught the fever that sent
him Home while paddling about after the *mallis* when the ground
was flooded.' 'Romayne gone Home! He said that he was going
to die out here. He had bought a place in the Hills, and settled
comfortably.' 'Yes, but he fell in love in his old age, and his
wife took him to England.'
    Now Romayne, as this battered peg-table could bear witness
if it had speech, was wont to lift up his voice and entirely,
unreservedly and unrestrainedly abuse, vilify and hold to
derision, Marriage and all that appertained to it. Is there no
consistency in man?
    Of course there is! The oldest and trustiest of all friends,
Shallardyce the Immutable, will not fail me. I missed him at
the Club, but he must be somewhere near here playing tennis.
And when the game is done, he will loaf up, his hat over his
left eyebrow, his racquet under his arm, both hands deep in his
pockets, and that quaint three-cornered smile on his ugly old
countenance. He will only nod, because this David and that
Jonathan understand each other without words, and he will
drawl: — 'Hulloo! Back again, old man?' Then he will pause
before he says: — 'I think we might do a drink together in
honour of the occasion. Eh? What shall it be?' And after we

have drunk brotherhood anew, we shall stroll off together and compress all the stored conversation of many months into a few fragmentary words helped out by much cigar-smoke. But we shall know that we are both unchanged; and he will explain why on earth he did not write to me all last month. The twilight is drawing in, and tennis should be ended. — 'Where's Shallardyce?'

'Dicky? Well you *are* behind the times! Dicky went out three weeks ago with something or other: I've forgotten what it was, but it was rather sudden. I bought that skewbald mare of his that pulls like a fiend. Poor old Dicky! Well, so you're back again. I think we might do a drink together in honour of the occasion, Eh? What shall it be?'

'Lethe — a *poor* a Lethe and bitters please.'

# 'Till the Day Break'

*Civil and Military Gazette, 19 May 1888*

**Attribution: Sussex Scrapbooks 28/4, pp. 64—5**

Heat and fever were among the things unchanged in Kipling's experience of Lahore.

The Brain-fever Bird had a secret to tell since the earliest morning. 'I'll tell you what,' said he confidentially. 'I'll tell you what.' But he never never told. Now he has gone to bed, taking the secret with him, and the little owls have come out to play bo-peep among the *bougainvilleas* and chuckle over the folly of the Brain-fever Bird.

Does an owl feel the heat? How can an owl hang head downwards for five minutes and talk politics to a neighbour at the same time. If an owl were to lose its balance. . . .

But the business of the night is to sleep. Once upon a time, there were one thousand sheep who came to a nullah, and the bell-wether jumped, and the second sheep jumped, and the third sheep jumped, and the fourth and the fifth and the sixth. . . . Whose cartwheels are those? Some man coming back from a dinner somewhere. Is it a two-wheeled cart or a four-wheeled? If the first, it may be Bathershin's — if the second, Nixey's. But *did* Nixey send his cart to be repaired, or was it Nixey's mare or Bathershin's that cut her hock upon the splash-board? It was a beast with two white stockings — no one, and a blaze on the nose. Or two. But *which* was it? A stocking and a blaze, or two white stockings and without a blaze?

If she had two *why* did not Nixey or Bathershin get rid of her, for the saw says:—

> One you may buy it,
>     Two you may try it,
> Three you may doubt it,
>     Four go without it.

But it may be, 'one you may try it, two you may buy it'. That can't be correct! It must be as first stated. The punkah is flapping to the cadence in the hot darkness. 'One-you-may' — a brisk kick — 'buy it'. 'Two you may' — No that was too slow. The next pull is correct 'Three you may doubt it.' He has altered the swing afresh. How can one go to sleep? 'The seventh sheep jumped it and the eighth sheep jumped it and the ninth and the tenth.' Angels and ministers of grace defend us, *what* is in the next room! Only Nixey's little terrier hunting for some cool spot to sleep in, and sniffing for rats.

He was very friendly in the day-time, but suppose he has gone mad since we last met and presently fixes his teeth in my throat, or, pattering up in the dark, nips me on the leg. Nothing will happen for weeks and weeks, months and years, and I shall have forgotten all about it. Then one fine day — a very fine day in England, most likely — there will be a funny little spasm in my throat that will grow and grow and grow, and I shall see a looking glass, just like the one that the moon is beginning to shine on now, and I shall howl like a jackal and hide myself in a corner of the room until I feel thirsty and want a drink. By the way there *was* a spasm in my throat just now. *Spoof* never bit me that I can remember, but he may have scratched me and that is just as bad.

I would throw a boot at him — he is still sniffing in the next room — but for fear that when I put my hand out of the bed, I should touch a *karait* that had been waiting there since the dawn of time.

That would be even worse than feeling *Spoof's* business-like little teeth in my leg, for when a man is bitten by a *karait* he dies in twenty minutes in excessive pain. There was a cow once bitten, by a *karait*, on the tongue, and she lowed without ceasing for an hour and then was dumb; and when the morning broke she was a swelled and shapeless mass upon the ground. The *gaoli* said he thought that she was crying for her calf. If a man lowed for half an hour without ceasing, no one could hear him in this place, and he would be able to swell in peace, just as the cow did.

Curious idea — a man's lowing. If any one heard him what would they suppose he was bellowing for? A khitmatgar? It would be amusing for a punkah-coolie to hear a Sahib bellowing and to know that the Sahib could do nothing, and so to fan that Sahib from this world into the next — if there is one; the punkah-stroke answering the last beat of the pulse just like the relentless *tick, tick, tick,* of the watch under the pillow.

By the way, what time is it? Two twenty-seven and the blessed sleep as far off as ever, the head throbbing like the drums behind the servants' quarters and the brain full of sick fancies. The outside world is worse than indoors. A choking dust-storm has wiped out the moon, and the air is full of flying rubbish. All the world is going down-wind together — beyond the girdling belt of trees, beyond the white road — straight into the copper-hued bosom of the sultry night. Everything would escape from the heat if it could — even the tortured writhing clouds of dust that must be used to it.

If a man returned to his couch and lay very still and religiously thought of nothing at all, he might surprise sleep unawares. But to think of nothing necessitates thinking very hard indeed, and this increases an already sufficiently lively headache. Not to think of nothing means that the uncontrolled brain will tie itself up in a helpless knot of doubt, perplexity, argument, re-argument, wonder and pain. The stroll into the open has brushed away the unwholesome cobwebs of groundless panic, but when will the rest come?

Nine hundred thousand sheep — all Australia full — tried to

jump through a hedge. And the first jumped, and the second jumped. . . . and the thirty hundred and forty first jumped. Never were such disappointing muttons! They jumped so merrily that I took an interest in them instead of dozing off. Happy thought! One hundred and fifty Bathershins once tried to crawl through a hedge on their hands and knees. And the first Bathershin — stuck 'like a fou-weltered yow'. I am so absorbed in his performances that I neglect all his followers. Fancy Bathershin with his head in a black-thorn bush and his feet kicking wildly over a ditch! And that is no use. The real thing is to think of nothing — of nothing — of nothing.

5.45 A.M. — As bitter a piece of work as ever was! And here with a cessation of the dust-storm and a few drops of tepid rain, breaks the pitiless day. The Brain-fever Bird is up and across the lawn, stammering the secret that he is forbidden to divulge. Sleepless, and you who have watched through the night, all the world over, good morning!

*Spoof* trots round the corner, his tail in the elements and his nose on the quiver for a rat. He looks as though few ill dreams had disturbed *his* rest. *Spoofkins*, come here and have your ears pulled for frightening a fool of a Sahib nearly into a fit last night!

# Glossary of Indian and Anglo-Indian Words and Phrases

Note: since there is no uniform system of transliteration of Indian terms into the Latin alphabet I have followed Kipling's spellings. Words that are followed by question marks I have been unable to define. Some are perhaps typographical errors, but others may be Kipling's own spelling.

| | |
|---|---|
| *archarji:* | teacher, priest |
| *aftaba:* | water pot with spout and handle |
| *almirah:* | wardrobe, chest of drawers |
| *anna:* | one sixteenth of a rupee |
| *Arains:* | ? |
| *Arayavarta:* | the Aryan race |
| *ayah:* | nurse, maid |
| *babu:* | clerk, especially one who knows English |
| *badlis:* | transfer (from one place/station/office to another) |
| *Badshah:* | king |
| *bahut accha:* | very good, all right |
| *bakshish, bukshish:* | tip, payment |
| *batcha:* | child |
| *bazar:* | market |
| *beetel:* | aromatic leaf for chewing |
| *Belait:* | England specifically, Europe generally |
| *Belaitee, Bilayut:* | natives of England; those from across the water (Europeans) |

| | |
|---|---|
| *benaoti:* | ? |
| *bhai-bund* | brotherhood; family and friends; community |
| *bhisti:* | water carrier (literally, one from Paradise) |
| *bhoosa:* | hay |
| *bokhar:* | fever |
| *budmash:* | rogue |
| *Budndming:* | ? |
| *buggalow:* | Arab vessel |
| *bund:* | dike, wall |
| *bundobust:* | arrangement, system, agreement |
| *bunnias:* | traders, merchants |
| *bus:* | stop, enough |
| *bustee:* | settlement, village (in the city, a slum) |
| *byle:* | ox |
| *bylewalla:* | ox driver |
| | |
| *chabil:* | ? |
| *chalder:* | perhaps *chader* = blanket? |
| *changar:* | earth workers |
| *chaprassi:* | messenger |
| *charpoy:* | cot |
| *chatty:* | earthern pot |
| *chick, chik:* | bamboo blind or screen |
| *chillum:* | part of the hookah containing the tobacco and charcoal; or, the whole arrangement |
| *chirag:* | clay lamp |
| *chit:* | note |
| *choga:* | loose upper garment, robe |
| *chop, chup:* | be quiet; shut up |
| *chor do:* | let go |
| *chota:* | small, little |
| *chota hazree:* | early breakfast |
| *chowki:* | toll house, police station |
| *chowkidar:* | watchman |
| *chudder:* | sheet, cover |
| *chumar:* | leather worker (low caste) |
| *chunam:* | lime, plaster |

| | |
|---|---|
| *chupper:* | thatched roof |
| *consumah:* see *khansamah* | |
| | |
| *dacoit:* | robber (in a gang) |
| *dak:* | post, mail, journey |
| *darogah:* | local (village) constable |
| *degchies:* | cooking utensils |
| *dekko:* | look, peep |
| *dhak:* | flowering tree of the Punjab |
| *dhobie:* | washerman |
| *dikked:* | troubled |
| *doabs:* | the territory between two confluent rivers |
| *doolie:* | a covered litter |
| *doomb; doomba:* | fat-tailed sheep |
| *duftar:* | office |
| *Durbaies:* | ? |
| *durbar:* | court, levee, public audience |
| *dustoor, durtoorie:* | custom, commission |
| | |
| *ekka:* | one-horse, two-wheeled vehicle |
| | |
| *ferash:* | menial servant |
| *fitton:* | phaeton, i.e., a four-wheeled carriage |
| | |
| *gaoli:* | perhaps an error for *goalla* |
| *ghariwans:* | drivers |
| *gharri:* | cart, carriage |
| *ghee, ghi:* | clarified butter |
| *goalla:* | cowherd |
| *godown:* | warehouse |
| *goor:* | molasses |
| *gorah log:* | white men |
| *gowallas:* see *goalla* | |
| *gram:* | chick-peas |
| *griffin:* | tenderfoot, newcomer to India |
| *gutkas:* | ? |
| *gureeb:* | poor, docile |
| *gurrah:* | clay water pot |

| | |
|---|---|
| *Hajii:* | one who has made pilgrimage to Mecca |
| *Hakim:* | doctor |
| *Hazur-ki-parwashti:* | thanks for the generosity of the powerful one |
| *holi:* | spring festival |
| *hookah:* | water pipe for smoking |
| *hookum:* | an order |
| *howdah:* | chair or seat carried by an elephant |
| *hulwaie:* | confectioner |
| *izzat:* | respect, honour |
| *jat:* | one of a peasant class; noted as big and strong |
| *jezail:* | heavy Afghan rifle |
| *jhampanies:* | sedan chair carriers |
| *jhool:* | horse blanket |
| *juldee ao:* | come quickly |
| *kabab:* | meat on skewers |
| *kafir:* | infidel |
| *kala admis:* | black men |
| *kamra:* | room |
| *kanats:* | canvas enclosures |
| *karait:* | small deadly snake |
| *karkhana:* | workshop, department |
| *kazi:* | Muslim law officer |
| *kerritch hogya:* | ? |
| *khansamah:* | butler, steward |
| *khinkhab:* | gold brocade |
| *khitmatgar:* | house servant |
| *khud:* | brink, steep hill side |
| *kivaste:* | for the use of, for |
| *kizilbashes:* | Persianised Turks, named for their red caps; a community of them in Afghanistan |
| *koil:* | small singing bird |
| *kubberdar:* | take care, look out |
| *kunkar, kunkur:* | small pebbles, gravel |

| | |
|---|---|
| *kutcha:* | makeshift, temporary, substitute, poor (antonym of *pukka*) |
| *kutcherry:* | court, administrative office |
| | |
| *lakh:* | 100,000 |
| *lathi:* | stick, club |
| *lon:* | red powder |
| *lotah:* | brass pot |
| | |
| *madressa:* | Muslim school |
| *maidan:* | open space, park, common |
| *mallee; malli* | gardener |
| *massala:* | spice mixture |
| *maulvis:* | learned men, professors |
| *maund:* | measure of weight, varying widely |
| *mehter:* | sweeper |
| *mela:* | festival |
| *mimbar:* | a maulvi's pulpit |
| *mistri:* | carpenter |
| *mochi:* | leather worker, shoemaker |
| *mohurrir:* | writer in a native language |
| *munsiff:* | native judge |
| *munzar:* | ? |
| *mussalchi:* | kitchen helper, scullion |
| *must:* | mad, drunk |
| | |
| *naib:* | deputy |
| *nats:* | jugglers |
| *nauker:* | servant |
| *netschies:* | ? |
| *nokri:* | job, employment |
| *nullah:* | watercourse |
| | |
| *ooplah:* | dried cow dung for fuel |
| | |
| *pagal:* | mad, foolish |
| *pagdundies, pugdundies:* | paths |
| *paisa:* | money |
| *pal:* | small tent |
| *palki:* | small compartment, box |

*pardahneshin:* see *purdah nashin*

| | |
|---|---|
| *phenyl-ki-diwai:* | phenyl-as-medicine |
| *pice, pie:* | small coin; money |
| *pipal:* | large fig tree |
| *poora:* | the whole, all of it |
| *poshteen:* | Afghan fur-lined coat or robe |
| *puggris:* | turbans |
| *pukka, pucca:* | genuine, substantial, permanent, superior: opposite of *kutcha* |
| *pummeloe:* | large citrus fruit |
| *punkah:* | large fixed swinging fan, pulled by a rope |
| *purdah:* | curtain, veil |
| *purdah nashin, pardah-nishin:* | woman secluded behind the screen or curtain |
| *raises:* | respectable natives |
| *rezai:* | a quilt |
| *rickshaw:* | two-wheeled passenger cart pulled by a coolie |
| *rupee:* | standard coin of the Indian money system |
| *saf-karo:* | clean it |
| *sais:* see *syce* | |
| *sahib-logues:* | Europeans |
| *saloo:* | red cloth |
| *saree:* | woman's dress |
| *serai:* | inn, rest house, built around a courtyard |
| *shabash:* | well done, bravo |
| *shamiana:* | tent |
| *shisham:* | tree, valuable for timber |
| *shroff:* | money lender |
| *sida:* | straight |
| *sirdar:* | leader, captain |
| *siris:* | acacia tree |
| *sirkar:* | government |
| *solah topee:* | pith helmet |
| *soor:* | pig |
| *soorkee:* | pounded brick used in paving |

| | |
|---|---|
| *sowar:* | horseman, rider |
| *spins:* | spinsters, young women |
| *sudder judge:* | chief judge under Muslim law |
| *sunnyasi:* | Hindu religious mendicant |
| *syce:* | groom |
| *tahsildars:* | native revenue officer; chief collector |
| *takkus:* | tax |
| *tamasha:* | show, spectacle, entertainment |
| *tar:* | telegram (literally *wire*) |
| *tat, tattoo:* | native-bred pony |
| *tazias:* | images of the tombs of Hussein and Hassan, carried in the Mohurrum procession |
| *teapoy:* | small tripod table |
| *tehsils:* | administrative district (cf. *tahsildar*) |
| *tharrahs:* | ? |
| *thermantidote:* | cooling device fitted in a window |
| *ticca gharri:* | hired carriage |
| *tiffin:* | lunch |
| *tikkah:* | ornamental mark on forehead |
| *tonga:* | light two-wheeled carriage |
| *vakil:* | attorney |
| *yaboos:* | breed of Afghan horse |
| *zemindar:* | landholder |
| *ziafut:* | ? |

# Index